PRIVATIZATION IN EASTERN EUROPE

A
Central European University
Privatization Project
book

PRIVATIZATION IN EASTERN EUROPE: IS THE STATE WITHERING AWAY?

Roman Frydman
Andrzej Rapaczynski

CENTRAL EUROPEAN UNIVERSITY PRESS
BUDAPEST • LONDON • NEW YORK

Distributed by Oxford University Press, Walton Street, Oxford OX2 6DP
Oxford New York Toronto
Delhi Bombay Calcutta Madras Karachi
Kuala Lumpur Singapore Hong Kong Tokyo
Nairobi Dar es Salaam Cape Town
Melbourne Auckland Madrid
and associated companies in Berlin Ibadan
Distributed in the United States by Oxford University Press Inc., New York

This collection © Central European University Privatization Project 1994

For the provenance in their original form of the papers appearing here, please see the opening page of each chapter.

First published in Great Britain 1994 by
Central European University Press
25 Floral Street, London WC2E 9DS

British Library Cataloguing in Publication Data
A CIP catalogue record for this book is available from the British Library.

ISBN 1 85866 004 1

Library of Congress Cataloging in Publication Data
A CIP catalog record for this book is available from the Library of Congress.

Typeset by Mayhew Typesetting, Rhayader, Powys
Printed and bound in Great Britain by SRP, Exeter

CONTENTS

To Halina, Rebecca, Julia, Kate, Marcella, and Tessa

PREFACE AND
ACKNOWLEDGEMENTS

The chapters of this book trace the development of our ideas on privatization and its role in the transition to a market economy in the countries of Eastern Europe. All but the last of them are slightly revised versions of earlier published papers, often written in response to events, debates with other observers, and the evolving formulation of policies in the region. In preparing these papers for publication, we faced the choice of retaining their original form or rewriting them as chapters of a tightly organized book. Given the importance of their historical context, we have decided to preserve their original flavor and not engage in extensive editing. But we believe that the papers included here naturally develop out of each other and present a rather coherent overall evolution of a theory of privatization in Eastern Europe.

The papers included in this volume contain separate acknowledgements of our specific debts to various individuals and institutions. Here, we would only like to add our general expressions of gratitude. Many of our research and policy advising activities, which enriched our understanding of the privatization process in Eastern Europe, would not have been possible without the generous support of George Soros, who also shared with us many of his insights into the nature of open societies and market economies. We are also very grateful to our colleagues in the CEU Privatization Project, and especially to John S. Earle and Joel Turkewitz, for their help and dedication to our common research efforts.

We also acknowledge the support for this book from the Lynde and Harry Bradley Foundation, CV Starr Center for Applied Economics at New York University, and Columbia University School of Law. Expert editorial help was provided by Heather Bliss. As always, Frances Pinter, of the CEU Press, has been most supportive of our work.

R.F.
A.R.

FOREWORD

Edmund S. Phelps

The building of economic and legal mechanisms to put in place of the fallen communist system in Eastern Europe is one of the great dramas of the century. All of us who are students of society and its choices of economic institutions are fortunate to be living in such exciting times. The authors of this volume, Roman Frydman and Andrzej Rapaczynski, have had the even greater luck of having the skills – in economics and in the law – and the background – both grew up in communist Poland – to get into the thick of it. In Frydman and Rapaczynski we have worldly philosophers who are actually worldly and philosophical.

This collection operates at several levels. It can be read as an account by first-hand observers of the uphill struggle in Eastern Europe to build capitalism on the ruins of communism. It is a brief for their own widely-discussed policy proposals by authors who are themselves major players in that struggle. Above all, it is a sustained analysis of the obstacles on the path to a successful market system and of the strategies most likely to overcome them. Our understanding of the mechanisms of capitalism is considerably deepened in the process. This volume will establish Frydman and Rapaczynski as the leading theoreticians of the transition – or non-transition – to capitalism.

The authors early understood that what is at issue in Eastern Europe is not a transition to the market. The liberal socialist theoreticians of the 1960s, whose ideas were increasingly tried in the 1980s over much of the region, all understood the benefits of a wide range of circumstances that come from reliance on market mechanisms – the freedom of each enterprise to set its own prices and make its own supply decisions. But markets, though necessary, are far from sufficient.

Enterprises must be under private ownership if there is to be any hope that they will not simply be arms of a powerful central government. Nor is private ownership enough. Private enterprise must be subject to the control of outside owners, whose main interest is the quick or distant buck, not by insiders whose bread is buttered on the side of job security or (if there is no such security) asset stripping. Market capitalism needs these special institutions to function. And this, the authors discovered, was just the beginning of wisdom!

This part of the struggle was played out in the fights over privatization. With the proposal they floated in Warsaw in the summer of 1990 Frydman and Rapaczynski were among the first to weigh in with a scheme to privatize existing state enterprises through the device of vouchers. Incredible as it may seem to sensible people today, in many an East European country it had been supposed that each enterprise ought to be sold for cash in the same way that a number of public-sector firms had been sold off in Britain and Mexico. Dreams of the proceeds that such sales would bring the government, strapped for tax revenues in most cases, made this a tempting road to start down. The authors, however, quickly saw how crazy and disastrous such a policy would be. The typical state enterprises would not fetch on the capital market the amount needed just to cover the fee that the investment banks would charge for their services in taking the enterprise to the market. And it would not have been feasible to achieve by this laborious means the massive scale of privatization that was desired in less than a decade, maybe two decades. Mass privatization would be vastly cheaper and much faster if the enterprises were given away. But how exactly? The devil is in the details.

The first idea that came to mind was to distribute shares in each enterprise equally over the population. Here too Frydman and Rapaczynski saw a difficulty. Simply showering an equal share of each enterprise on each qualifying adult might seem both just and expedient, but it would risk cheating everyone of whatever promise a private enterprise system might offer. Having only the standard miniscule allotment of shares, no shareowner would have a sufficient stake in any enterprise to warrant spending time and money thinking about the best direction for it to take. Nominating and electing a board of directors under these circumstances would have been a strange and haphazard process. Such an allocation of shares, as long as it lasted, could not be serviceable from the point of view of enterprise control: enterprises would not have outside owners with powers to govern.

With time, very possibly, the market might evolve solutions. Some people would become rich enough through small businesses to buy a large enough assemblage of shares in a large enterprise to take it over. In the pattern likely to become more prevalent, some people would borrow enough – borrow the shares or borrow the cash to buy them – to obtain a stake of the necessary size to exercise control of the enterprise. We could expect the emergence of financial intermediaries – banks and investment funds – that would attract depositors and use the resources obtained to amass a decisive stake in one or more enterprises. It might be hoped that these funds would become the operative capitalists, dominating the board of directors and setting the strategy of the enterprises they control. Frydman and Rapaczynski view this strategy as subject to several perils. Who would control the enterprises before private interests gained effective control (if indeed they ever did)? The government? The workers? The managers? The authors have no illusions about the sort of job they would do. Worse yet, there might be a period in which none of the above would enjoy sufficiently secure ownership rights to be able to benefit from any moves that would be profitable for the enterprise.

The unique thrust of the Frydman–Rapaczynski proposal was that it embedded a provision for concentrated ownership in the privatiz-ation machinery. In the proposed arrangements, a number of 'investment funds' would be licensed to acquire the privatizing enterprises: The citizens would deposit the vouchers issued to them with the investment funds of their choice, and the investment funds would use the deposited vouchers to bid for the enterprises – or a controlling stake in the enterprises – of their choice in a series of auctions for vouchers. Through this device there was the prospect that each of the investment funds would be led to perform the role of capitalist: Using its large stakes to gain control of management in order to restructure and, if necessary, reorient the enterprises under its control. As it has turned out, only the Czech Republic and the Slovak Republic have opted for a scheme close to this blueprint. Governments have preferred to remain indirect owners of the enterprises they auction through ownership of the investment funds! The managers of the funds are hired under a short-term contract. But the authors will tell that story.

There was more bad news about outsider control. In most countries the insiders – workers or managers or both – were often judged so powerful that, to buy their support, the privatization plans provided the lion's share of each privatizing enterprise to its insiders, leaving little to outsiders. In Russia, the great majority of the shares in the newly privatized enterprises were made available on attractive terms to the insiders. In Poland, the tussle over the rights to go to insiders, especially the powerful workers, has held up mass privatization for more than three years. The result is that there is no country, save the Czech Republic, in which the state enterprises are well on their way to control by outside private interests.

Evidently the great experiment in Eastern Europe is not really the transplantation of a living, beating capitalist heart into a once-sick but potentially healthy economy. Instead the experiment is the creation of a *mutant* capitalism in which insiders – in some countries the workers, and in other countries the managers – will wield control of the enterprises and do so in the interest of their jobs rather than the profitability of the enterprise. What is being artificially constructed, it would seem, is not a super-creature but a defective creature in a life-imitates-art parallel to Dr Frankenstein's well-remembered slip-up. (We hope that it will never be so frustrated and provoked as to go on a rampage, but there is that danger.)

Conceivably this assessment is much too pessimistic. First, it is conceivable that enterprises that never existed before – new start ups – will prove to be the salvation of the Eastern European economies, those that have the good sense to permit free entry of new enterprises at any rate. Some see in Poland and in China the possibilities for growth of aggregate real income despite continuing stagnation and decay of the old state sector. Here too, however, the authors have seen a problem: Insofar as the new enterprises feed off the existing state sector, and the latter is stagnant, how far can they go? (China may be a special case, as there is a Chinese diaspora with which the newly emerging private sector in China can trade and make financial deals.)

Second, with regard to the privatized enterprises, it could be argued that the insiders in the enterprises they dominate will see that they cannot survive without compromising with outside interests. Workers and managers might give up large amounts of enterprise control to outsiders in return for infusions of equity finance from new share purchasers or loans from new private lenders. However, as we shall see, the authors have doubts whether outside investors will be willing to come in. In this event, the Eastern European countries will be unable to make up the ground lost from starting in the wrong place.

Clearly the problem arises in the power of vested interests. Musing on this problem, Douglass North, the latest Nobelist in economics, writes that:

the individuals and organizations with bargaining power as a result of the institutional framework have a crucial stake in perpetuating the system. Paths do get reversed (witness Argentina from growth to stagnation in the past half century or Spain the reverse since the 1950s). But reversal is a difficult process about which we know all too little – witness the ongoing fumbling efforts at such reversal in central and eastern Europe. The reason is that we still know too little about the dynamics of institutional change and particularly the interplay between economic and political markets.[1]

The premise that vested interests can block even a reorganization of the economy so powerful that it could make everyone better off does raise a puzzle. Why don't the potential gainers buy off the potential losers, so everyone will gain? The *system* could be reformed, it would seem, without any redistribution of wealth *away* from anyone – only a Pareto improvement. But there are difficulties. In some cases the losers know they will never be identified or located, of course. The other difficulty is that many of the gainers would rebel at a proposal for a surgical redistribution, in the form of cash bribes, to the vested interests, tarred by their connection with the old system in disrepute. The polity has to find other, inefficient ways by which to obtain the acquiescence of vested interests in a degree of reform (barring a resolution of the problem by force). Such a redistribution is indeed happening. In Eastern Europe we see that numerous interest groups feel well entitled to help themselves to a generous amount (perhaps as much as they can get) of the vaunted gain that the emergence of market capitalism is expected to deliver: Bureaucrats helping themselves to bribes, the officials of the dinosaur state enterprises helping themselves to state subsidies, the workers at enterprises helping themselves to enterprise profits and, with privatization, a big allotment of shares. The trouble is that these inefficient mechanisms of redistribution are killing the goose that was expected to lay the golden egg.

Frydman and Rapaczynski, in the last essay especially, dig deeply into precisely this area – the force of political power in shaping and limiting the scope for economic reforms. In a short time they have gone well beyond the existing wisdom. I will not attempt to do justice to their discussion here, only to cite a couple of their points.

Even as early as the second essay, the authors pointed out that it is

---

[1] Douglass North, 'Institutions and Economic Theory,' *The American Economist*, Spring 1992.

not at all the former commissars and the generals once at the top of the old communist system who are the main impediment to rapid and extensive progress. With the broad-based reforms of the communist system that began decades ago in some countries and in recent years in others, new interest groups were unleashed – workers, farmers, managers, civil servants – all able to pursue their own interests in new ways without the boot of the central master. It is a paradox (reminiscent of a theme of Gershenkron in another context) that it is in a country where relatively slow and belated reforms of this type took place, namely the former Czechoslovakia, where the class of newly empowered groups was not created, that a transition to ownership of enterprises largely by outside interests could go swiftly and smoothly.

With the last essay, however, the authors move to a higher plane in beginning to assemble the basic elements of a political-economic theory of the sort of private-ownership economy that is likely to evolve from the initial conditions present in Eastern Europe. They argue, first, that any attempt to use privatized assets for market-driven purposes may be frustrated by the absence in Eastern Europe of a set of self-enforcing expectations concerning the respect of property rights. Second, they argue that little attempt to use the assets for these purposes may be made owing to the absence of incentives discouraging dependence on the state. The analysis serves to flesh out and improve upon the old themes that an equilibrium of distrust and rent-seeking may emerge to block the economic development of a (substantially private-ownership) economy.

On the first theme, the authors' discussion leads to a new point on the likelihood of equity financing by minority interests in Eastern Europe. Unless a goodly number of people are willing to invest real money in the newly privatized enterprises, not just the sparse capitalists willing to take a large stake, equity financing of new investment by these enterprises will be difficult (and a similar conclusion might apply to loan financing). But to do so these buyers of a minority interest in enterprises will require confidence that the majority owners will honor their commitments to the minority without need for costly arrangements for monitoring and sanctions. Furthermore, the authors note that this confidence is in turn supported by the majority's need to go back to financial markets to raise capital in the future. Such a need is substantially diminished when the enterprises are given soft budget constraints by the government and hence do not have to go to the capital market. Thus a hitherto unrecognized connection between macroeconomic stability and genuine property rights is brought to light.

On the second theme, the authors are led to the view that, where the capital stock of a privatized enterprise is of low quality, the privatized resources may be more profitably deployed for rent-seeking than for market-oriented activity. In what must have been a painful realization, the authors have seen the downside of concentrated ownership in those economies where a substantial proportion of the privatized capital stock is of low economic value: when ownership of an enterprise is dispersed among many shareowners, there is the famous difficulty of gaining control of the management. But, on the other hand, there is also a balancing difficulty if – as will be the case when the capital stock is of low economic value – the owners would like to organize a rent-seeking expedition to the government in order to gain subsidies and contracts. It could be, in something of a nightmare scenario, that the investment funds set up to exercise enterprise control will be perverted into agents lobbying on behalf of the enterprise for a share of government largess.

Thus the authors have gone well beyond the usual conclusions – that the transition to capitalism requires the replacement of state management with private owners operating under effective corporate governance, the clarification of property rights, and the development of financial markets.

When benighted observers exclaim that the inferiority of socialism to capitalism remains unproved empirically, they often cite the stellar performance of the state-owned enterprises operating in a predominantly private-ownership economy founded on a capitalist ethos. Soon, if the analysis in this collection is right, these same observers will be able to point to the miserable performance of private enterprise embedded in several state-dominated economies, and they will conclude that this poor performance proves the ineffectualness of private ownership. It is perhaps the authors' most valuable contribution in this volume to have shown how simplistic such observations are. Frydman and Rapaczynski have laid out for us how to begin thinking about capitalism and socialism in systemic terms, with an empirically founded sense of all their political and economic workings.

INTRODUCTION

The papers presented here were born from a very practical involvement in policy debates concerning privatization in Poland in the first half of 1990. In fact, when we started our work, we had not at all expected it to become our primary preoccupation for the next several years and result in an extensive empirical and theoretical research agenda.

For unrelated reasons, we were spending a significant amount of time in Poland during the first few months of 1990, after the introduction of the stringent stabilization program associated with the name of the then Deputy Prime Minister, Leszek Balcerowicz. The expectations among the Polish people with respect to the short-term efficacy of this reform program were quite clearly unrealistic, and the pain connected with the transition was beginning to generate serious political difficulties. As a result, the unity of the Solidarity movement was disintegrating, and the sustainability of the reform movement was being threatened. On a more personal note, many of our old friends were in the government, and we wanted to help them prepare for the approaching elections. One of the themes of the political and economic discussions was the question of privatization.

From the beginning, we were of the opinion that, given the deeply distorted nature of the communist development, macroeconomic stabilization alone would be insufficient to bring about genuine recovery and restructuring. We believed that much more emphasis should be put on the question of privatization and microeconomic reforms. At the same time, the discussion of privatization proceeded along the lines we quickly came to see as entirely inappropriate. The Polish government, with support from some international organizations, was embarking on a rather ambitious program of sales of state companies modeled on the British privatizations during the years of the Thatcher government. Our first thoughts on the problem of privatization in Eastern Europe were connected with showing that the situation in the region was entirely different from that in the West and that the solutions adopted there could not be transplanted to Poland.

In trying to develop an alternative to the sales program, we began with the idea of giving away the assets in the hands of the state, and asked ourselves the question how that could be accomplished in a way that would lead to a serious change in the *modus operandi* at the enterprise level. The result of this effort was a series of memoranda to the Ministry of Finance and other government agencies, as well as a paper, written in Polish, under the title 'Privatizing Privatization: A New Proposal for Social and Economic Reform in Poland.'[1]

We advocated a mass privatization of state assets that would eschew the problems inherent in the sales program, including the shortage of capital and the difficulties in valuation of state enterprises. Our proposal was to distribute special privatization vouchers to every Polish citizen and invite them to participate, directly or indirectly, in auctions at which shares of state enterprises would be sold for the vouchers. While some citizens might want to make their investment decisions for themselves, most, we argued, would prefer to diversify their holdings and avail themselves of the expertise provided by specially formed privatization intermediaries.

The privatization intermediaries were the nub of our proposal. We envisaged that the state would announce a proper regulatory scheme and invite foreign and domestic fund managers, investment bankers, venture capitalists etc. to establish privatization funds in Poland. The funds would first compete for the vouchers received by the population (in exchange for which they would offer their own shares), and then invest their 'voucher capital' in the shares of the privatized enterprises. The vouchers would lose their validity after the auctions, and the funds would be expected to exercise necessary monitoring and supervision over the management of the enterprises in their portfolios. This, we hoped would result in the creation of a novel form of institutional investor, somewhat similar to a Western mutual fund, yet like a German

---

[1] This paper appeared in Polish in September, 1990, in *Res publica*. Subsequent issues of the same periodical featured comments from a number of Polish economists and policymakers, including the future Minister of Privatization, Janusz Lewandowski.

bank or an American venture capital fund, actively participating in the corporate governance of the privatized enterprises. We also hoped that, in the long run, the intermediaries would bring in other investors and thus be able to accomplish what the government wanted but could not do, namely, sell large amounts of equity in the privatized enterprises to both foreign and domestic investors. We therefore coined the phrase 'to privatize privatization' – which we were happy to see become a part of the standard vocabulary of future discussions – to underscore the fact that our approach involved not only a privatization of state assets, but also the use of market mechanisms in the very process of implementing the reform.

In the summer of 1990, we were invited to present our ideas at a conference devoted to the problems of economic transition, organized by the World Bank. The first chapter in this volume is a slightly abridged and revised version of the paper we prepared for that conference, and it was the first work in which we tried to give a systematic and more theoretical expression to our approach. The paper lays down the main requirements of a successful privatization program: the speed of implementation, social and political acceptability, establishment of working corporate governance arrangements, and the facilitation of access to foreign capital and expertise. We also provided our own account of the role of valuation of enterprises in the process of privatization. Previously, we had argued that one of the main obstacles to a sales program was an extremely time-consuming and unreliable method of estimating the market value of state enterprises, and we insisted that valuation should be left to the parties who bear the consequences of their estimates, rather than to consultants hired by the state. In 'Markets and Institutions,' we recognised that valuation plays a very important role in the initial restructuring process, and we explained how the use of vouchers, rather than money, simplifies it by restricting the universe of available investment alternatives.

The bulk of the first chapter, however, is devoted to a systematic taxonomy of mass privatization proposals and the structural interconnections among their various elements. In particular, we stressed the importance of investors' choice, free entry of intermediaries, and the general competitiveness of the new institutional arrangements. We also emphasized the potential conflict between the economic and political incentives of the main players in the privatization process and the resulting dangers of bureaucratization. This theme came to pervade most of our later research and is visible in all the subsequent chapters in this volume.

The work on 'Markets and Institutions' started a process of reflection that made us increasingly realize the complexity of the issues with which we were dealing. Indeed, we have come to see that the problems we were discussing had serious implications for our understanding of the role of market mechanisms not just in Eastern Europe, but also in the developed Western societies. In particular, while most observers had treated the goal of the transition to a market economy as axiomatic, we were coming to the conclusion that the complexity and diversity of the institutional arrangements of capitalist economies raised the question of an appropriate direction for East European reforms. Moreover, in light of the uncertainty concerning the inner workings of the various market economies, we were led to an even greater emphasis on open-ended arrangements, containing self-correcting mechanisms that could substitute for the inherently missing human foresight.

These themes are developed at length in the next two chapters in this volume. In 'Privatization and Corporate Governance', which was initially presented at a conference organized in Baden, Austria, by the International Monetary Fund and the Austrian National Bank, we investigate the question of what will fill the gap created by the withdrawal of the state from the position of control over East European enterprises. Privatization, we argue, should entail much more than a mere transfer of title; it is an establishment of a private system of enterprise control which provides an appropriate structure of incentives for the economic actors functioning within the institutional setting of Eastern Europe. Having reviewed the types of institutional arrangements characteristic of the main Western economies, and shown that economic analysis is incapable of coming up with a blueprint of the optimal set of such arrangements that could be used as a model in Eastern Europe, we nevertheless caution against leaving the future structure of East European corporate governance to purely spontaneous developments. The most important danger of spontaneous developments, we argue, is the capture of control by various special interests (especially labor and management), which have evolved as a consequence of previous reform attempts, and the subordination of economic to political concerns. We therefore stressed that a good privatization program should facilitate the establishment of a firm system of managerial accountability and external control.[2]

---

[2] Our arguments concerning this issue were honed in numerous discussions with Jeffrey Sachs, with whom we were otherwise in far-reaching agreement about the need for speedy mass privatization.

The question of the appropriate mixture of evolutionary and design elements in the various privatization proposals became at that time a focal point in our thinking about East European transformation. Since we were very concerned about the structure of post-privatization enterprise control, we may have at that point somewhat over-emphasized the details of the design side and ignored the extent of the political difficulties involved in making mass privatization a reality. This was, in part, made clear to us by our discussions, at the Baden conference, with Dusan Triska and Vladimir Rudlovcak, who had been involved in the preparation of the then-just-adopted Czech mass privatization plan. The Czech plan was similar to the one we had proposed. But while our proposal attempted to assure that each privatized enterprise would have at least one large stakeholder, the Czech plan left the control structure free to emerge as a result of the citizens' and intermediaries' choices concerning the use of their voucher capital. This may have lessened political opposition to the Czech plan and facilitated its implementation, since company managers expected that voucher privatization would lead to a wide dispersion of owner-ship and allow them to maintain control. In the event, the Czech plan seems to have produced a significant concentration of ownership in the hands of the new intermediaries; although time will tell whether the post-privatization enterprise control structure will result in a sufficiently substantial involvement of the intermediaries in the restructuring process.[3]

While our previous work focused on the changes to be brought about by privatization on the level of individual enterprises, the paper on 'Evolution and Design,' prepared for the Villa Mondragone Seminar in Rome, Italy, attempted to link the changes at the enterprise level to the broader context of inter-enterprise relations. In particular, we argued that the structure of the capital stock inherited from the communist command economies involved numerous links among enterprises ('asset specific investments') that could result in a great increase in transaction costs of negotiating new relations among these enterprises in the wake of privatization. In the same paper, we also refined our understanding of the issues involved in determining the appropriate speed of privatization. We argued that the speed of privatization should be endogenously determined, depending on the quality of the capital stock of the enterprises involved. We especially emphasized that nonviable

[3] The Czech plan also differed from our proposal by requiring that each participating citizen pay a nominal fee for his vouchers.

enterprises should not be privatized together with the viable ones, since their inclusion in the portfolios of the intermediaries heightened the danger of the intermediaries' politicization.[4] We also proposed a method by which viable enterprises could be separated from the nonviable ones under the conditions of the postcommunist economies, in which the governments have no access to reliable information concerning the value of individual companies.[5]

The chapter on 'Corporate Control and Financial Reform,' originally published under the title 'Needed Mechanisms of Corporate Governance and Finance in Eastern Europe,' was written with Edmund Phelps and Andrei Shleifer at the request of the European Bank for Reconstruction and Development. It traced the different points of departure of the economies in the region and proceeded to analyze the role of financial institutions in the future governance structure of East European enterprises. In addition to discussing the role of privatization intermediaries in the monitoring of enterprise performance, we also looked into the possibility (raised in some of our earlier papers) of their developing into full-fledged banking institutions, similar to German 'universal banks,' involved in the provision of a whole range of commercial, investment, and consumer banking services. The same paper also contains a rather pessimistic assessment of the East European banking system, and proposes a scheme for combining its recapitalization with its simultaneous shrinkage and the creation of new banking institutions.

In the meantime, since the spring of 1991, we had become involved in the growth of a unique educational and policy institution, the Central European University, created in Prague and Budapest by the American financier of Hungarian descent, George Soros. The support we received from the CEU allowed us to conduct research and policy advising activities throughout the region. As a result, we gained access to large amounts of empirical information[6] and acquired considerable practical experience of the privatization process in a number of countries. This encounter with the practice of privatization made us particularly conscious of the political nature of the process, and we began to explore the issues related to the interplay between politics and economics in a

---

[4] This theme is also developed at length in the last chapter in this volume.

[5] Another, more political aspect of the question of speed with which privatization can be accomplished is discussed in the chapter on 'Insiders and the State.'

[6] The results of our research have been published, with John S. Earle and other collaborators, in two volumes of CEU Privatization Reports and a volume of papers by East European researchers (see Frydman, Rapaczynski and Earle, 1993a and b, and Earle, Frydman and Rapaczynski, 1993a).

paper, entitled 'Insiders and the State,' originally published in *Economics of Transition*, and reproduced as the fifth chapter in this volume.

The choice of privatization policies and their outcomes is to a large extent influenced by the balance of political strength between enterprise insiders (workers and management), on the one hand, and outside investors and the state, on the other. Moreover, the relative political position of these players is, in turn, partly a function of the previous reform efforts during the communist period. This issue had occupied us already in the paper on the 'Needed Mechanism of Corporate Governance and Finance in Eastern Europe,' where we explained how different historical conditions resulted in a dominant role of different interests in different countries: managers in Hungary, labor in Poland, and the state in the Czech Republic. In 'Insiders and the State' we examined the influence of these initial arrangements on the process of adoption and the outcomes of various privatization programs, and we argued that the dominance of insiders may create serious corporate governance problems and lead to increasing politicization of future economic decision making. In this paper, we also turned our attention for the first time to the special problems of so-called 'small privatization,' i.e. the transformation of the retail trade and service sectors.[7]

The sixth and last chapter brings together many strands of our previous work and sets a new research agenda. This final chapter was written especially for this volume in collaboration with John S. Earle. The crucial new concept introduced in the last chapter is that of the 'private property regime.' This concept refers to the social and economic order defining a set of expectations that individuals may have with respect to their ability to dispose of the assets recognized as 'theirs' by the legal system. As such, the concept is much broader than that of corporate governance upon which we had previous focused, and includes the political and legal determinants of economic behavior, as well as the implications of macroeconomic policies on the establishment and maintenance of property rights. Indeed, we argue that a private property regime has its material basis as well, rooted in the nature of the capital stock of a given economy, which poses very special problems for the establishment of such a regime in Eastern Europe.

In contrast to the usual emphasis on the creation of legal rules and a stable political system providing a framework for private economic

---

[7] The reflections begun here matured in a separate study, done under the joint auspices of the CEU and the World Bank, on small privatization in Poland, Hungary, and the Czech Republic (Frydman, Rapaczynski et al., 1994), which in turn served as a basis for our participation in designing an appropriate small privatization program in Russia.

activity, we argue that the nature of the private property regime relies primarily on a set of self-enforcing, decentralized arrangements, and that laws and regulations are at most capable of enforcing marginal infractions in an already functioning system of private property. In this context, we analyze a number of situations, in which the attempts to establish by design the foundations of property rights in the absence of an already existing private property regime lead to reversals and paradoxical results.

As part of our analysis of the private property regime, we pay particular attention to the tenuous balance between private economic activities and the state. In this connection, we propose a somewhat more developed political theory of privatization as a reallocation of resources leading to a new configuration of political forces. Within this framework, privatization does not necessarily lead to a lessening of political interference in economic decisions, and we provide a number of suggestions as to how such politicization may be mitigated.

Given the obsolete state of the capital stock in Eastern Europe and a hypertrophy of certain parts of the economy (heavy industry), we have come to view privatization as not simply a restructuring of the existing institutions, but as a far-reaching reallocation of resources across different sectors of the economy, and a concomitant shrinkage of the overgrown sectors. This 'creatively destructive' function of privatization gives rise to particularly acute political problems in the period of transition and poses special dangers of a reintroduction of state power into the economic domain. Thus, the political chances of a successful transition in different countries of Eastern Europe may depend on the extent to which such reallocations have to take place. Here, again, the design elements of transition policies become important, and we therefore end by examining the various available paths of development, with a view to determining their political sustainability.

1 Markets and Institutions in Large-Scale Privatization: An Approach to Economic and Social Transformation in Eastern Europe*

We attempt to provide here a systematic approach to the problem of privatization in the context of East European economies. The approach we adopt will be 'systematic' in the sense of providing a theory of what privatization is supposed to accomplish and supplying the means of evaluating the relative advantages and disadvantages of each privatization strategy. While the case of Poland will serve as the focal point of our discussions, the analysis is intended to have more general significance, applicable to the region as a whole.

* This chapter is a slightly revised version of a paper which appeared under the same title in Corbo, Coricelli, and Bossak (1991). The first version of our privatization proposal, suggesting an institutional setting analyzed here, appeared under the title 'Privatization in Poland: A New Proposal' in June, 1990. A revision of that article has been published in Polish in *Res publica* in September, 1990, under the title 'Sprywatyzować Prywatyzację: Nowa Propozycja Przemian Własnościowych w Polsce' ('On Privatizing Privatization: A New Proposal of Ownership Transformation in Poland').

We are grateful to Ned Phelps for his comments and interest in the ideas presented here from the very beginning of this project. We thank Professor Bronisław Geremek, Minister Jacek Kuroń, Drs. Marcin Król and Aleksander Smolar, Messrs. Lejb Fogelman, Damian Kalbarczyk, and Henryk Wujec for their early encouraging reactions. We also thank the following persons for discussions and comments: Professors Bruce Ackerman, William Baumol, Bernard S. Black, John C. Coffee, Marek Dąbrowski, Owen Fiss, Harvey J. Goldschmid, Jeffrey Gordon, Irena Grosfeld, Stanislaw Gomułka, Henry Hansmann, Cezary Józefiak, Barbara Katz, Alan Klevorick, Grzegorz Kołodko, Michael Montias, Joel Owen, Mark J. Roe, Susan Rose-Ackerman, Roberta Romano, Jacek Rostowski, Jeffrey Sachs, Alan Schwartz, Ferdinando Targetti, William Vickrey, Stanisław Wellisz, Charles Wilson, and Messrs. Andrew Berg, Ian Hume, Grzegorz Jędrzejczak, Stefan Kawalec, and Jacek Kwaśniewski.

Why privatize?

The first thing to understand about the privatization process in Eastern Europe is that, in contrast to other countries, privatization, in the environment of the transitional economies, is not a simple transfer of ownership from the state to private individuals. It is rather a process by which the very institution of property, in the sense in which lawyers and economists employ the term, is reintroduced into East European societies.

At the core of every socioeconomic order is the problem of the efficient use of socially available resources. Whenever the use of these resources is not restricted, there arises the so-called 'problem of the commons.' Consider the case of a primitive society in which no one has exclusive rights to land and every member of the community is free to use it for his own purposes. In this society, every time a person invests his time and energy in cultivating the land, he bears all the costs of producing the new crop, but can only derive a small part of its benefits; conversely, whenever any person removes something from the commons, he derives all the benefits of what he removes, but bears only a fraction of the costs of producing it. In a regime of this kind, there is a systematic incentive to underproduce and overconsume, and the resources become depleted at a rate that may not be socially desirable.

There are two standard ways of dealing with the problem of the commons: regulation and the creation of property rights. In the first case, a communal decision is made concerning the use of the common resources, and this decision is then coercively enforced against those who attempt to free ride on the efforts of others. In the second case, resources are assigned to the exclusive use of individual agents, who, having to pay all the costs and deriving all the benefits from the use they choose to make of the resources assigned to them, have the appropriate incentive to choose those uses which yield the greatest net benefit. In the first case, the social use of resources is made on the basis of political decisions; in the second, it relies on individual interest maximization, in conjunction with the market as a resource allocation mechanism.

While all societies use political decisions to regulate certain aspects of the economy (in particular those in which market mechanisms are vitiated by persistent free riding and externalities), the socialist systems of Eastern Europe made practically all decisions concerning production[1] through the political system, with factory personnel playing the role of state functionaries. What the name 'command economy' conveys is precisely this eschewing of market mechanisms, but also the fact that all property-related arrangements in general have been replaced by an administrative system in which the state preferred to control the behavior of each agent directly, rather than relying on his own pursuit of self interest. In this sense, the socialist economies of Eastern Europe did not have *any* property system (including state and not just private property) governing their productive activities. It is not surprising, therefore, that in all East European countries it is nearly impossible to answer the simple question of who owns what in the state enterprises: the legal determination of ownership was simply irrelevant under the old system, which relied instead on directly prescribing the conduct of factory officials.

The need to reintroduce the very institution of property in the productive resources of East European societies means that the structural reform of the economies of these countries cannot proceed primarily on a macroeconomic level. This realization, given the recent reform efforts in a number of East European countries, is of great importance.

The case of Poland is quite instructive. The first stage of the economic reform there, known as the 'Balcerowicz Plan,' consisted in a series of macroeconomic measures – such as credit restrictions, wage restraints, and reduction of subsidies – designed to arrest inflationary pressures in the economy. The effects of this series of moves were in part quite predictable: prices at first shot upwards, then inflation slowed down quite dramatically and prices remained relatively stable (although not as much as had been hoped). Among other expected effects was a fall in production and a rise in unemployment. Both of these did indeed happen, though to an extent differently from what had been expected and perhaps for reasons that had not been foreseen.

The authors of the Balcerowicz Plan also expected, however, that the macroeconomic measures undertaken since January 1990 would result not only in the elimination of the strong inflationary pressures evident at the end of 1989, but also in the creation of the basic conditions of a market economy. It was expected that the lifting of subsidies, together with other monetary measures, would result in a readjustment of prices. By bringing out a more realistic assessment of costs and revenues of each particular enterprise, this in turn was

---

[1] Agricultural production in Poland was the most significant exception.

supposed to provide proper incentives for the management and put state enterprises on a sound footing. Privatization would merely complete the process begun by the macroeconomic reform: when the real viability of individual enterprises was going to be determined by the market, the enterprises could then be valued and gradually sold off through a variety of well-known techniques.

It is a relatively safe proposition that, without some fairly dramatic steps on the microeconomic level, the hopes for a structural adjustment of the Polish economy through the macroeconomic stabilization program could not be fulfilled. The reasons for this are related precisely to the absence of an appropriate legal and organizational structure at the enterprise level.

The structure of the Polish enterprises, like those of the other countries in the region, is still largely a function of the old regime, and the behavior of their managers is determined by the conditions in which they operate. Polish enterprises are not even structured as joint-stock companies. They are governed by state-appointed bureaucrats – so-called *nomenklatura* – who used to respond to other bureaucrats higher up in the mammoth hierarchy of the planned economy. This hierarchy has been by and large dismantled and the enterprises were said to go it alone. But in the absence of any new external control over management, the *nomenklatura*, instead of maximizing the enterprises' returns, are scrambling to find the best deal for themselves. Some are trying to convert state enterprises into their own fiefdoms, which could then enter into joint ventures with foreign participants, whereby the management would get a hefty payoff and the foreigners would get the enterprise for a song. Others are attempting a home-grown 'privatiz-ation' by which, without any capital input or another legitimation, they might end up as owners of the formerly state companies. But most of them, by now deprived of their traditional bureaucratic support, are trying to maintain themselves by forging a new alliance with their workers, to whom the reform has given an inordinate amount of power at the enterprise level. The managers are thus willing to decapitalize their firms and neglect all measures that may require sacrifices from the work force, while maintaining the highest possible levels of salaries and employment.

In this situation, the freeing of prices and the emergence of markets for the products manufactured by state enterprises are by themselves not sufficient to discipline the managers' behavior. Without the pressure of shareholders, who can cashier the management that does not produce high enough rates of return on the firm's investments, the only remaining sanction provided by the product market is bankruptcy. Before that happens, however, a state enterprise can continue for a long time in its traditional inefficient ways by using up the available sources of credit, cutting back on investment, or at best coasting along on the borders of profitability. And when a bankruptcy does happen, there is no mechanism of restructuring available to put things aright. Thus, the reliance on the product market, with its threat of bankruptcy as a disciplining mechanism, is potentially very dangerous. To be sure, there are some enterprises that should simply be closed down. But a large number of bankruptcies might be caused by inefficient management of potentially viable enterprises, and many resources might be wasted, without there being any clear way of moving out of the depression.

The only way of remedying the crippling inefficiency of post-socialist state enterprises is to move as fast as possible toward a genuine property regime. An immediate move, of a limited scope but considerable practical importance, is to introduce a new legal system of genuine *state* property, even before a transfer of ownership from the state to private hands can take place. This process of 'corporatization' or, as it is sometimes called, 'commercialization,' would consist of an immediate transformation of all state enterprises into joint-stock companies (with the state treasury being the sole shareholder) and the appointment of outside directors. While the establishment of a genuine form of state property, especially in a society without a significant private sector that could shape the behavior of state-appointed directors, should not be expected to result in a far-reaching improvement in the functioning of the enterprises, it could provide a remedy for the worst cases of mismanagement and abuse now common in the Polish economy.[2]

But nothing will remove the need for speedy privatization. Privatization should not be seen as just the last stage in the process of transition from a centrally planned economy to capitalism, a stage at which final touches are applied to an already functioning system. On the contrary, insofar as privatization consists in a transfer of control into the hands of private shareholders, who, in a mutually competitive environment, are trying to maximize the returns on their investments, it is an indispensible condition of an efficient control of management performance. This control over management is, in turn, the essence of a genuine restructuring process, i.e. a process of transition from a command economy to a true market order in which not only the value

---

[2] Professor Jeffrey Sachs has been among the main advocates of immediate 'corporatization.'

of particular products, but also that of the enterprises producing them, is determined by the relation of supply and demand. Unless this process is completed, the reform efforts in Poland and the other East European countries will probably fail, and the economic situation is likely to deteriorate even further.

The general principles of privatization

There are four main requirements that must be satisfied by any privatization plan that has a chance to work.

1. *Privatization must be accomplished quickly.* This should be evident from what was said already. If privatization, as we have argued, is the core of the process in which the state enterprises become restructured, the economic reform in Eastern Europe cannot proceed without a radical ownership transformation.

2. *Privatization must be socially acceptable.* The East European industry, antiquated and inefficient as it is, has been built at the price of enormous sacrifices by the general population over the last forty-five years. The industrialization program of the 1950s has been pursued at the cost of drastic cuts in consumption, and although the austerity was somewhat relaxed in later years, the rise in standards of living was constantly retarded by the policy of investment in heavy industrial infrastructure. If this industry is now sold at prices which are seen as very low, popular opinion might turn against the privatization program as a whole.

The people of Eastern Europe also have a somewhat ambivalent attitude toward privatization and market economy as a whole. On the one hand, nearly everyone understands that the move in the direction of capitalism is necessary and can be expected to yield, in the long run, significant improvements in standards of living. On the other hand, it is also clear that, in the short run, the move toward a market economy means further sacrifices, involving potentially high rates of unemployment with which the people of Eastern Europe are not familiar.

Finally, while a certain amount of wealth differentiation based on risk taking and superior business acumen is usually socially acceptable, an extremely unequal distribution of wealth, which creates a permanent division between the haves and have-nots, is inherently destabilizing. This might be especially dangerous in Eastern Europe, where people have been accustomed to a certain amount of equality and where the political climate is not very stable. Great attention must therefore be paid to choosing a strategy of privatization that will not exacerbate the anxieties of the population, but rather give it some tangible stakes in the success of the undertaking.

3. *Privatization must assure effective control over the management of privatized enterprises.* The move away from bureaucratic control over the economy cannot mean a simple removal of all control mechanisms with respect to the functioning of the enterprises. This important point does not appear to be widely understood and was apparently responsible for the belief that the removal of price controls and the emergence of markets would by themselves usher in a significantly more efficient system of production at the enterprise level. In fact, however, a system of decision making in a complex modern economy, involving vast amounts of information necessary for even the most trivial decisions and a complicated system for allocating responsibility, requires a whole panoply of institutions that properly structure the incentives of the actors involved and reduce the complexity of real-world situations to a manageable number of relatively simple rules. In other words, when the control mechanisms of the command economy are eliminated, something else must be put in their place that will play the same role as the historically evolved, and often taken for granted, control institutions of a Western market economy.

Prime among these institutions is a system that provides incentives for managers of enterprises to maximize the interests of the shareholders which, in a properly competitive environment, correspond to the interests of the consumers. In the developed capitalist societies, this task is accomplished, with varying degrees of effectiveness, through a variety of institutions, such as takeover mechanisms (with the whole legal, financial, and organizational infrastructure of the stock market which they require), markets for managerial talent, or an elaborate banking system that supervises company management in countries such as Germany and Japan. Without something that fulfills a similar role in the East European economies, privatization might result in an extreme fragmentation of holdings, and replace the stifling system of bureaucratic control with a system that leaves managers without any effective external supervision. This in turn would undermine the whole meaning of privatization, which, as we have argued, involves not just a simple change of ownership, but also a radical restructuring that transforms the incentive system of the economic agents at the enterprise level.

4. *Privatization must assure access to foreign capital and expertise.* Nearly everyone understands that the capital-starved and heavily

indebted East European economies badly need an infusion of Western funds in order to modernize their aging industrial infrastructure, introduce new technologies, etc. It is equally clear that Eastern Europe also needs Western know-how and management expertise, without which it will not be able to use properly whatever Western financial aid is made available and to bring its production up to the standards of the developed world. What is less often realized, however, is that Western expertise is most needed in the effort to construct the general infrastructure of a modern market economy, and particularly the already mentioned control institutions necessary for the supervision of the management at the enterprise level. Moreover, in order to be effective, the entry of foreign capital and expertise into Eastern Europe cannot take place through a provision of advisory and consulting services. The only way in which Western financial institutions can play a truly creative role in the region is to have their entry based on sound business principles, so that they stand to gain or lose by their activities. This in turn means that privatization policies must create conditions that make entry attractive from a business point of view and that the entry must take place in a properly competitive environment.

While serious Western participation in the construction of the infrastructure of the market economy in Eastern Europe is a condition of a successful move away from the bureaucratic command systems, the entry of foreign capital also gives rise to special political problems and raises additional questions of legitimation. The people of Eastern Europe very much want to catch up with the Western world and they expect to be helped in their efforts to do so. At the same time, however, they are afraid that their societies will come to be dominated by foreign capital and that their economic and political interests will be jeopardized in the process. In order to succeed, therefore, a privatization plan for Eastern Europe must, on the one hand, provide a clear avenue for the entry of foreign capital and expertise, but, on the other hand, must place this entry in a setting that makes it acceptable from the point of view of the East Europeans' own perception of their interests.

The problem of valuation

It is clear that privatization requires a valuation of the enterprise about to be privatized. It might be possible, of course, for the state to convey the title of a company to some private party without engaging in an assessment of its value, but such a naked transfer, quite apart from the legitimacy problems that might arise, would not, by itself, accomplish anything of economic significance. The purpose of privatization, as we have argued, is not to transfer title, but to initiate a restructuring of enterprises and a rationalization of the East European economies. In order for this to take place, someone *must* evaluate the potential of each enterprise to be privatized, i.e. assess its relative value as compared with other possible investment opportunities. Only in this way is it possible to decide where best to invest the limited resources available for the upgrading of the economy.

Given the absence of a developed market economy in the environment of Eastern Europe, there are, however, seemingly insuperable obstacles to traditional forms of enterprise valuation.

Traditional valuation methods used in the developed market economies essentially aim at an 'objective,' i.e. intersubjectively recognized, assessment of an enterprise. In the case of a publicly traded company, the intersubjective element is self-evident, since it is equal to the price obtainable on the market at any given point, although even then individual valuations may differ from the market price.[3] In the case of a privately held company or a fully state-owned company, where the market price is not available, different individuals may have different subjective assessments of the company's value, and the subjective element cannot be separated from the valuation process. In the general context of a market economy, however, it is possible to come up with some approximation of the price that would be arrived at by the market itself, since the agent doing the valuation may base his estimates on a number of analogies to the methods commonly used by investors in the market under similar conditions, such as relying on price–earnings ratios, the firm's performance over the last few years, the average prices of similar enterprises on the market, etc.

The very idea of an objective valuation does not make much sense, however, under the conditions in Eastern Europe, since the absence of markets makes it impossible to establish any reliable benchmarks against which the value of the enterprises could be measured. Data from the past, when the enterprises functioned within the regime of a command economy, tell us nearly nothing about a firm's present value.

---

[3] One of the reasons for this difference may be due to a premium that an investor may be prepared to pay for a certain block of shares that would give him control of the company. Another may be due to an individual assessment of the company's future that differs from the one implied in the market price.

The peculiarly East European institution of 'interfirm credit,' i.e. a chain of mutual indebtedness among the companies along the production process, introduces a further element of uncertainty into the already clouded company books: around 40 percent of the book value of some of the companies being prepared for privatization in Poland is in the form of outstanding liabilities from other enterprises, much of it of very long standing. Without evaluating the soundness of all of the enterprises involved, it is thus impossible to predict what portion of these funds will ever be recovered. The absence of capital markets makes it impossible to reason by analogy with other enterprises of the same type. Given no reliable track record, it is impossible to make any informed guesses about how a given firm would do in the conditions of a free market economy. Moreover, the economic situation in Poland changes all the time, and it is impossible to predict the state of the whole economy or even of its particular segments a few months ahead. The long-term interest rate, some assumptions about which are necessary for a calculation of the present value of future streams of income, is still simply set by the state, and its future course, if only for the next few months, is largely unknown, even though relatively small variations in the interest rate may radically affect the estimated value of an enterprise.[4]

All of these factors put together mean that the objective elements of valuation are, in the conditions of Eastern Europe, *de minimis*, and the subjective elements, which are present in any valuation process, must dominate the assessments of the companies during the transition to capitalism. First, given the absence of reliable benchmarks for an objective assessment, the agents who perform the valuation must make more or less arbitrary guesses about such things as the real value of fixed assets, the appropriate price–earnings ratio, or the interest rate for the next few years, and these guesses will, of course, differ from person to person. Second, when the market does not convey certain types of information through the pricing system, the informational differentials among individuals will increase dramatically. Thus, for example, someone involved in shoe manufacturing will have information about the conditions of the shoe industry, which would normally be conveyed

---

[4] In order to show the difficulties and the arbitrariness of valuation of East European enterprises, Appendix I discusses the case of an enterprise valued by a prestigious British accounting firm for the Polish government in connection with the privatization program there.

to the world at large through the price system, but which remains private in the absence of a market economy. Third, when assets are largely illiquid (because there is no established market), certain assets, quite apart from any informational disparities among agents, will have very different values to different people. A beer producer, for example, might put a high price on a ton of yeast, but the same yeast will be useless to a shoemaker, who, if he cannot readily resell the yeast to someone who needs it, will not offer any price for it. Fourth, by the very fact that an agent has certain plans with respect to some assets for which he is bidding, he is in possession of some information which other people, such as accountants or outside consultants, who would not be involved in the exploitation of the assets in question, are lacking, and again, the informational disparity is compounded by the absence of a historical knowledge concerning the most predictable uses of even the most standard resources. Finally, every valuation process contains some elements of skill or 'hunch' or 'tacit knowledge,' which are not quite arbitrary (since it may be shown that some people, using their 'hunches,' do consistently better than others), but which cannot be explained in objective terms, understandable to a third party. Thus, for example, a good venture capitalist does not base his assessment of a given firm's prospects exclusively on the value of its assets, price–earnings ratios etc.; he attaches the greatest importance to his 'feel' of the managerial skills of the people involved, which, while intangible and often impossible to explain, may be decisive for the venture's success.

The predominance of the subjective aspects of valuation poses significant problems for a privatization program, primarily because even to the extent that valuation is not arbitrary, it is impossible to explain or legitimize it in objective terms. As a consequence, any help or advice that might be gained from even the most reputable consulting or accounting firms is likely to be worthless, since advisers of this kind must explain their conclusions to their principals, and this task is, under the circumstances, simply impossible. This in turn means that a privatization model that has a chance to work must avoid the situation in which the duty of valuation rests on the state (which, in order to legitimize its decisions, must use outside consultants and try to arrive at an 'objective' valuation). The only way to avoid this is *to place the burden of valuation on those parties who, like an ordinary investor in a market economy, will bear the consequences of their own decisions, since only the parties in this position can rely on their subjective estimates, without having to explain their reasons to anyone else.*

But even if the burden of valuation is placed on the party that will bear the consequences of its decisions (deriving extra gains from having arrived at a more precise valuation than other parties and losing by making errors greater than the others), the remaining high degree of uncertainty may make agents reluctant to place their assets at risk on the basis of what must be at best very imprecise guesswork. If, for example, an investor must decide whether to purchase some shares of Nowa Huta (a somewhat antiquated steel mill in Poland) or a piece of real estate in Switzerland, the uncertainty attendant on making any assessments of the value of Nowa Huta will make the investor choose the safer investment in Switzerland, unless the price of Nowa Huta is discounted to such an extent as to make it competitive. But then the price may be perceived as too low and serious problems of ligitimation may arise. To deal with this problem the agents must be put in a position in which either their risk or the uncertainty of their judgments is reduced. A way to accomplish both of these objectives is *to reduce the universe of competing opportunities relative to which the agent must evaluate the enterprise in question.* Thus, in the example just given, if the agent has no choice but to invest some of his assets in one of the privatized enterprises in Poland, his valuation problem is reduced to an assessment of the value of Nowa Huta relative to other Polish enterprises, and no longer to all other possible investment opportunities. Not only is the problem of the size of the discount due to uncertainty lessened in this way, but the uncertainty itself may be reduced as well. The reason for this is that large areas of uncertainty, which make the valuation of Polish enterprises so difficult, pertain to all of these enterprises in the same way and may therefore be ignored for the purposes of internal comparisons. It is precisely this reduction of the universe of competing investment opportunities that is accomplished through the device of issuing special privatization vouchers. Making the agents bid for the privatized companies in a specially restricted form of currency (vouchers), which cannot be used for any other purpose, rather than in money, which is a universal medium of payment, eliminates all the other options which compound the already serious valuation problems.

The sale model

The imperative of a speedy privatization of most of East European industry, together with the already discussed problems of valuation, mean that privatization in Eastern Europe cannot follow the models elaborated in recent years in such countries as Great Britain or France. In these highly developed West European countries, privatization had an entirely different significance from the process to be embarked upon in Poland: there, the task was not a restructuring of the national economy, but merely a sale of a few state-owned enterprises, functioning in a fundamentally market environment dominated by private property. Already prior to their privatization, state enterprises in, say, Great Britain had to operate in competition with other private companies and their managerial system (even if often less efficient than that of their private analogs) was basically a product of the surrounding capitalist business culture. If some of these state enterprises were in the red, it was relatively easy to provide a measure of subsidies and reform, so as to bring them, within a relatively short period of time, to profitability and to put them up for sale. The sale itself was also rather easy: in a full market economy, in which most of the industry is in private hands, in which there exists a developed stock market, and in which all enterprises use modern accounting methods, the sale of a state enterprise does not differ very much from the process by which a private closely held corporation 'goes public' by issuing shares to investors at large. It is enough for the state to hire the services of an investment firm (or a consortium of such firms), which underwrites the issue and sells the shares to the public.

This simple description of privatization in the West is enough to show that it cannot serve as a model for privatization in Eastern Europe, where capital markets do not yet exist and the very structure of market economy is to be introduced precisely through the process of privatization. First, the very idea that most enterprises can continue to be owned by the state until they are profitable, in order to be sold off afterwards, is not to be taken seriously: the state has been unable to run these enterprises efficiently for forty-five years and it is not likely to change now, even if it is no longer communist. Indeed, if the state had been at all able to take care of the enterprises it owns, there would be no need to privatize them. Second, even if we abstract from this problem, we immediately come up against the already discussed difficulties of valuation which make the ordinary sale through a public offering (with or without an underwriter) impractical, insofar as no objectively acceptable price can be put on the shares of the enterprises to be privatized. And third, if we ignore this problem as well, valuation, even when the existence of a market economy makes such an undertaking meaningful, is a costly and time-consuming proposition. The process of valuing over 6,000 state enterprises in Poland (or even the 500 or so of the biggest firms) would take decades and make the whole exercise completely futile.[5]

But, even if one were to assume all these problems away (by proposing, for example, to auction off all the state enterprises without any preliminary valuation and hoping that the buyers would be able to make some decisions on the basis of the scarce information available), there still remains one more crucial argument against large-scale privatizations through public sales, especially in those countries in which a stabilization program eliminated the accumulated 'overhang' of local currency. Taking Poland as an example, we have calculated that, under the very optimistic assumption that people are prepared to spend 20–30 percent of all their savings to buy shares in the privatized enterprises, the amount of money available for the purchase of the state companies would equal between 2.4 and 3.6 percent of their book value. While this last number says relatively little about the 'true' value of the state enterprises, the discrepancy is staggering enough to make clear that, if purchases by foreigners are left aside for the moment, privatization through so-called sales would in fact be a form of give-away, which would increase the existing inequalities by a factor of several scores. And given the fact that the public does not perceive the existing wealth inequalities in Poland as a legitimate reward for thrift or industriousness, but as spoils distributed to its loyalists by the old regime, the giveaway would cause tremendous political problems for the new authorities.[6] (If, on the other hand, the government were to try to avoid the accusation of giving away the national wealth to the old *'nomenklatura'* and set the prices too high, it would then run the risk of not finding enough buyers, which might, in turn, have the harmful effect of lowering the general level of confidence in the Polish economy.)

For these and similar reasons, it is just about clear to most people, at least in Poland, that large-scale privatization cannot be accomplished through sales. Nevertheless, the state is still trying to sell at least a part of the state enterprises through one or another form of a public offering, with a hope that a significant portion of the shares might be sold to a foreign investor who would become an active participant in the restructuring efforts.

---

[5] A look at the number of enterprises reprivatized in Britain during the ten years of the Thatcher administration gives one an idea of how time consuming is the process of valuation and sale.

[6] It should also be considered whether it is really a good policy to suck out all the capital reserves still kept by the people in Poland in order to feed the state treasury, instead of utilizing them for other badly needed investments.

We shall not return here to the already discussed technical difficulties related to valuing the enterprises to be sold through a public offering of the British kind. But there is still a number of political issues that have to be considered. Let us note the following coincidence. According to the Polish privatization law, a considerable portion (up to 20 percent) of the shares of state enterprises will be sold to employees at discount prices. The existing management is also frequently interested in buying a large block of shares that would allow it (perhaps in coalition with the workers) to maintain control. Both of these groups (which have key access to information and are often in a position to keep it secret) are therefore interested in having the enterprises valued as low as possible, since they would then strike the best deal for themselves. The Ministry for Ownership Transformations is also interested in not setting the price too high, since otherwise the enterprise might not sell and this, after months of preparation and hundreds of thousands of dollars spent in the process, would be regarded as a proof of the Ministry's inefficiency. The end result might, therefore, be that, if a foreign buyer is not found for a significant block of shares, a substantial portion of the ownership of the privatized enterprises will end up in the hands of an alliance of workers and the old *'nomen-klatura,'* with the rest being held by small shareholders (if they are found) who would be too insignificant to interfere. All in all, therefore, the situation might not be very much different from the present one, in which there is no significant outside control over the enterprises.

The preservation of the status quo could be avoided, of course, if a foreign investor were to be found for a significant block of the shares of each privatized enterprise. That is why bringing in foreign capital would have to be an integral part of any program of selling selected state enterprises for cash. But it is by no means obvious that foreign capital is willing to enter Poland under the conditions that are offered. If a foreign investor can buy no more than 10 percent of an enterprise (and this is the portion he is allowed to hold without special dispensation under the Privatization Act), 20 percent of which is controlled by the employees, and a significant portion of the rest by the *nomenklatura* management, the enterprise does not seem to be a promising investment. In order to make it more attractive to the foreign investor, he must be given an opportunity to buy a larger block of shares (that would assure him of some influence) at a price that would be low enough to outweigh the uncertainty involved.

While the entry of foreign capital is of crucial importance for the restructuring process in Eastern Europe, it is not clear that this way of bringing it in is the most advantageous one. First, the capital brought in from abroad in this manner does not come in the form of a productive investment, but is fed into the state treasury. Not only is this likely not to be the best use of the money, but also, given the very high external debt of most East European states, large inflows of the proceeds from privatization might result in an intensified pressure for an increase in debt repayment (which would make the money flow right back out of the country). Second, the fundamental rule of trading is not to sell before the prices go up. In view of the general political and economic situation in Eastern Europe, the price of the privatized enterprises is likely to be very low. After several years, if the general situation improves and the enterprises are restructured, the same companies may be worth several times more. If the state of the East European economies cannot be improved without selling a very substantial portion of the existing assets to foreigners, perhaps the price is worth paying. But if there are other ways of utilizing foreign expertise, without mortgaging the country, the restructuring of the East European economies should bear fruit for the people of the region.

Finally, let us assume that in spite of all the difficulties it will be possible to privatize a portion of state-owned enterprises through traditional forms of sale. Since only the most profitable enterprises are likely to find buyers, the companies selected for the British-style privatizations will be the few most attractive plums of the East European economies. What, however, will happen to the rest (and with them, to the economy as a whole)?

Free distribution models

The inviability of the sales model of privatization means that the restructuring of the East European economies must proceed through more unconventional means. An important element of this strategy is rapid privatization through a program of free distribution of the shares of the state-owned companies. There are basically three variables along which free distribution plans can be analyzed. The first concerns the *beneficiaries* of the free distribution: to whom is the ownership given away? The second variable concerns the *mode of distribution*: the shares can be distributed directly, or through some intermediaries, or the beneficiaries may receive some form of currency (vouchers) with which they can choose which shares to acquire. (The mode of distribution is decisive with respect to the question of whether the beneficiaries will have some say over which shares they will receive.) The third variable concerns the *role of the beneficiaries in the governance of the privatized companies*: are the beneficiaries to become active or passive owners, and if they are to be passive, who will monitor and control the management on their behalf?

Labor ownership

The most deeply flawed free distribution proposals envisage a giveaway or heavily subsidized sale of the shares of state-owned enterprises to the workers employed in them. From the point of view of social justice, free or subsidized distribution to workers involves fundamental inequities, since some workers, who happen to be employed in the most valuable factories, will receive an undeserved windfall, while many other citizens, including those employed in state administration or the private sector (potentially the most dynamic and entrepreneurial segment of the population) will be left with nothing. Moreover, quite apart from equitable and distributive considerations, the proposal to give to the workers the ownership of enterprises in which they work would constitute a step in a radically wrong direction from the economic point of view. The interest of the workers, who care, above all, about their employment and remuneration, is not at all parallel with the interest of the public (which wants the best product at the lowest possible price) or with the long-term requirements of the economy as a while (which requires long-term investment and productivity growth). Moreover, if the individual workers were to be in some ways restricted in their ability to sell their shares, the plan might impede a transfer of control to an outsider whose input could discipline management behavior. Effective supervision would have to come from the workers themselves, and there is very little evidence that such supervision, especially in an economy in which worker-owned firms do not compete with firms organized along more capitalist lines, can produce desired results. In other words, like some of the flawed sales plans, a program of free distribution to workers threatens to leave things much as they are and to impede the economic restructuring efforts. (This is not to say, of course, that the interests of the workers are not very important or that they should not be protected by some institutional arrangements. The appropriate institutional protection of the workers' interests, however, should come in the form of trade unions and governmental regulation of employment conditions, rather than worker ownership.)

Despite the dangers involved in worker giveaways, many East European countries face considerable political pressure to move in this direction. In Poland, this pressure had resulted, despite the initial resistance of the government, in a series of provisions in the privatization law that allow the workers to buy up to 20 percent of the shares of the companies in which they are employed at seriously discounted prices. Thus, any privatization program in Poland will probably have to be reconciled with a significant element of worker participation. If possible, however, the potential damage resulting from this giveaway should be contained in some way. One method would be to give the workers a choice between their right to acquire the shares of their companies through this avenue and benefiting from any other forms of free distribution to which they may be entitled (*qua* citizens, for example), rather than allowing them to avail themselves of both opportunities. Another method of containing damage from worker giveaways is to restrict the shares acquired in this way to beneficial ownership, without the right to appoint directors or otherwise actively participate in the governance of the company.[7]

Free distribution to the general public

While a giveaway of shares to workers presents both justice and efficiency problems, a program of free distribution to the citizenry at large offers the promise of an equitable and potentially efficient solution to the problem of speedy privatization. The main advantages of a free distribution program are twofold: first, it reduces the problems of valuation and, second, it eliminates the problems related to the shortage of domestic capital or the reluctance of foreign investors to enter.

It would be a mistake to say that a giveaway program eliminates the valuation problems entirely. To be sure, it might be possible to execute a free transfer ownership to some party, without worrying about valuation at all. But, as we have stressed already, if privatization is to result in restructuring, and not just an ownership transfer, someone will have to value the enterprise involved in order to make decisions concerning the best way in which each company could be restructured. Similarly, the choice of who should be entitled to exercise the control powers associated with ownership (and not just enjoy its benefits) requires some method of discovering the party best able to supervise

---

[7] [Our views of the pros and cons of limited worker ownership have evolved significantly since this early position. See Chapter 2 in this volume.]

the restructuring process, and the best (indeed, probably the only) way of determining this is to find the party who puts the greatest *value* on the enterprises in question. But a free distribution program potentially reduces the valuation problems, because at least some of the most troublesome aspects of valuation are eliminated. The prime among them is the need to express the value of the privatized companies in monetary terms – which requires establishing their value relative to all other investment opportunities, such as real estate in Switzerland or paper mills in Sweden. Instead, the allocation problems may be dealt with using valuation in some form of restricted currency, such as vouchers that can be used only for the purchase of the shares of the privatized companies – thus narrowing the universe of opportunities to the set of the companies to be privatized.

Even more obviously, free distribution programs eliminate the problem of capital shortage: regardless of whether the shares of the privatized companies are distributed directly to the beneficiaries or whether the beneficiaries are given vouchers with which to 'buy' them (either at a preset price or at an auction), there is no danger of the state being unable to 'sell.'

Free distribution to the public at large also solves most of the legitimacy problems associated with selective giveaways and the sales model. Selective giveaways are, by their very nature, suspect: the question why someone is more deserving than others is one to which, in this context, there can be no satisfactory (sufficiently objective) answer. Similarly, given the valuation problems, sales in the East European context inherently raise the question of whether a given asset is sold at a price that corresponds to its 'real' value (whatever that means) and give rise to accusations of covert selective giveaways. If, on the other hand, the privatization program distributes state-owned assets in some demonstrably equal manner, the giveaway needs no special justifica- tions. This is especially true in the East European context, in which it makes eminent sense to say that the whole society has paid a very heavy price for the construction of the national industry in the last forty-five years.

The main problem with free distribution to the public at large is to ensure that the new owners, either directly or through some represen- tatives, exercise sufficient control over the management of the privatized enterprises. Otherwise no change in the status quo can be accomplished and the industry will not be restructured. It is for this reason that some free distribution schemes can be immediately eliminated from the realm of acceptable possibilities. Suppose, for example, that the state wants to distribute the shares of the privatized enterprises directly to the population at large. Clearly, without determining the relative value of each company with respect to every other company to be privatized, any attempt to give different portfolios of shares to different people must raise serious problems of equity, since there is no way of ensuring that one portfolio is worth as much as another. A direct distribution of shares to the population at large must therefore imply that every person receives exactly the same portfolio. But this means that each person must receive the same number of shares (say, one) of each company to be privatized. This, in turn, means that, in a country like Poland, each company must issue at least 35 million shares and end up with 35 million shareholders. The coordination problems facing the shareholders in their efforts to supervise the management would then be so staggering that no supervision would be possible, and the management would be subject to no external control.

Problems of this kind are endemic to many other free distribution schemes. Suppose that, given the difficulties just described, the state decides not to distribute the shares directly to the population, but rather to issue special vouchers that are distributed in equal numbers to all citizens who can then use them to 'purchase' (either at a preset price or through an auction of some kind) the shares of the privatized companies of their choice. Through such an indirect distribution, it is possible to avoid the extreme outcome of companies with 35 million shares, but still the voucher 'capital' of any individual purchaser is insufficient to allow him to acquire more than a small fraction of any one enterprise.[8] This means that the ownership of all the privatized companies will still be extremely fragmented and no effective shareholder control mechanisms will arise (at least for some time). It is this problem that needs to be solved if free distribution is to constitute the basis of a viable privatization program.

The problem of control

The core investor

One way to deal with the problem of control, proposed by some in connection with the privatization discussion in Poland, is to combine

---

[8] Appendix II discusses the problems involved in the attempts to combine the use of vouchers with ordinary sales and the question of whether privatization vouchers should have monetary denominations.

free distribution to the population with a sale of a significant block of shares (around 10 percent or more) to a 'core investor' who would assume an active role in the restructuring process and subsequent management supervision.

We have already discussed some of the difficulties related to the core investor idea in connection with our analysis of the sales model. The core investor must, for a number of reasons, be a foreigner: there are very few East Europeans who could afford to buy a significant block of shares in a large company, there are not many people in Eastern Europe with sufficient expertise to facilitate and supervise the introduction of modern production and management techniques, and only a foreign investor could facilitate contacts with potential foreign joint venture partners or an entry into foreign markets. Also, despite his holding a relatively small block of shares, the core investor will be the only significant investor in the company. He may thus be rather hard to dislodge in a system in which corporate raiders are not likely to appear for some time. This means, in turn, that, unless other shareholders have large enough stakes in the same enterprise to act as a restraining force, the core investor will be basically uncontrolled, and if he does not supervise properly or exploits the company in favor of other (foreign) entities in which he has a higher share of ownership, there will be no one in a position to do anything about it. But the most troublesome aspect of the core investor idea is that, as we have noted, it may be very difficult, for both political and economic reasons, to bring foreign investors into the Polish market, and a privatization plan that relies on finding a core investor for every company to be privatized does not offer a realistic chance of moving with enough speed to restructure the Polish economy.[9]

Financial intermediaries

The other, more promising, way of resolving the control problems associated with free distribution is to *separate ownership from control* and to vest the latter with special intermediary institutions. These inter-mediaries are usually envisaged as holding companies or mutual funds, which would be the legal owners of the shares of the privatized enterprise, although they may also hold these shares in some looser form of trust accounts on behalf of individual small investors. If the

---

[9] This does not mean that core investors would not be helpful for many companies. But the appropriate moment to bring one of them in is probably at a later stage in the process, when other important players are already present on the company boards and the price at which he enters is likely to be higher.

intermediaries are the legal owners of the shares of the privatized enterprises, the individuals hold, in turn, the shares of the intermediary institutions themselves and are therefore indirect beneficial owners of the assets held by the intermediaries. The intermediaries may then perform various services on behalf of the small investors, from pooling their resources for purposes of diversification, to making all kinds of investment decisions on their behalf, to, most importantly, exercising supervisory functions with respect to the management of the enterprises in which they are invested.

There are a number of privatization proposals involving financial intermediaries of one kind or another. We shall attempt to provide a systematic way of analysing their respective advantages and disadvantages.

Again, there are several variables along which a taxonomy of the intermediary institutions can be devised, and it will be helpful to begin by listing them separately before coming to the discussion of concrete proposals.

The first variable concerns *the relationship between the intermediaries and the state*, including the role of the state in their formation and later functioning, the conditions of entry which determine the existence of the intermediaries, and the nature of their regulation.

The second variable concerns *the relationship between the intermediaries and the small investors* for whom the intermediaries perform a variety of services. Of particular importance here is the way in which small investors acquire the shares of the intermediaries and the degree of choice they have concerning such issues as entry and exit.

The third variable concerns *the relationship between the intermediaries and the companies in which they are invested*, and particularly the way in which the intermediaries acquire the shares of the companies in which they invest and their level of involvement in the supervision and control of the management of these companies.

The fourth variable concerns *the relationship between the intermediaries and other kinds of financial institutions*, especially banks and investment banks.

Finally, the fifth variable concerns *the relationship between the intermediaries and foreign and international financial institutions*, in particular the role of these institutions in organizing and managing the intermediaries, as well as assisting the Eastern European participation.

The intermediaries and the state. Several privatization proposals for Poland envisage financial intermediaries which would be set up by the state. The state is envisaged in some of these proposals as appointing the directors of the funds (in one of the plans, they would be nominated by the Ministry of Ownership Transformations and confirmed by the parliament) and the intermediaries would receive the shares of the privatized companies directly from the state according to a set formula (one of the plans, for example, proposes that each of the five funds receives 4 percent of the shares of each privatized enterprise). In many of these plans, the government would strictly control the number of the intermediaries and would use them as an exclusive medium to distribute the free shares (so that, at least initially, individuals would be limited to owning the shares of the intermediaries and would not be able to acquire directly the shares of the privatized enterprises themselves).

Plans of this kind run very serious risks of making the intermediaries into essentially new bureaucratic institutions which would be closely associated with the state and dependent on the state for their existence and functioning. A foreseeable effect of such an arrangement would be a dramatic reduction in the funds' readiness to make decisions on the basis of ordinary business principles, their reluctance to take risks, and, above all, their security in the assurance that the state, closely identified with the intermediaries in the minds of the public, would have to come to their aid if either they or the companies in which they were heavily invested were ever to find themselves in danger of going under. Another obvious risk is that the small number of the intermediaries might encourage their collusion and empire-building tendencies.

The only way of making the intermediaries perform genuinely business-oriented control functions with respect to the management of the companies under their supervision and of making their interest closer to that of their shareholders, rather than of the state bureaucracy, is to make them into private, profit-driven institutions functioning in an environment which forces them to compete for the favor of their shareholders. This does not mean that the intermediaries should be unregulated, but they must be independent from the state. Among the most important areas to be regulated is the structure of management compensation, so as to tie the managers' interests as much as possible to their performance on behalf of the funds' shareholders and the long-term interest of the economy.[10] Similarly, the state may limit the

---

[10] The design of such a compensation structure, as well as the control structure of the intermediaries themselves, is one of the most complex and important tasks of any privatization proposal which envisages a significant role for the intermediaries.

number of the intermediaries, but the right to operate should not be issued on the basis of an administrative, bureaucratic decision; instead, the state should, in such a case, auction off a certain number of licenses to operate an intermediary to private parties satisfying certain basic conditions.

Clearly, the matter of state regulation of the intermediaries is a very broad subject, related to the totality of their operation. We shall discuss some aspects of this problem as we go along, but the issue requires a special treatment touching on nearly the entire field of securities regulation.

The relation to the small investor. The main question regarding the relation between the intermediaries and the small investors is whether the latter would have a choice of the intermediaries in which to invest or whether they would automatically receive a certain number of shares of the intermediaries. A corollary to this question is whether individuals would be able to invest in the shares of the privatized enterprises directly or whether they would be limited to acquiring the shares of the inter- mediaries.

There is a certain appeal in restricting the individual beneficiaries of a free distribution to the shares of the intermediaries, rather than devising ways of allowing them to acquire shares in the privatized companies themselves. Similarly, there are some advantages to not giving the beneficiaries, at least initially, the right to choose the intermediaries of which they are going to hold shares. The reasons for all these restrictions are always the same: administrative simplicity (which eliminates much of the transaction costs involved in other solutions) and the informational barriers facing small investors which would limit their ability to avail themselves of the benefits of the choice, were it available. Thus, for example, if the shares of the privatized enterprises are somehow distributed among the intermediaries (and we shall deal with constraints on this allocation later), it might be administratively much simpler to give every citizen one share in each intermediary, rather than worry about devising a scheme that would allow individual beneficiaries to choose among the intermediaries or to acquire directly the shares of the privatized enterprises, especially since any such scheme would have to involve a costly distribution of vouchers to all the individuals involved, who would then choose between using them to purchase shares of the privatized enterprises or to acquire an interest in the intermediaries. It might also be argued that, if given this choice, most individuals would not know how to use it, and to find out might require more effort than the choice itself, given the small investments involved, would be worth.

A decision to restrict investor's choice in these matters is not, however, without its costs. To be sure, investor's choice might be quite uninformed in a situation in which, as is the case in all East European countries, there would be no reliable information concerning the relative value of the alternatives among which the investor is supposed to choose. Nevertheless, the elimination of investor's choice also means the disappearance of an important factor that could potentially provide a significant element of external control over the intermediaries' performance. If the intermediaries have to compete for the vouchers to be received from the public at large or if they have to 'sell' their shares in some other way, their success will in part at least depend on the satisfaction of those very persons whom they are supposed to serve. If, on the other hand, the shares of the intermediaries are automatically distributed to the beneficiaries, the dependence of the intermediaries on the beneficiaries must diminish and that on the state must increase, if for no other reason than because the decision concerning their very creation would have to be made not by the consumers of their services, but by the state. (If the consumer has no choice about which intermediaries he will invest in, the entry of the intermediaries must be a function of a state decision.) To be sure, some forms of consumer approval could still play a role in the intermediaries' behavior; it would be possible, for example, to tie the managers' compensation to the price of the shares of the intermediaries. But the fact that at least the initial position of the intermediaries would be independent of investors' choice might allow some intermediaries to entrench themselves, especially if their origin in a state decision were to lead to their having a leverage on state assistance in times of adversity.

Another, and perhaps more significant, cost of disallowing the beneficiaries of the free distribution to own directly the shares of the privatized companies is a long-term concentration of all shareholding in very few hands. While some concentration of holdings is undoubtedly desirable (since it allows for effective shareholder control), the exclusion of the small investor has the consequence of making a genuine securities market less likely to arise. If there are ten, twenty, or even one hundred shareholders in the country, especially if most of their holdings are large blocks of shares giving them privileged access to inside information, the volume of trading is certain to be small; indeed so small that all trading is likely to be private and most holdings are likely to remain illiquid. This, in the long run, might not only seriously impede the creation of stock markets, but also make the intermediaries difficult to value and forever 'closed,' i.e., incapable of moving to a system in which they would have to redeem their shareholders' shares on demand.

The closed nature of the funds is related to another possible means of investors' control over the management of the intermediaries: the possibility of exit. As long as the fund remains closed, exit is possible only through a sale of the intermediary's shares to a third party, and the illiquid nature of the intermediary's assets might make the market price of the fund's shares a rather unreliable indicator of how the fund is doing. To be sure, the illiquidity of the fund's assets is, under the East European conditions, entirely unavoidable, at least for the time being: it will be a while before the privatized companies, in which the intermediaries are invested, have a reliable market price. Still, it is a consideration to be kept in mind that a move to 'open' funds (i.e., those obliged to redeem their shares through a sale of a portion of the fund's assets) might be desirable in the future, since this will not only make the funds' valuation more reliable, but also might allow for the dissolution of at least some of them and a move away from a system in which the same intermediaries are a fixture of the economic landscape of Eastern Europe.[11]

The relation to the privatized companies. There are two main issues under this heading: how active is the role of the intermediaries in exercising the control functions on behalf of the small investors, and how will the intermediaries acquire the shares of the companies to be privatized.

The two questions are, to some extent, related, since the mode of acquisition may determine the suitability of the intermediaries for the exercise of the control functions. In fact, the most important question concerning the allocation of the shares of the privatized enterprises to the intermediaries is to ensure that the intermediaries take an early interest in examining the potential of the companies to be privatized and compete among themselves to spot the most effective ways of restructuring them. This can only occur if the intermediaries can determine, at least in part, which companies they will acquire and if they can then acquire sufficiently large blocks of shares in the companies of their choice, so as to be able to influence their

---

[11] The process of the formation of the stock markets may also be helped by either forcing the intermediaries or giving them an incentive to divest themselves of a part of their holdings through public offerings in the future. [Our views on the relationship between the liquidity of privatization intermediaries and their role in monitoring management performance have later evolved along the lines proposed in Coffee (1991) and Chapter 2 in this volume.]

management and prod the restructuring in the direction that appears to them the most promising. For this reason, unlike the case of the allocation of holdings to the individual beneficiaries of free distribution, the simplicity of a solution which allocates the shares of the privatized companies to the intermediaries in some random or mechanical fashion has very little to recommend it. To be sure, one may say that the initial mode of distribution does not matter, since the intermediaries will later trade among themselves in order to reach an allocation that they most desire. But this is not the right approach. To begin with, one would want the intermediaries to begin their research into the companies to be privatized as soon as possible, and there is no better way to ensure this than to force them to make important allocative decisions by a certain fixed date (as is the case when the allocation takes place through an auction, for example). Second, once an initial allocation is made, some intermediaries are immediately put in a better position with respect to an evaluation of certain companies than others because they have access to inside information. But then, the informational asymmetries among the potential traders put some parties at a distinct disadvantage and, as a result, they may be reluctant to trade.[12] Third, trading presupposes a number of institutions which facilitate it, such as stock markets with well-established prices for the shares to be traded, specialists who help effectuate certain transactions by underwriting them, etc. In their absence, trading may be very difficult. Consider, for example, the fact that in the East European context, especially in conjunction with a privatization plan relying on free distribution, the funds may not have at their disposal any large amounts of cash with which to trade. But if most transactions are to take the form of barter arrangements, trading will be slow and the needed reallocation of resources may take a long time (during which the East European economies will languish and the reform movement might collapse under populist political pressures). Finally, back-door transactions among a small number of agents are an open invitation to collusion among the intermediaries.

The design of a proper allocation mechanism by which shares of the privatized companies are initially assigned to the intermediaries is among the most complex and difficult parts of any privatization plan involving free distribution. In order to understand the difficulties involved, it is necessary to remember that the free distribution is

---

[12] We are indebted for this point to Bulent Gultekin's and Gavin Wilson's Memorandum of August 10, 1990, to Messrs. Krzysztof Lis and Stefan Kawalec (of the Polish Ministry of Finance).

necessary because the traditional sales mechanism will not work under East European conditions. This mechanism, with respect to large issues of shares (as opposed to isolated transactions among individuals) normally involves the institution of an underwriter who assumes the risk of selling the whole issue for a small percentage of the sale price. Whatever the considerable advantages of this solution, it cannot be used, without some very significant changes, in the context of Eastern Europe, and, in a free distribution system, the best way of allocating shares to the intermediaries is a special auction during which the intermediaries (as well as private individuals, if they are allowed to do so) bid for these shares with the vouchers they receive for this purpose (depending on the plan) from the state or from their own shareholders.

The main challenge of the privatization plan involving inter-mediaries is to design an auction that will accomplish, without the use of real money, the following objectives:

1. Allocate the shares of the privatized companies to reflect the relative valuations by the intermediaries.
2. Allow the bidders to acquire significant blocks of shares of the privatized companies, which will permit them to implement their restructuring plans and make sure that every privatized company has at least one (and optimally more than one) large shareholder (so that none are left with no effective outside control).
3. Reveal information about the relative valuation of the privatized enterprises by the bidders, both to the other bidders during the auction (so that they can adjust their bids to what they learn about the emergent market prices) and to the general public.
4. Ensure that the shares-for-vouchers market will clear (at least approximately), so that no unsold shares are left and no bidders are left with worthless paper at the end.

Design of an auction that would satisfy all the above conditions is beyond our scope here.[13] But the following sketch provides the main outlines of an auction design.

The enterprises to be privatized should be divided into several groups, each comprising no more than 150–200 companies. Each of these groups should be auctioned off separately. After the first group is sold, there will be an intervening period, during which the new

---

[13] [We return to the role of auctions in the mass privatizations in Chapter 3. The appendix to that chapter also contains a more developed auction design.]

shareholders will elect the boards of directors of the enterprises, and the policymakers and the public will be able to assess the initial consequences of the chosen strategy of privatization. In order to avoid intertemporal problems related to the bidders' trying to apportion their vouchers among all the enterprises scheduled to be privatized in the future, there should be a separate emission of vouchers for each privatization phase and the validity of the vouchers should expire at the end of a given phase. In effect, the vouchers are a form of self-liquidating credit extended by the state to the public for the duration of each privatization phase.

The preliminary design for the auction of each group of companies privatized at a given phase involves a multistage process in which the agents are asked to rebid several times. The actual sale will take place according to an appropriate rule designed to facilitate convergence and limit the agents' strategic manipulation. A key feature of the proposed auction is that the enterprises *will not be auctioned off seriatim*; all of them will be bid for *simultaneously* at every stage.

There will be two basic components of every auction which will be handled separately. In the first one, the agents will be able to bid for, say, three large blocks of shares in each company: one of 20 percent, and two of 15 percent. (This is designed to ensure that each company will have some large shareholders who will exercise effective control). In the second one, the remainder of the shares will be sold through a different procedure: the agents will apportion their remaining vouchers among the companies of their choice, and they will receive a number of shares determined by the level at which the prices will clear.

Following the auction and the allocation of the shares in the privatized companies, the intermediaries may be viewed as fulfilling a number of roles, from relatively passive to very active. At one end of the spectrum would be the institutions modeled on the American ones, which, as a rule, must diversify very broadly and cannot hold a large stake in any single company, thus taking no active part in supervising the management of the companies in their portfolios. Intermediaries of this kind allow their shareholders to pool assets for the purposes of diversification and access to expert advice. Institutions of this kind would not be suitable for the restructuring needs of the East European economies.

At the other end of the spectrum are the financial institutions prevalent in Germany and Japan, which have significant stakes in the companies in which they are invested and play an active role in management supervision. While we believe that the East European economies need precisely these kinds of institutions to supervise the restructuring effort, there are clear agency problems that must be guarded against when one shareholder controls the whole corporation and has the opportunity of exploiting the other owners. While it would take us too far afield to explore in detail the legal framework and the incentive mechanisms which might be the most appropriate to reconcile the requirements of management supervision with the protection of minority shareholders, the importance of such an exploration needs to be signaled here. It is, for example, likely that a deeper analysis will yield a number of restrictions on the intermediaries' relations with the companies in which they are invested, the prime among which might be a cap on the percentage of the shares an intermediary may own in any one company (35 percent seems a good candidate in light of research on American companies), and a host of self-dealing and conflict of interest restrictions. Another result of such an analysis may call for mixing the intermediaries with other significant investors (such as the 'core investor'), whose incentives may be structured in a different way, so as to minimize the agency problems involving the intermediaries.

The relation to other financial institutions. A corollary of the matter just discussed is the relation of the intermediaries to other financial institutions, especially banks and investment banks. Again, it is possible to follow here the American model, in which fiduciary institutions, like mutual funds, are forbidden by law to engage in the provision of other financial services, on the theory that the conflict of interest problems may lead to abuses of fiduciary duties to their shareholders. At the other end, once again, is the German model, in which banks engage in supervising companies on their own behalf as well as on behalf of their trust account clients, in the process also lending money to the companies under their control (thus further increasing their leverage). Somewhere in the middle is a standard investment house, which may arrange for the financing of companies short of capital, place directors on their boards to guard over the lenders' interests, and provide expertise to the management of a company in which the investment firm's clients have a stake.

It will be an important part of the regulation of financial intermediaries in Eastern Europe to determine the degree of their separation from the other types of financial institutions. It is clear that the less of this separation is required, the greater is the potential for conflict of interest situations, and the greater the need for other kinds of regulation (such as restrictions on self-dealing, etc.). On the other hand, one of the greatest lacunae in the East European economies is the absence of a modern banking system, as well as of the other types of modern financial institutions. Moreover, setting up the infrastructure of an intermediary, which involves among other things the establishment of local branches and opening up of accounts for individual beneficiaries, is not unlike the setting up of an infrastructure of a standard bank. The absence of restrictions on the provision of banking services by the intermediaries may thus greatly facilitate the establishment of a modern banking system as well as aid the privatized enterprises in obtaining finance for their operations. Similarly, the lack of stringent restrictions on combining the fiduciary services of the intermediaries with merchant and investment banking services may allow for the intermediaries to become a flexible source of funds for the privatized enterprises: funds could be transferred among the companies in the same intermediaries' portfolio, domestic savings could be channeled into investments, and financing could be solicited from outside investors. These services may be particularly important if the intermediaries are linked to Western financial institutions, since they may then provide a transmission belt for foreign banking expertise, and open a window to the Western sources of debt financing.

The relation to foreign financial institutions. We have noted several times the importance of the entry of foreign capital and expertise into Eastern Europe. We have also indicated their reluctance to enter some of the East European countries, such as Poland, and the reciprocal fears in those countries of foreign domination. For all these reasons, the entry of foreigners in their capacity of investors presents a serious political problem, while their entry as advisors is of little use.

We believe that the entry of foreign banking and investment banking institutions in connection with the setting up and running of the financial intermediaries related to a privatization program is particularly appropriate. First, foreign expertise may be most needed in the establishment of the infrastructure of a modern capitalist economy, with which the East Europeans have practically no experience. Second, this infrastructure is particularly important, since its presence liberates the forces of the market and makes possible a chain reaction of growth and development. Third, foreigners would be entering here primarily not as buyers of East European industry (although some part of their compensation may, and should, include stock options), but as managers of the funds working on behalf of the local owners of the underlying assets. Since their success would directly contribute to the increase in the value of equity in the local hands, their presence might be more easily acceptable than in other contexts. Moreover, if the relations between the funds and their shareholders are structured in such a way that the capital under the intermediaries' management is directly proportional to the number of local citizens who chose that fund over others, the degree of foreign influence over the running of the local company could be seen as also exactly proportional to the welcome of the local population.

While foreigners have a very important role to play in East European intermediary institutions, it may be for many reasons appropriate to effectuate their entry in the form of joint ventures with local partners. This would speed up the transmission of expertise to the local population and further legitimate the foreigners' role in the privatization process. In order to facilitate the formation of such joint ventures, international banking institutions could aid the local partners through grants and subsidies, and if the local governments require some payments from the intermediaries (in the form of security deposits or license fees), special reductions in those payments, in proportion to the degree of local participation, could be introduced.

Conclusion

Privatization in Eastern Europe is not a mere change of ownership: it is rather a complex social and economic transformation, which is supposed to change the way every company is run and every business decision is made. Without a rapid transition to private ownership and the dismantling of the rigid communist structure of the industry, the East European communities will continue to decline.

Moreover, privatization is not just a goal of a market-oriented economic reform. It is also a process which should be itself privatized, so that competition and market mechanisms are used from the very beginning to decide who should be in charge of the restructuring process. Otherwise, the state will try to decide what to do with each enterprise and the economy will be bogged down in the same bureaucratic quagmire which has paralyzed it for the past forty-five years.

While the restructuring should be done exclusively by private institutions, the state could influence the process by providing a general regulatory framework. Among other things, the law would regulate the incentive structure of the intermediary institutions, prescribe antitrust rules and tariffs, as well as provide a safety net for the work force in transition.

What distinguishes the approach advocated here is its combination of several seemingly incompatible features. It combines widespread ownership and a measure of social justice with concentrated control and economic efficiency. It avoids the initial monetary valuation of enterprises, while immediately allocating the existing productive resources to private agents who value them most. It confers ownership on the citizens of East European countries, while providing a link to foreign financial institutions capable of ensuring access to world financial markets and expertise in management supervision. And above all, it offers a chance to move rapidly to a novel system of economic governance which could provide an effective private control of East European industry.

Appendix I: Valuation of state enterprise in the Polish economy

We shall discuss here the case of a valuation of a Polish state enterprise, which we shall call X. The government planned to offer X for sale to the public in the Fall of 1990. Our discussion is based on a preliminary appraisal, prepared by a prestigious British accounting firm, which we shall call A. However, even our brief discussion of the preliminary appraisal brings out the fundamental problems inherent in the so-called 'objective' valuations performed by independent experts on behalf of East European governments. What we hope to show is that valuations of East European enterprises necessarily involve predominantly subjective judgments, and thus, to be really legitimate, should be performed by agents having a genuine stake in the future of privatized enterprises.

Firm A uses three standard methods of valuation: the first one is based on the book value of the enterprise's assets, the second on the price–earnings ratio, and the third on the discounted value of future cash flows.

Firm X has assets in the form of buildings (partly under construction), machinery, tools, equipment, motor vehicles, outstanding receivables, and inventories. The pro-forma balance sheet as of December 31, 1989, displayed in Table A, shows that fixed assets have been valued at $3.7 million and represented 52 percent of the appraised net asset value. The absence of a real-estate market and the secondary markets for machinery and equipment forced the government to value these assets in an apparently arbitrary manner. Firm A reports that the government recently revalued the fixed assets of the firm by $2.2

million, that is, by 146 percent. This revaluation (presumably due to inflation adjustment) accounts for 31 percent of the company's whole net asset value. The valuation of the fixed assets is further clouded by the inclusion of the unfinished Center for International Cooperation, a white elephant in the process of construction, intended to serve as a meeting place for international conferences in the provincial (and not especially attractive) Polish town of Kielce. In the absence of markets, firm A reports having understandable difficulties in valuing the Center. Together, government revaluation of the fixed assets of X and the value of the Center assigned to it by form A amounted to $3 million, which represented 81 percent of the appraised value of X's fixed assets and 42 percent of its net asset value.

Table A   Pro-forma balance sheet of firm X as of December 31, 1989 ($ million)

Fixed assets	3.7
Inventories	1.8
Cash and bank deposits	4.8
Debtors	7.9
	18.2
Bank loan	(0.8)
Creditors and provisions	(9.7)
Welfare fund	(0.6)
	(11.1)
Net assets	7.1

The balance sheet also shows that so-called 'interfirm credit' (the result of a notorious practice of intercompany lending) represented 43 percent of X's assets ($7.9 million due from X's debtors) and 87 percent of X's liabilities ($9.7 million due to X's creditors). Prevalence of such credit and substantial uncertainty associated with its repayment add an additional level of complication to the valuation exercise. As we explained earlier, to value such credit, one would have to evaluate the financial position of the enterprises which are the debtors and the creditors of a given enterprise. In turn, however, those enterprises are also likely to be burdened with their own interfirm credit arrangements, and so on.

The second method used to value company X based on the price–earnings ratio, is, according to firm A, more applicable, because the main business of firm X is the export of labor services, and the value of the firm primarily depends on the quality of its management. However, typically for the East European economies, firm X derived a considerable portion of its earnings from exports to COMECON countries. The artificial nature of the historical prices and exchange rates in these countries makes the computation of meaningful earnings figures highly problematic. This computation is also further complicated by the already mentioned prevalence of interfirm credit.

The absence of securities markets in Poland forced firm A to fix the applicable price–earnings ratio arbitrarily at 3, which resulted in the value of firm X of (at least) $17 million, with potential margin of error of $8 million. A simple check of the robustness of this calculation shows that uncertainty about whether the price–earnings ratio should be 3 or 4 would have increased the potential valuation error to $16 million, that is, to 94 percent.

The third method, based on the value of discounted future cash flows, requires projections of cash flows and the proper discount rate. Here, firm A had to resort to making several 'key assumptions.' First, the future rate of profit of firm X has been assumed to be the same as in 1989. This was the year before the Balcerowicz plan, and, again typically for East European economies, pre-reform data are very unlikely to be relevant in forecasting the future. The dangers of such extrapolations are rather nicely illustrated by the fact that the 1990–91 and 1992–93 sales in East Germany (sic!) have been projected by firm A to lie between 30 and 120 percent of the 1989 figure, whereas sales in the Soviet Union, Czechoslovakia and Hungary have been assumed to amount to between 30 and 75 percent of the 1989 sales. Furthermore, inflation rates in all countries in which firm X operates have been assumed to be unchanged in the future years. Finally, faced with an impossible task of determining the applicable discount rate in the absence of financial markets, firm A used the figure of 25 percent – supplied to it by the Polish Ministry of Finance.

Perhaps the peculiar outcome of these procedures is that despite the arbitrariness of all the numbers used by firm A, the discounted future cash flows yielded the value of firm X virtually identical to the one obtained by the price–earnings ratio method. The only way to explain this outcome is that seemingly arbitrary assumptions have been carefully tailored to yield the reported coincidence of results.

Appendix II: Money and the question of voucher denomination

One of the issues which often arise in conjunction with proposals to use vouchers as a part of free or subsidized distribution programs concerns the question of whether the use of vouchers should be combined with the use of money in the privatization process, and whether vouchers distributed to the population or the financial intermediaries should have some monetary denominations. This Appendix explains why this is not a good idea.

1. Combining vouchers with the use of money means that the price of the shares of the privatized enterprises must be expressed in regular currency. This in turn means that some of the valuation problems involved in the ordinary sale of the privatized companies continue to create obstacles on the way of the privatization program.
2. Combining vouchers with the use of money also means that vouchers must have money denominations. This raises several additional issues.
   • The amount of the vouchers to be issued presents a serious problem. Insofar as the state is concerned, the vouchers are like money: the state must accept them as payment for equity *in lieu* of local currency at face value. The total value of the vouchers to be issued must thus remain in some relation to the total value of the enterprises to be privatized. This makes the problem of valuation even more daunting: not only must each enterprise be valued separately, but also the value of all of them combined must be estimated at once.
   • Even though the vouchers will be denominated in a certain amount, their market value (either explicit, if trading is allowed, or illicit, if it is not) is certain to be much less than that amount. The discount is likely to be significant, since not only is the use of vouchers (unlike money) restricted to long-term investment, but also the 'real' (i.e., market) value of the shares bought for them is very uncertain. The psychological effect of this might be that people will feel cheated: the government will be telling them that they are getting, say, Zl 1,000 subsidy, while people will look at the voucher as worth, say, 300. The resulting political liability might erode the political gain from the free distribution.
   • Given that the (real or hypothetical) market value of the vouchers will be less than the nominal value, the use of the vouchers in an auction will only confuse the nascent price system. Nominally, shares will be bought for, say, Zl 1,000, but since the payment will be in some

combination of cash and vouchers (which will be worth less than their nominal value), market value of the shares outside the auction will be less.

3. In the face of all these troubles, one should ask, what is to be gained by combining the use of money with vouchers? We can think of two such reasons.

• The budget will be hurt if the state cannot sell at least a part of the enterprises for cash. This is a serious argument, but the state has alternative means of raising funds. A consumption tax (such as VAT), for example, will increase the savings rate rather than absorb the savings available for investment. A corporate tax provides an opportunity of a steady flow of revenue, instead of a single injection to cover budgetary expansion that will have to be financed from other sources in later years.

• People who have money will not be able to use it to acquire greater than average shares of the privatized enterprises. This is not a good argument. If trade in vouchers is allowed, people who want to invest more than their allotment will be able to buy more vouchers on the open market. Also the shares of the privatized enterprises (or at least those of the intermediaries) will be traded on the stock exchange soon after the initial privatization auction. Those who want to invest their savings in long-term investments will thus have the opportunity to do so, and the process (more orderly and extended in time) will contribute to the establishment of genuine market prices of the privatized enterprises. (It should also be noted that the price of the vouchers or the shares acquired for them will be higher if the vouchers are the only means of payment at the initial auction. This will mean that the population will be more likely to feel that it has received something valuable, and the level of confidence in the privatization process as well as in the economy as a whole may be enhanced). Finally, the sale of state enterprises for cash might soak up savings into the state treasury instead of allowing them to flow into other, more needed investments (such as the opening of small businesses).

2 Privatization and Corporate Governance: Can a Market Economy Be Designed?*

It is quite common to be somewhat skeptical about the chances of a smooth transition to a market economy in Eastern Europe. The standard fear is that the cost of the transition may be so high that the process will be thwarted by political obstacles and the popular resistance that faces the still fragile democratic institutions.

The usual view of the problem is that the industrial plant of Eastern Europe is technically obsolete and the countries involved lack many of the technical and managerial skills necessary to run a modern production process. In addition, the absence of a rational price system causes great misallocations of resources and creates wrong incentives for the people in control of enterprises. The transition is thus envisaged to entail enormous social costs, since, as subsidies are cut and prices are freed, many enterprises will have to be closed, workers will have to be dismissed, and a great amount of social dislocation will occur.

While we share some of these fears, we believe that the analysis of the difficulties facing the East European economies is often flawed by insufficient attention to what constitutes the most basic systemic obstacle to the growth of the region's economies. For, in addition to all these problems, and beyond the political crisis they may generate, there remains what we consider to be the most challenging question of the whole economic reform: What will fill the gap created by the

* This chapter is a slightly revised version of a paper which appeared under the title 'Privatization and Corporate Governance in Eastern Europe: Can a Market Economy be Designed?' in Winckler, ed. (1991). Martin Gargiulo and Markus Kreuzer were very helpful with their research and comments. Rebecca Berlow kindly went through the original paper and improved its style.

withdrawal of the state from the position of control? Indeed, without solving this problem, the process of modernization is bound not only to be costly, but also to fail.

The paradox of designing a market economy

Markets and institutions: the case of Poland

It is a commonplace that what the economies of Eastern Europe need most at this moment is a free market. The introduction of a rational pricing system, it is believed, will force companies to sink or swim. Those that will be able to transform themselves into viable entities will survive; the others will either be liquidated or have to restructure in bankruptcy proceedings. In this context, privatization is often understood as the state's withdrawal from the running of the firms, thereby subjecting them to a genuine discipline of the market.

In our opinion, this view is based on two essential misunderstandings: it misses the main purpose of privatization in Eastern Europe, and it represents a very simplistic view of what the market economy is all about.

The common feature shared by market societies is a pricing system that results from a large number of transactions among producers and consumers of goods and services. This pricing system in turn coordinates private activities and directs the available resources to their more profitable uses. However, in any developed economy, agents who act in the market are, for the most part, not individuals, but *institutions*, such as corporations, which comprise a large number of individuals acting in a coordinated fashion. If this *internal coordination* process does not work properly, the information conveyed by prices will be very imperfect (leading to a host of misallocations), and the agents themselves will be unable to react properly to the cues provided by the price system. In other words, markets function well (provide an effective *external coordination* of economic agents) only when they have embedded in them a system of institutions that provides a socially desirable internal coordination mechanism, including a complex set of incentives for individuals to respond in a particular way to the information conveyed by the market environment. In all known market societies, such an effective mechanism involves a certain definite *control structure*, that is, a mechanism that ensures both that someone *within the institution* (the management) is in charge of the coordination process and that those who are in charge within are in turn controlled by someone *outside the institution*, so that they serve the interests of the owners (shareholders) and indirectly of the society at large. It is this rational structure of *corporate governance* that the state enterprises in Eastern Europe are lacking, and the main task of privatization is to introduce it. Without it, no amount of deregulation and decentralization will produce a well-functioning market economy.

The history of the economic reforms in Eastern Europe up to this point illustrates this rather nicely, since nearly all of these reforms, both before and after the demise of the communist regime, were also based on the belief that a decentralized system of decision making was going to release the productive energies thwarted by central planning. What happened instead, however, at least in Poland, was a release of a completely different kind of force: that of special interests.[1]

The earliest attempts to reform the control mechanisms of the East European economies were undertaken by the state bureaucracies under the mounting pressure of popular discontent. In Poland, by the mid-1950s, it became clear to many that the very size of the enterprises created by communist authorities in the preceding decade, together with the sheer complexity of the resulting coordination problems, posed insurmountable technical difficulties for the totally centralized planning system. As the public became increasingly dissatisfied with the economic outcomes of rapid industrialization, and as the discontent erupted in the popular uprising of Poznan (in June 1956), the uppermost echelon of the Stalinist party hierarchy was eased out of power and the new leadership undertook the first efforts at decentralization. The previous system, in which government ministries controlled entire industries according to the requirements specified by the Central Plan, was replaced by a system of so-called branch associations (*zjednoczenia*) within each industry. These branch associations were still subordinated to the ministries and had to adhere to the requirements of the plan, but they were endowed with some discretion to reallocate the available funds among their constituent enterprises, so as to enable them to introduce some badly needed flexibility into the productive system.

Not surprisingly, the results were quite disappointing. The

---

[1] In this chapter, we use the example of Poland to illustrate the development of the corporate governance structure in Eastern Europe over the last forty years. But we believe that the story, *mutatis mutandis*, is quite similar in Hungary as well. The case of Czechoslovakia perhaps deserves separate treatment, but it would lead too far from our main subject. [We pick up this theme in Chapter 4.]

allocative decisions made by the branch associations were, by and large, politically motivated and on the whole detrimental to the national economy: the association came to represent a new special interest, intent on entrenching its own power and control. Thus, for example, instead of strengthening the most productive enterprises and cutting out the 'losers,' the associations were more interested in maintaining output and employment levels for the branch as a whole. As a result, they often reallocated 'excess' funds from the more efficient enterprises to those that were threatened with failure. Individual enterprises continued to have no autonomy, and the interactions among all layers of the state sector remained governed by administrative decisions and political bargaining. In the ultimate reckoning, this first attempt at decentraliz-ation – instead of creating a new control structure conducive to a more efficient economy – created a new powerful layer of the state apparatus and had the perverse effect of further strengthening the bureaucratic control over individual enterprises.

The next major attempt to decentralize the economy came in the wake of the workers' unrest in December 1970. The branch associations of the earlier period came to be replaced by the so-called Great Industrial Organizations (*Wielkie Organizacje Gospodarcze*). Enterprises grouped into these organizations were granted limited autonomy. New incentives were introduced, which attempted to link the compensation of workers and the management to the enterprise's performance, and the level of investment funding became tied to profitability. At the same time, however, the state did not release its centralized grip over some of the most important decisions at the enterprise level: in particular, it continued to set prices in a centralized fashion and to exercise indirect control over the amount and allocation of profits retained by the enterprises. A system of progressive taxation was introduced, which penalized those enterprises that retained more than the mandated proportions of profits or allocated them for investment, bonuses, and working capital in proportions different from those recommended by the center. In fact, the key feature of the new economic mechanism was the embedding of the enterprises within a structure of external coordination and control based on a system of arbitrary restrictions, directives, and centrally mandated prices, which made the newly increased autonomy of the enterprises incapable of influencing the overall performance of the economy. The illusory improvement, owing to the influx of foreign debt capital, disappeared together with its cause: when the loans stopped flowing at the end of the 1970s, the economy collapsed.

Following the collapse, and the rise of the Solidarity labor union, the evolution of the economic control and coordination mechanisms entered a new stage. In a desperate attempt to introduce some elements of a market economy into the production system based on state ownership, the state for the first time allowed individual enterprises to set prices of some goods through a bargaining process, although the prices of such basic inputs as coal and energy were still determined administratively. Even more important, the structure of the state's control over individual enterprises began to disintegrate. In September 1981, in an effort to allay workers' dissatisfaction, the state, under pressure from Solidarity, allowed the creation of workers' councils in individual enterprises and endowed them with considerable influence over the choice of management, the allocation of bonus funds between labor and management, and over the employment policies of the enterprise. Unlike previous efforts to introduce, in a cautious and controlled fashion, limited autonomy for the enterprises, the rise of the workers' councils initiated a process of genuine decentralization, with the state progressively losing its ability to make decisions at the enterprise level. Moreover, while the state was able, at least temporarily, to reassert its political control during the period following the introduction of martial law in December 1981, its loss of economic control was never reversed: in fact, the Jaruzelski government continued the policy of supposedly market-oriented decentralizing reforms, which freed an increasing proportion of prices from the dictates of the center.

The results were, again, far from encouraging. Centralized state control continued to wane, and prices of many goods were being liberalized, but no new mechanisms of external accountability of the enterprises were substituted for the old system of bureaucratic control. Consequently, the forces of management and labor, both committed to the defense of their (often interdependent) vested interests, came to dominate the productive and allocative decisions at the company level, causing an explosive spiral of price and wage increases. At the same time, the state, still committed to full employment and accepting the responsibility for the success or failure of each enterprise, continued to maintain an ever-increasing system of subsidies and other payments designed to appease one or another special interest group. The original model of the active communist state was thus progressively reversed: the state became a basically reactive force, increasingly responding to pressures from below, and financing its responses through an expanding budget deficit. The resulting macroeconomic imbalance and the monetization of the deficit ultimately led to hyperinflation and the demise of the communist rule.

The basic presupposition of the economic reform program of the first post-communist government in Poland was that the failures of the economic policy of the old regime were due to the absence of a commitment to genuine market discipline. Among the main goals of the Balcerowicz Plan, therefore, were the elimination of the macroeconomic imbalance, price and trade liberalization, and the stability and convertibility of the currency. The reform freed most prices and eliminated the bulk of subsidies that had bloated the previous budgets: before January 1990, administered prices applied to an estimated 50 percent of the nominal value of legal transactions; the reforms reduced this proportion to 10 percent.[2]

Despite the unquestionable achievements of the Balcerowicz Plan in terms of creating some of the necessary conditions of a long-term transformation of the Polish economy, a number of observers have noted that, contrary to initial expectations, few state firms failed to survive the effects of the introduction of free market prices and the elimination of most subsidies, tax abatements, etc. Nor is there much evidence that this fact is due to any large-scale rationalization of the production process at the enterprise level. What is more likely – and more ominous from the longer-term perspective – is that most firms have been able to weather the effects of the recent reforms by cutting down on reinvestment, increasing various forms of mutual indebtedness, and generally decapitalizing themselves and the economy as a whole. Very significantly, despite dramatic cuts in production, layoffs have been relatively rare, indicating that labor's control over the enterprises continues undiminished.[3]

While it may be too early to draw any definitive lessons from the experiences of the Balcerowicz Plan, it is by now quite accepted that, without the next stage of reform, designed to reintroduce the concept of external accountability into the everyday life of the enterprises, there is relatively little hope that the market forces released so far will rapidly lead to the profound structural transformation required to move Poland out of the doldrums of a post-communist economy. In some sense, unless followed by rapid privatization, the economic order introduced

---

[2] For an analysis of the Polish reforms, see Calvo and Coricelli (1991); and Frydman and Wellisz (1991).

[3] For a discussion of this point, see Hinds (1991); and see also Chapter 1 of this volume.

by the recent reforms only completed the process of decentralization initiated under the old regime, and retained many of its structural deformities, because of the absence of a system of ownership and of monitoring the performance of the enterprises on a daily basis and the entrenchment of special interests (especially those of labor and the *nomenklatura* management), united in their resistance to a fundamental reorientation of the production process. Thus, although free market prices are certainly necessary for a proper functioning of the economy, the processing of the information conveyed by prices and the economically desirable responses to market signals at the enterprise level require the existence of an appropriate corporate governance structure.

Economic theory and the designing of corporate control

Privatization, as understood here, is thus a way of constructing a new corporate governance structure in Eastern Europe designed to fill the gap left by the withdrawal of the state from the management of the productive assets of the society. That imposing such a new structure may be difficult is not hard to see. To begin with, there is the already diagnosed problem of deficient managerial expertise, without which the job of coordinating and supervising the large number of people composing a corporation is unlikely to be accomplished. But this is just the beginning, for while Eastern Europe may not have very good managers, it has at least some experience in running large enterprises. Where the corresponding experience is almost completely lacking is in controlling the managers themselves: the past experience of political control is quite useless in this respect, and a new breed of capital owners, company directors, supervisory board members, financial experts, etc. is still missing.

But even if we were to abstract from the fact of the missing personnel, the East European countries would still be facing a monumental problem in their restructuring effort: how to choose the precise form of corporate governance that might work in the conditions of their economies. For if one considers the institutions of capitalism, such as corporations, banks, institutional investors, and stock exchanges, as an integral part of a market economy, then there is not *one* market economy, but *many*, each with its own peculiar mode of operation, financing, and a set of complex institutional interrelationships that determines the incentives that make the managers respond to signals conveyed by the market.

Even a cursory look at a few developed countries shows how significantly they differ among themselves with respect to the institutional arrangements through which the behavior of the management is subject to external control. In the old days the owner and the manager may often have been the same person. As the size and complexity of the modern corporation grew over the last century, however, and as its capital requirements began to be satisfied in large part through the sale of stock to the public, there arose a large degree of separation between ownership and control, with the concomitant need for new ways in which the behavior of the management could be supervised on behalf of the owners. In Germany, for example, most of the supervisory functions came to be exercised by big financial institutions that held, on their own behalf or on that of their customers, a very large portion of the shares of German corporations. In the United States, by contrast, most financial institutions are either legally precluded from playing such a role or they are unwilling to play it. Consequently, in the age of dispersed ownership, the control functions have largely devolved on the stock market: when management does not perform sufficiently well, a company may be subject to a takeover and the management will be dismissed.[4]

In both Germany and the United States, the institutions of control evolved slowly over the course of history, and the resulting economic order is exceedingly complex: in fact, as the many disputes among the economists and policymakers attest, we are far from understanding fully the way it really works.

The importance of this last point is not to be underestimated. The institutions of the market economy have been a subject of much study recently, and a number of attempts have been made to account for them from a full-fledged theoretical perspective. The most fruitful of these efforts has attempted to explain the need for institutions in terms of the so-called transactional approach.[5] When parties come together in a market, their relations are often of such complexity and duration that the cost of regulating their interactions through a system of explicit

---

[4] There are, of course, other ways of facilitating owners' control over the management. For further discussion, see Chapter 4.

[5] The classic text in this tradition is Commons (1934). The historical evolution of economic institutions has been discussed by Shonfield (1965). More recently, transaction cost economics has gained increasing attention among organizational theorists, and Williamson (1975) is largely credited for its development. For a review of later works, see Williamson and Ouchi (1981). See also Williamson (1985).

contracts (the normal structure of a market interaction) would involve prohibitively high transaction costs. It is said that institutions economize on these costs by establishing an alternative system of coordination, involving hierarchies, routines, etc.

Despite the undoubted accomplishments of the transaction costs approach to the theory of institutions, it is doubtful whether such a theory could ever hope to be able to decide that one or another set of institutional market arrangements is the 'best,' in the sense of best solving the coordination, supervision, and other contractual problems facing agents in an economic market. The institutional theorists who believe that the best institutional arrangements can be identified are inspired by neoclassical economics, and they view the optimal arrangement as an equilibrium in the 'market' for competing institutional forms.[6] Each one of these forms is, in turn, related to optimal individual behavior subject to constraints that include transaction costs and the structure of property rights.[7] In essence, this approach assumes that an external observer would in principle be capable of making all the calculations necessary for selecting the optimal institutional setup in any given situation.

But such an assumption is questionable in several respects. To begin with, even if the necessary calculations could be made in theory, it is quite clear that in fact we lack sufficient knowledge and information, as well as neoclassical models of sufficient specificity, to be able to make the relevant judgments in the actual world.[8] As we have seen, the advanced economies have developed quite different institutional solutions to what are arguably quite similar problems, and it would be fatuous to pretend that the literature contains any decisive arguments why this or another system is the 'optimal' one. Furthermore, even if the observed institutional arrangements correspond to some neoclassical equilibria it would be a case of *multiple equilibria*, and if such is indeed the case, the choice facing the East European countries may not have a determinate theoretical solution.[9] But in fact, the continuous evolution of the institutional arrangements of the advanced economies makes it doubtful whether any of these economies have

---

[6] Exposition of this view is contained in Eggertsson (1990).

[7] For an argument in support of this approach and further references, see De Alessi (1983).

[8] This is just a special case of the view elaborated in Simon (1957).

[9] Adding to the theoretical difficulties is the equally plausible possibility that there may be *no* equilibrium solution to the standard problem of the institutional setup of the capitalist corporate governance structure.

actually reached an equilibrium of the kind talked about by the neoclassical economists. Moreover, even the more ardent supporters of the neoclassical school recognize that this approach encounters serious difficulties in explaining institutional change;[10] indeed, if the historical evolution of institutions were to be fully explicable with the help of the neoclassical approach, we would be dealing with no less than a scientific theory of history.[11]

Recognizing problems such as these, much of the literature on transaction costs does not in fact rely on the economic optimality paradigm; instead, it argues that institutions arise to solve problems stemming precisely from the impossibility of performing the complex calculations that would be required to form optimal plans and to compute the resulting institutional equilibria. Consequently, every actual institutional arrangement is seen as an adaptation mechanism of a different kind, often relying on a number of contingently present cultural milestones around which the agents habitually orient their behavior.[12] This presence of an irreducible element of contingency, idiosyncrasy, and cultural specificity, deriving from the fact that individual decisions lying at the basis of any specific institutional setup contain certain rationally nonreconstructible components, indicates that a genuine equilibrium theory of the capitalist institutions, which would be grounded in a rational reconstruction of the Western models to be transplanted in Eastern Europe, is likely to be impossible.[13]

Compounding the problems already mentioned is the question of transition: even if the institutional equilibrium models were to be available, it is clear that the East European economies are starting from different (and obviously nonequilibrium) conditions, and have to be moved to an equilibrium over time. To have a genuine theory of how to get there, one would also need to have a theory of what economists call the 'convergence' to an (institutional) equilibrium. As is known from the literature, however, such transitions cannot be described in terms of fully optimal decisions; in fact nonoptimal individual decision rules

---

[10] North (1981).

[11] For a discussion of the implausibility of such a theory, see Popper (1961) and Hayek (1955).

[12] For a classic exposition of this view, see Alchian (1950). For an alternative approach that still eschews the optimality postulate, see Williamson (1975).

[13] This may explain why much of the comparative literature concerning the corporate governance structure of the various advanced economies is so largely dependent on 'soft' *ex post* explanations, full of references to 'the way Japanese (or Germans) do it,' rather than on hard-nosed economic analysis.

appear to be the basic assumption of all stylized models of convergence to equilibria.[14]

The significance of all this for the East European situation is the following: The complicated institutional framework that ensures the proper governance of the corporation constitutes the very core of the capitalist infrastructure that is completely missing from East European societies. The task of privatization is to construct such a governance structure and institute it in an environment in which there is a pronounced lack of available personnel and a potentially unfavorable political structure. But even assuming that, by some feat of magic, Eastern Europe were somehow to become overnight populated by Harvard MBAs and that the political system were to be completely resistant to the opportunistic pressure of special interests which, at least in the short run, may have much to lose from the restructuring process, the problem of providing a new institutional structure of control for the existing productive sector would still be monumental. For while decisions have to be made now that may predetermine much of the developmental chances of the East European economies, the choice is largely not determined by any firm knowledge of what will work. Devising entirely new and untried institutional arrangements carries with it an enormous risk of failure. But trying to learn from the experience of other countries, while safer, is also dangerous: we do not reliably know which of the existing institutional models are the best, and we cannot confidently say why they work (to the extent they do) in the countries that use them. And perhaps most important of all, it is by no means clear that the institutional setup of any particular market economy can be made to work outside its own specific context, so that we cannot be sure how to transplant the tried models into the unique environment of Eastern Europe.

It might be said perhaps that the countries of Eastern Europe should not embark on the road of designing the corporate governance structure of their economies, any more than the Western countries did: after all, the known successful institutional arrangements arose in a way that was, to a large degree, spontaneous and unplanned.[15] Why shouldn't, say, Poland follow the same path?

---

[14] For a discussion of these issues, see Frydman and Phelps, eds (1983).

[15] It should be noted, however, that the state played a far from neglible role in this development. It has been claimed by some, for example, that the move away from management supervision through the banking system and toward a system of stock market control in the United States was largely determined by political decisions. See Roe (1991); see also Herman (1981), especially chap. 4. The German system of control through banking is also thought to have

Unfortunately, spontaneous development of new institutional arrangements is not a solution. The East European economies are not virgin territory, where capitalism would be able to develop over a long period of time, starting with small owner-controlled enterprises that would gradually expand into larger and more complicated units. On the contrary, Eastern Europe has a specific industrial infrastructure, for the most part composed of large industries, which it took decades to build and which should not facilely be assumed to be fit only for the garbage heap. And the physical structure of this industry corresponds to the nature of the command economy within which it was constructed: a typical enterprise is very large (in Poland, for example, a hundred enterprises are responsible for 40 percent of industrial production), and no attention whatever has been paid to diversifying the sources of supply (so that competition is difficult to introduce). In order to set the economy on the right footing, the state must withdraw from its position of control. But the gap created by the state withdrawal will have to be filled by the privatization program, and the infrastructure of the market society will have to be *created* for the market forces to begin to operate.

We have thus the makings of a genuine paradox that constitutes the most fundamental systemic obstacle to the economic transformation in Eastern Europe: the most important aspect of the transition to a spontaneously functioning market economy cannot be initiated by market forces themselves. Indeed, the only force powerful enough to set the market forces in motion is the very state that is supposed to remove itself from the picture. And for a number of reasons, the state may be unable to accomplish this task.

The first major reason is one of potential intellectual failure, a failure linked not just to the individual limitations of those in charge, but to the inherent limitations of human knowledge. The task before us is nothing less than creating a 'market by design.'[16] But despite the economists' ambitions, there exists no economic theory of sufficient scope to tell us how to design a market economy; indeed, we know too little, and we may in principle never know enough, about markets

---

resulted from a conscious decision at the end of the last century. See Esser (1990). See also Shonfield (1965) chap. 11, and Kocka (1980). Finally, the Japanese system of *keiretsu* developed out of the prewar *zaibatsus*, which were broken up by the stringent divestiture measures imposed by the American occupation authorities after World War II. See Hirschmeier and Yui (1981), and Sato and Hoshino, eds (1984). For an assessment of the specific role of the banks in the emergence of the *keiretsus*, see Goldsmith (1983).

[16] We would like to thank Mr Peter Dougherty for coining this phrase for us.

themselves[17] (and especially about the institutions embedded in a market economy) to make the East European transition a matter of applying proven economic theories to new material. Thus, it would be fatuous to expect that any design can be failure-proof; the only promising strategy is to try to set up an institutional arrangement that contains in itself some *self-correcting mechanisms*. Such mechanisms must, of necessity, be imperfect, in the sense that the achievement of an optimal solution cannot be assured. Indeed, the very working of a self-correcting mechanism of this kind cannot be precisely known in advance; this is just a special case of our earlier general point about institutional design. For this reason, the task of the designer of these mechanisms is in many respects more like that of a constitutional 'founding father,' attempting to institute something in the nature of 'checks and balances' or 'separation of powers,' than that of an economist devising, say, a scheme of airline deregulation or another policy designed to improve the competitiveness of a failing market arrangement.

The second major danger is one of a failure of will: the state, in addition to lacking the requisite knowledge, may be unwilling or unable to resist the political pressures of the special interests bound to lose their privileged position as a result of the required changes in the control structure of the national economy. Given the absence of any existing powerful constituency that is likely to gain by the process of privatization in the short run, a democratic system directly responsive to popular pressures may be simply incapable of securing enough support for the required radical transformation, despite its being in the long-term interest of the nation. Paradoxically, it may be only because the East European democracies are still very young, and because the normal channels by which organized interest groups exert political influence in the more mature democratic systems are not yet fully crystallized, that the governments of the region may be able to accomplish the task before them.

But even if such a chance exists, it is only a narrow window of opportunity, which is bound to close within a relatively short period of time. For this reason, the only way to prevent the state power from being captured by the forces of special interests intent on undermining the process of transition is to create a situation in which the state, having set the stage for further developments, can credibly claim to

---

[17] For a classic statement of this too often neglected point, see Hayek (1948). For contemporary analysis of this issue, see Frydman (1982), and Soros (1987).

have no further direct influence on the decisions of the most important economic agents. This the state can do only if it initiates the process of transition by setting up the rules of the game, and then goes on to play as minimal a role as possible within the newly created structure of control. Furthermore, while market forces cannot be relied upon to initiate the process of transition by themselves, they should be set in motion from the very beginning in structuring the new institutions of control. This means, above all, that the various private agents in favor of whom the state withdraws from its role in the running of the enterprises should be both diverse and placed from the start within a firmly competitive environment. This would allow for a self-correcting and spontaneous evolution to take over as quickly as possible, thus mitigating the problems arising from the imperfection of the initial design and strengthening the credibility of the state's commitment to a withdrawal from participation in the corporate governance structure.

Privatization proposals and the reform of corporate governance

In the remainder of this chapter, we will try to use the theoretical insights sketched so far to analyze and evaluate some of the privatization proposals recently suggested for Eastern Europe. In particular, given our understanding of privatization as, above all, a mechanism for the reform of institutional governance, we shall concentrate on the solutions proposed by each plan to the problem of corporate control.

Three *types of privatization proposals* have received the most attention in recent discussions. The *first* type, modeled after the United States and the United Kingdom, aims at the creation of viable stock markets and a system of external financing of corporate investment; it is believed that the resulting market for corporate control would have the desired disciplinary effect on the behavior of company managers. The *second* type, inspired by the German or, to a lesser extent, the Japanese model, advocates a so-called internal market, that is, a system in which banks and other financial institutions play a crucial role in supervising corporate management and the financing of corporate investment. Finally, the *third* type advocates so-called spontaneous privatization, to be initiated by the present management with the support of the workers; this type of proposal favors the preservation, indeed strengthening, of the present control structure.

The stock market model

The East Europeans often view the stock markets as the ultimate symbol of capitalist maturity. For this reason, as well as because of the inherently nonbureaucratic *modus operandi* of the market, many East Europeans see stock markets as attractive devices for exercising a measure of external control over corporate management. Creation of a market for corporate control can be attempted in a number of ways. At one extreme, one can try to sell state enterprises to foreign and domestic investors, hoping that each firm will end up with at least one significant large owner who will take an active interest in the way it is run. At the other extreme is a 'naked' giveaway plan: the population at large (or some fragment of it) might receive special vouchers that each holder can exchange (either at a predetermined ratio or through some kind of auction) for the shares of a corporation of his or her choice. Through later trades, a market for the shares of the privatized companies is expected to develop and, because of the possibility of takeovers, create some pressures on company management to improve performance.

The problems with the stock market approach are well known by now and need not be rehearsed here in detail. In brief, the sales model of privatization appears both economically and politically infeasible. If the prospective buyers are to be domestic, there is not enough capital available internally in Eastern Europe to make the sale of most state enterprises a realistic possibility. If foreign investors are to be relied upon, however, the uncertainty concerning the stability of the region and the high cost of monitoring foreign investments there are likely to make the prospective buyers impose a politically unacceptably high discount on the price of East European corporations.[18] Insofar as the giveaway plans are concerned, they would lead, at least initially, to extreme fragmentation of ownership, with the concomitant inability of the investors to exercise any meaningful control over management. As already explained, the quintessential type of discipline exercised by the stock market is the possibility of a hostile takeover, which is likely to result in the management's dismissal. Takeovers would not be likely to occur, however, until ownership was fairly highly concentrated. As time goes by, this could happen, of course, but given the initial fragmentation of holdings, any effective restructuring of East European

---

[18] See Chapter 1.

enterprises, which is the main purpose of privatization in the first place, would have to wait for years before a sufficient pressure could build up.[19]

While the problems with the capital-market approach are quite well known, it should be noted that even if a realistic possibility existed of instituting a viable stock market system in Eastern Europe, some people have argued that the resulting increase in the liquidity of investments would have certain deleterious effects that should not be ignored, perhaps especially in the context of Eastern Europe. First, the high degree of liquidity that developed stock markets introduce is said to lessen the incentives of investors to monitor their investments, even if these investors do not face the coordination problems facing small players: the very fact of easy exit may provide a sufficient incentive for selling the stock of companies that are perceived to underperform, rather than engaging in the costly process of monitoring and fighting the management trying to ward off external interference.[20] Second, reliance on takeovers for external monitoring increases the job uncertainty of company managers and may be responsible for a tendency toward 'short-termism': managers who fear being dismissed in the wake of a takeover may lose the incentives to postpone part of their compensation in exchange for greater security and may be reluctant to develop firm-specific skills that can become useless if they are not retained by the new owners.[21] Both of these potentially negative consequences of the market-oriented approach toward corporate control may be particularly dangerous in the context of the East European economies, which badly need strong commitment from the new owners toward the costly restructuring effort and the long-term improvement of corporate management.

Spontaneous privatization

Before moving on to the discussion of the proposals oriented toward the model of corporate control through financial institutions, we should briefly pause to consider the proposals advocating so-called spontaneous privatization. The first thing to observe here is a pitfall

---

[19] See Chapter 1.
[20] We owe this valuable observation to Coffee (1991), who, in turn, builds upon Hirschman's (1970) seminal work.
[21] See Franks and Mayer (1990).

that awaits those who would too mechanically transplant into Eastern Europe institutions that may have had a large degree of success in the West, but which acquire an entirely different meaning in the East European context. The idea of spontaneous privatization looks, at first sight, like an East European equivalent of a management buy-out. To begin with, even if the managers were in fact to acquire control of their enterprises, having been chosen by the largely negative selection of the old regime, they would be extremely unlikely to reveal the level of entrepreneurial drive and competence characteristic of their Western counterparts, to say nothing of the understandable social resistance to this kind of *'nomenklatura* privatization.' But in reality, the managers are in fact very unlikely to gain genuine control through spontaneous privatization. The pressure for this type of ownership change comes instead from an alliance between the workers and the management who are intent on resisting significant departures from the status quo: it is precisely the opposition to a restructuring that is likely to result from genuine privatization that motivates the alliance. In addition, in the Polish context at least, the change is unlikely to lead to increased efficiency; quite the contrary, one of the primary incentives toward spontaneous privatization is an attempt by the workers to get around the stiff tax on wage increases that applies to the employees of state enterprises, but which may be relaxed for companies that privatize. Thus, the pressure for spontaneous privatization is primarily political, and as such it may turn out to be a threat to genuine restructuring. Apart from pure worker ownership, it is the only form of privatization for which a considerable constituency exists, and the analysis of the nature of spontaneous privatization may only strengthen our previous conclusion concerning the peculiar importance of the initial role of the state in the privatization process: if the state turns out to be incapable of resisting the political pressure in favor of spontaneous privatization, and does not assert its power in setting up the genuine forces of competition at the very start of the ownership transformation process, the withdrawal of state power will leave intact the stifling structures created by the old regime.

Corporate control by financial intermediaries

To make our discussion of the privatization programs oriented toward the control of management by financial institutions more concrete, we shall analyze one special version of this type, namely, the plan adopted by the Polish government for its so-called mass privatization program, involving the largest 500 state enterprises in Poland.[22] However, we intend to use this plan, which follows the lines advocated in our earlier work,[23] as a springboard for making some points of more general significance.

The main features of the Polish government plan are the following: each of the 500 largest enterprises scheduled for privatization will be first converted into a joint-stock company. Following this 'corporatization,' 10 percent of the shares will be given (free of charge) to the workers,[24] and the state will retain another 30 percent, while the remaining 60 percent will be transferred to new owners with the help of privatization vouchers.

The 500 enterprises will be disposed of in several phases, with 150–200 to be privatized in the first phase. An appropriate number of vouchers will be issued for each phase, with two-thirds most likely going to the public at large (each citizen receiving one voucher), and one-third to the social security office (to capitalize the state pension fund).[25] (Thus, the citizens will receive vouchers equivalent to 40 percent of the value of the privatized enterprises, and the state pension fund 20 percent.)

The state will then invite the creation of a number of intermediary institutions (investment and restructuring funds), which will offer their shares in exchange for vouchers. (Entry will be free, so that any person or institution, foreign, domestic, or mixed, will be able to create an intermediary, as long as the minimum conditions specified in a special law are satisfied.) The vouchers received by the citizens will have to be used to 'purchase' the shares of the intermediaries, with each person having a choice among the intermediary institutions in which he or she wants to invest. The social security office will have a choice of depositing all or some of its vouchers with the intermediaries or of creating one or more special pension funds of its own.

---

[22] [This plan was one of the branches of the overall privatization program for Poland at the time this chapter was written (1990). The other branches dealt with so-called small and medium-sized companies (some 2,000 industrial companies and 3,500 others) that were scheduled to be privatized through sales or liquidation. For a description of the plan as originally announced, see *Rzeczpospolita*, November 21, 1990.]

[23] See Chapter 1 of this volume.

[24] The Privatization Law foresees that the workers should receive up to 20 percent of the shares of the privatized enterprises at half price, but not to exceed the value of their last year's wages. The present plan proposes giving up the idea of selling at half price and the limitation relative to last year's income because of valuation difficulties. It is not clear, however, that this proposal accords with what the Privatization Law requires, and may be abandoned.

[25] As initially announced, the plan had foreseen that the public would receive half of the vouchers and one-sixth would go to a number of state banks. The idea of the banks' share now appears to have been abandoned, with the vouchers presumably going to the public.

Once the vouchers are transferred to the intermediaries, the 150–200 companies privatized in the first phase will be sold at a specially designed auction.[26] The state will also deposit the 30 percent of the shares it owns in the intermediaries according to some predetermined formula.[27] However, the state will not become an ordinary shareholder of the intermediary institutions; its share will be apportioned to the intermediaries, and the state's role in them will be limited to appointing one director on the board of each intermediary. The intermediaries will be charged with selling the state's shares in each privatized company to other investors, either by private placement or in the open market, and once a certain percentage of the total state holdings administered by a given intermediary is sold, the state director will disappear from the board of the intermediary.

When the transfer of ownership and control has been completed, new directors will be appointed by the intermediaries and other shareholders for each company, and the business of restructuring will begin. The new owners (with, it is hoped, the intermediaries in the dominant position) will be free to change the management of the privatized companies, to split them up (or perhaps combine them, insofar as no antitrust violations would result), to sell a part of their holdings, to approve various joint-venture arrangements between the privatized companies and other entities (foreign or domestic), etc. The sale by the intermediaries of the 30 percent of the shares held by them on behalf of the state will, it is hoped, allow for an introduction of 'core investors' into a number of the privatized companies, as well as (together with the transactions involving the 10 percent of the shares held by individual workers) create a market for a sizeable proportion of the shares of the privatized companies (thus allowing for a market valuation of the privatized companies and the intermediaries, and for the possibility that some of the funds may become 'open').

Although we favor many of the features embedded in the Polish government's plan, as we have argued already, the limitations on what we do or can know about markets make it in principle impossible to construct *a priori* an optimal institutional design of an advanced market economy. The best we can do is to try to set up institutions containing

---

[26] The type of auction to be used has been described in Chapter 1. See also Appendix to Chapter 3.

[27] Beyond specifying that the state will not be able to hold the shares of the privatized companies directly and will have to use the intermediaries, the formula for the distribution of the state holdings is not clearly specified in the government plan. Presumably, vouchers may be used in this connection as well.

within themselves appropriate self-correcting mechanisms that may mitigate some of the problems resulting from the limitations of our knowledge, and to use market forces as much as possible from the very beginning.

Potential institutional failures

The first step in designing an institutional arrangement containing an appropriate self-correcting mechanism is to identify, insofar as it is possible, the most likely failures, or types of failures, of the design, and then try to make sure that there are some forces operating that will make the failures less likely or effectuate the appropriate *ex post* corrections.

With respect to the Polish plan (as much as any other plan involving control through financial intermediaries), the most likely dangers appear to us to be the following:

- The plan may turn out not to be attractive enough for the type of entrant who would be the most desirable from the point of view of his ability to contribute to the restructuring process. In the case of the Polish plan, this would mean, above all, the failure to attract in sufficient number and caliber the foreign financial institutions interested in, and capable of, forming effective and active intermediary institutions.
- Under certain conditions, the intermediaries, instead of becoming aggressive, mutually competitive institutions, devoted to the idea of profitmaking, could become sluggish and entrenched bureaucracies, in some respects not unlike the old industrial branch associations that had controlled much of the industry under the communist regime.
- The financial intermediaries charged with supervising the corporate management of the privatized enterprises may opt for a strategy of passive investment and, rather than devoting their resources to exercising their supervisory functions, attempt to free ride on the efforts of others.
- The management fee of the managers of the investment funds may not assure sufficient incentive compatibility between them and the shareholders of the intermediaries (the public at large), so that the people in control of the intermediaries may develop conflicts of interest with respect to the fiduciary obligations vis-à-vis their shareholders. It might be very important in this context to identify particular types of possible opportunistic behavior on the part of the

intermediaries through which they may use their power over the companies in their portfolio in order to extract extra profits through self-dealing, loans paying above average interest, insider trading, etc.

• Finally, the system may not provide for an effective allocation of finance for the developing economy. The financial markets might not develop properly, regulation (including that designed to deal with the conflict of interest problems discussed above) may stifle the intermediaries' ability to move funds among the different parts of their portfolio or to procure sufficient access to external financing, or the intermediaries may engage in empire building, rather than allocate the available funds according to a formula designed to maximize shareholder returns.

Remedies

To deal in detail with even the rough and incomplete list of the possible institutional failures identified here, a whole implementation design for the Polish plan would have to be presented. Clearly, this would be outside the scope of this chapter. What we shall do here, therefore, amounts to no more than an overview of the main issues that need to be addressed.

The incentives for entry. The most desirable entrant, crucial to the success of the Polish plan, is a combination of a foreign financial institution – such as a universal bank of the German type, an investment bank, a venture capital fund, or perhaps even a pension fund with significant experience of shareholder activism – with a Polish institution, such as a bank with local contacts and familiarity with a large number of Polish enterprises. Clearly, a foreign entrant of the kind described here would bring a wealth of experience in financial management and monitoring of investments, contacts in the foreign financial and industrial communities, etc. But equally important is the foreign entrant's very ability to recognize and interpret market signals for the purpose of both identifying investment opportunities and alerting the companies in its portfolio. Of similar importance is the foreign entrant's familiarity with the standard devices for improving enterprise performance. Much of this kind of knowledge is not fully articulated, and in fact resists articulation. Indeed, this 'tacit knowledge'[28] is one of the main elements of the

---

[28] Polanyi (1962).

entrepreneurial skill that constitutes the driving force of the market, and enables it to outperform even the most knowledgeable planners. And, being in principle 'tacit,' this knowledge can be acquired only by a process of socialization into an existing environment of a market economy, rather than by a more formal learning process. For this reason, it is almost entirely absent in Eastern Europe and can probably only be transplanted from outside. (The role of the Polish partner would lie not only in providing some elements of a ready-made infrastructure of financial operations, such as local branches or contacts, but also the indispensable information about, and perhaps more important, an intuitive 'feel' for, the local conditions.)

To ensure the entry of these kinds of actors, the entrants must, above all else, have a reasonable expectation that the funds that they are invited to organize will have sufficiently large assets under their management, and that their ability to exercise influence on the boards of the privatized companies will not be unduly impaired. The regulatory structure should also permit them to engage in a wide range of activities, as well as to derive a sufficient return on their investment. This means, among other things, the following features:

(1) To allow the intermediaries to have sufficiently large assets under their management, the assets that cannot be acquired in exchange for vouchers (which will be the sole 'currency' available to the inter-mediaries) will have to be limited. This underscores the importance of the fact that the social security office will receive its allocation of assets in vouchers rather than shares of the privatized companies, and that at least a substantial portion of these vouchers should find their way to the intermediaries. Similarly, the state share must be either apportioned in vouchers or otherwise left under the manage-ment of the intermediaries.

(2) The intermediaries' ability to exercise proper influence on the boards of the privatized enterprises is dependent, among other things, on the role of other institutional actors. While some counterweights to the financial institutions may be desirable, the presence of a significant continuing involvement of the state on the boards of the privatized companies will make them quite unattractive. This again underscores the need to transfer to the intermediaries the manage-ment of a large portion of the assets of the state and the social security office, since otherwise these two institutions, together with the share of the workers, will control 60 percent of the shares.

(3) A number of steps might be taken to allow the intermediaries to engage in a sufficiently wide range of activities. If the regulations do not limit the intermediaries too stringently to their functions as fund managers, they will be able to branch out into such areas as consumer, commercial, and investment banking, brokerage, and insurance. Quite apart from other benefits that may accrue to the economy from the development of these important services, the possibility of this type of expansion may make entry much more attractive to the most desirable foreign participants.

Maintaining the competitiveness of the intermediaries. Among the devices designed to assure the competitive nature of the intermediaries and to prevent their bureaucratization are the following features of the plan:

(1) It is most important that the competitive nature of the intermediaries be attended to from the very beginning. The best way to do this is to assure, as does the Polish plan, relatively free entry, limited only by clearly specified legal requirements, and leave no discretion to the state to pick and choose among the possible participants. This can be done only if the intermediaries must compete for the vouchers to be received from the population, and if their obtaining of the assets controlled by state institutions proceeds according to a more or less mechanical formula. If, on the other hand, the state limits entry to a few firms, or deposits its assets on a discretionary basis, it will encourage political selection, identify itself with the success of its choices, and create an atmosphere of bureaucratic protection.

(2) In addition to ensuring free entry, the fact that the intermediaries, from the very beginning, compete with one another for vouchers also has a direct competitive effect. Similarly, the fact that the intermediaries will acquire their portfolios at an auction will force them early on to compete in their evaluation of the companies to be privatized and to attempt to maximize the attractiveness of their holdings in anticipation of the further privatization tranches. If, on the other hand, as some earlier proposals envisaged, the intermediaries were to acquire their holdings according to some predetermined mechanical formula and be encouraged to trade afterwards, they could in fact, especially if their number is small, be tempted to collude rather than compete.

(3) The design of the compensation structure of the intermediaries is a crucial aspect of the properly competitive character of their activities.

While this component of the plan is extremely difficult to devise, especially in the absence of market prices that would determine the value of the assets under the intermediaries' management (and thus also allow for a proper evaluation of their performance), the tying, however imperfect, of the fund managers' compensation to their performance is, of course, a fundamental feature of every healthy incentive structure. In particular, making the compensation in part dependent on the value of the intermediaries' own shares may introduce a dose of competition for clients on whose behalf the funds manage the privatized companies.[29] What may be less obvious is the degree to which the state should regulate the fund managers' compensation. While it is clear that the state should regulate their compensation *structure* (to make sure that it creates a proper set of incentives), the regulation of the *size* of their compensation (by, say, fixing it at a certain specific percentage of the funds' assets or of some other benchmark values) should probably be left to the market. Not only will this increase competitive pressures, but also avoid significant mistakes. For if the state sets the amount (rather than the type) of compensation, it is extremely unlikely that it will get the numbers 'just right,' that is, so that only transfer earnings and no rents are included. But then if the state sets the amount of compensation too low, the appropriate actors will not enter; if the compensation is set too high, the funds will derive unnecessary superprofits (rents).

(4) The composition of the boards of the privatized companies will also have an effect on the degree of the intermediaries' competitive attitudes. If the company boards are dominated by the state or by other state-controlled actors, the intermediaries are likely to try to devote a substantial amount of their energies to gaining political influence rather than to pursuing a competitive advantage.

(5) Adequate antitrust regulations will undoubtedly be necessary to prevent the intermediaries from excessive concentration in a particular area of the industry and from attempting to extract monopoly rents instead of achieving competitive advantages.

Supervision of company management. Active supervision of company management is a costly proposition: it requires research, close

---

[29] This aspect of the intermediaries' compensation may make it less desirable to force them to run 'open' funds. See fn. 32.

involvement with the company, assertions of power that may invite retaliation, etc. While an active investor pays the full cost of his monitoring activities, other shareholders can automatically free ride on the efforts of those who do the actual monitoring. It is thus tempting for many institutional investors to adopt a passive posture. On the other hand, the whole purpose of privatization in Eastern Europe would be defeated if the new owners did not actively contribute to the restructuring process. Among the measures limiting passivity and encouraging activity are the following:

(1) The design of the auction at which the intermediaries acquire their portfolios in exchange for vouchers collected from the population will have a decisive influence on the nature of the intermediaries' interest in the companies in their portfolio. If the auction were to allow the intermediaries to diversify very broadly, thus taking only relatively small stakes in any particular company, it would make monitoring very expensive and the chances of its bringing sufficient benefits to any given intermediary rather small. Thus, the auction must be designed (probably through a sale of a certain proportion of the shares of each privatized company in large blocks of, say, 15–30 percent) so as to assure that each privatized company has some very substantial shareholders, for whom the returns from monitoring are sufficiently high to make a significant investment of time and resources worthwhile.

(2) As we have mentioned already, there may be an immediate inverse trade-off for an investor between the ease of 'exit,' made possible by the existence of a market assuring the liquidity of his investment, and the attractiveness of 'voice,' in the form of asserting his power as a shareholder within the company itself.[30] This relationship is important but often not appreciated, especially by those East Europeans who are attracted to the idea of unobstructed markets. For what follows from this observation is that the increased liquidity associated with the rapid development of a stock market may come at a significant cost in terms of the effectiveness of the restructuring process. This does not mean, to be sure, that the privatization plan should try to create obstacles to liquidity in general. Quite to the contrary, there may be some definite advantages in creating a market

[30] See Coffee (1991) and Hirschman (1970).

for a certain proportion of the shares of the privatized companies, since such a market may, among other benefits, permit a better evaluation both of the assets under the intermediaries' management and of their performance.[31] Such a market could be achieved, for example, through a sale of the state share to the public within a certain period of time after the initial auction. But it must also be noted that if the intermediaries themselves could easily sell their stakes in the privatized companies, their incentive to monitor may be significantly decreased. The best way to prevent this from happening may be, again, to ensure that the intermediaries take sizeable blocks of shares in particular companies, so that their trying to sell would be likely to entail a significant discount on the price of their shares.[32] Among other ways of 'locking' the intermediaries into the companies in their portfolio may be regulation against excessive diversification and the fostering of other ties between the investment funds and the companies in their portfolio (such as cross-ownership and provision of banking services).

Limiting managerial abuse. The potential conflicts of interest faced by the managers of the intermediaries are among the most serious problems arising from the Polish privatization plan. The very taxonomy of such potential conflicts and the resulting agency problems is a task that requires more attention than we can give within the scope of this chapter. The fund managers may have all kinds of perverse incentives, beginning with maximizing their own power, and ending with trying to syphon off profits from the companies in their portfolio to the funds themselves or (even worse) to their foreign 'mother' institutions. Moreover, even an

---

[31] Japan, among the industrialized countries, has this type of divided ownership structure, since many Japanese companies (forming the so-called *keiretsu*s) own substantial portions of each others' shares and do not trade in them, while the remainder of their shares is owned by outside investors, who trade very actively. Cross shareholdings among companies in three of the *keiretsu* groups (Mitsui, Mitsubishi, and Sumitomo) are between 55 percent and 74 percent. This figure is somewhat lower for the other groups, but still ranks between 32 percent and 49 percent. While the holdings by institutional shareholders in Japan are estimated at between 60–80 percent of all the shares on the Tokyo Stock Exchange, these institutions account for only 10 percent of transactions on Japanese stock exchanges. See Gerlach (1987).

[32] Many people familiar with the Polish plan believe it would be desirable to make the intermediaries into open funds as soon as possible. If what we claim is correct, this view might be problematic, since the opening of the intermediaries might force them to diminish their stakes in the companies in their portfolio, in order to preserve liquidity. As a result, they are likely to stop being active. On the other hand, having closed funds might make the control of the fund's management more difficult.

abbreviated catalog of these possibilities of abuse makes it clear that, while properly structuring the fund managers' compensation may be an important way of lessening the agency problems, it would be fatuous to hope that all the potential abuses could be taken care of through these means. The variety and complexity of the situations in which the agency problems can arise make the writing of a perfect management contract – ensuring full incentive compatibility – into a dream. In fact, even attempting to write such a contract might make us too cautious and, by an excessive curtailment of the fund managers' discretion, limit their ability to operate too strictly.

Thus, it is very important to devise further mechanisms that could be used to control the possibility of these kinds of abuse:

(1) A principal means of limiting the possibility of abuse by the managers of the intermediaries is to make sure that there are other 'players' who may be relied on to monitor and control their actions. Thus, for example, it may be advisable to have other types of directors on the boards of the privatized companies in addition to those named by the financial institutions. Among them may be some 'independent' directors or the 'core investor' brought in through the sale of the state share, or even the workers' representatives, who are likely to defend the management against strong shareholder intervention.[33]

(2) The Polish plan envisages one state representative on the inter-mediaries' boards, at least as long as the intermediaries manage the

---

[33] One can observe widespread hostility to worker participation among the commentators writing on East European privatizations. The Polish authorities have also strenuously opposed giving workers a significant share of ownership or a voice on the boards of the privatized companies. On the one hand, this resistance is quite understandable: after all, much of the present inefficiency of the Polish firms derives from the influence of the workers' councils on the management. There are also widespread, and probably justified, fears that a large amount of worker participation would make Polish enterprises less attractive to foreign investors. On the other hand, worker participation, if kept within appropriate limits, often amounts to a degree of support for the management against external shareholders intent on 'ruthless' profit maximization at the expense of worker privileges. This support may be of value in a situation in which a dominant outside shareholder with a potential conflict of interest (such as a supplier or a banker who is also the company's creditor) attempts to pressure the management to accede to some measures that may not be in the company's interest (such as buying goods or taking a loan at above market prices). Some observers have noted such countervailing effects in Germany, where workers' participation on the executive boards of companies is required by law. See Franks and Mayer (1990) p. 19; and Monissen (1978).

state portfolio. Such a representative, if indeed his voice is not for some reason out of proportion to his number, may not be a disturbing presence, but may at the same time exercise some useful function in monitoring the intermediaries themselves.

(3) The existence of open financial markets, and an unobstructed access to international sources of credit may provide some counterweight to the financial power of the intermediaries, and make a company manager less likely to be entirely dependent on a director representing a potentially exploitative intermediary.

(4) A set of properly designed disclosure rules may make exploitative behavior by the intermediaries more difficult, without excessively limiting their freedom of legitimate action.

Development of flexible financial institutions. Finally, insofar as the creation of an effective system for the allocation of finance is concerned, the intermediaries must be ensured of enough flexibility, and not be unduly restricted to a narrow range of activities. To be sure, the wider their powers, the more likely it becomes that they may find ways of engaging in exploitative or opportunistic practices and hide this fact from the public (or the appropriate authorities). If the intermediaries are allowed, for example, to arrange loans from their mother companies (foreign banks or other financial institutions) to the companies in their portfolio or to force them to use suppliers who are affiliated with the intermediary or its mother institution, the possibilities of abuse are substantially increased. Unfortunately, however, there is no foolproof way of preventing all such abuses, without at the same time making the intermediaries incapable of fulfilling one of their crucial tasks, namely, the facilitation of the financing of the companies in their portfolio. On the whole, it seems to us that it would be quite desirable for the East European countries to encourage the transformation of the intermediaries into something akin to the German 'universal banks,' and not to hem them in with American Glass–Steagall-type restrictions. In this context, the intermediaries should be able to influence transfers of funds among the enterprises in their portfolio, combine their monitoring activities with investment and merchant banking activities, and engage in consumer banking operations. This may be particularly important in Poland, where the banking system is woefully inadequate, and foreign banks do not seem overeager to enter. Should it turn out to be desirable in the future to scale down the intermediaries' role and influence, a set of standard divestiture techniques is likely to be available. But it might very well turn out that the more diversified the role of the intermediaries, the more likely they are to develop a lasting commitment to the development of the country and to become increasingly stable, good citizens of the local economic community.

3 Evolution and Design in the East European Transition*

Most of the work on privatization in Eastern Europe to date has concentrated on the change of ownership issues and their importance for the restructuring process.[1] In our earlier work, we have linked these issues to the broader question of the future corporate governance structure in Eastern Europe.[2] So far we have looked at the impact of privatization primarily in terms of its effect on each enterprise taken as a unit, which is also true of the literature in general. The aggregate effects of privatization are usually left out of account, presumably on the assumption that the interaction among firms and the effect of their restructuring on the economy as a whole has no particular bearing on the appropriate method and scope of privatization to be pursued on the enterprise level.[3]

Here we shall begin to fill this gap in the literature and link the discussion of the various approaches to large-scale privatization with other problems of economic transition, such as the absence of a general infrastructure of the capitalist economy (the banking system and capital

* This chapter is a revised version of a paper which appeared under the same title in *Rivista di Politica Economica*, 81 (November 1991), pp. 63–103. The authors thank the following persons for stimulating conversations on the topics related to this paper: Bruce Ackerman, Fabrizio Coricelli, Irena Grosfeld, Edmund Phelps, George Soros, Stanislaw Wellisz, and Charles Wilson. Martin Gargiulo and Markus Kreuzer were helpful with their research assistance.

[1] See Blanchard, Dornbusch et al. (1990), Grosfeld (1991b), Grosfeld and Hare (1991), Lipton and Sachs (1990).

[2] See Chapters 2 and 3 in this volume.

[3] The only exception in this respect is the common exhortation that privatization should be accomplished quickly and that this precludes certain traditional forms and requires new ones. As we shall argue later in this chapter, the problem of the appropriate speed of privatization is in fact much more complex.

markets) and the state of the existing capital stock, which may make many post-communist enterprises nonviable in a competitive environment. The example of East Germany since German unification makes this last subject particularly important. To be sure, the disastrous performance of East German enterprises following unification may be due to a number of factors that are not shared with the other parts of Eastern Europe.[4] Nevertheless, the East German example is potentially quite chilling for the rest of the region. One of the informational constraints under which the East European reformers operate is the absence of any reliable knowledge as to what percentage of the capital stock of their countries is hopelessly obsolete or otherwise nonviable. In this context, if the failures of the East German economy are in fact largely due to the state of its capital stock, a rapid and effective method of privatization, introducing true competition and genuinely hard budget constraints in the rest of Eastern Europe, may lead to a similar string of bankruptcies and to levels of unemployment that none of the countries involved, without the cushion of enormous transfers from the West, would be able to afford. The analysis of privatization should therefore encompass not only issues related to corporate governance structure, but also the relation between privatization plans and the information concerning the quality of available capital stock and the aggregate effects of microeconomic reform. Only then will the full policy implications (including the appropriate speed of privatization) of the various proposals for change come to the fore.

In our earlier work we stressed that the economic transition in Eastern Europe involves a very complex interaction, between a 'planned' element of economic design, aiming at a change in the direction of further development, and an array of spontaneous forces defining the context within which the change will be taking place. On the one hand, the material and organizational structure of East European economies, reflecting the bureaucratic command system which had set it up, does not allow for the transition to be left to spontaneous developments alone: a deliberate intervention by the reformers is necessary to overcome the inertia of the old and to initiate a genuine process of change. At the same time – and this, in our view, is a crucial aspect of the transition – the reformers operate under a tremendous

---

[4] The rise of wages to a level equal to half of those in West Germany is often blamed for the failure of many East German enterprises. Immediate unlimited entry of West German goods, uncertainties concerning titles, and flawed policies of the Treuhandanstalt are also cited. For an analysis of these issues see Siebert, Schmieding and Nunnenkamp (1991).

handicap: not only do they not know the future, which makes all planning risky; they do not even know the past, in the sense of not having genuine information concerning the existing state of affairs which a gradual evolution of the market economies makes naturally available to policymakers in the West. In this situation, the reformers' design is bound to fail, unless at least two conditions are met: (*i*) the process of change is set up in such a way as to generate by itself enough information which, when fed back into the reform process, can allow for a proper adjustment of the design, and (*ii*) the design is flexible enough to leave sufficient room for spontaneous future developments.

We shall adopt here the same perspective of the relation between design and evolution which we used previously.[5] We shall begin, therefore, with the points of departure of East European reform and diagnose the particular handicaps faced by the reformers due to the peculiar developmental history of Eastern Europe. We shall then discuss the problems this poses with respect to designing a reform program and point to a few factors that may make this process somewhat less overwhelming.

The point of departure

The condition of the capital stock – the real side of the economy

It would be a mistake to say that the command economy did not have an evolutionary dimension, independent of the planners' decisions and intent. In fact, there existed a number of mechanisms that asserted themselves over and over against the planners' design. But the evolution of the planned economy had its own perverse dynamics which blocked the weeding out of nonviable enterprises and contributed to the creation of enterprises that had no *ratio essendi* from the very beginning. As we have mentioned already, this raises the possibility that the proportion of nonviable enterprises in East European economies may be so large as to put a question mark over the state's ability to afford a rapid exposure of the whole state sector to genuine discipline of the market.

While this aspect of the problem of the capital stock in Eastern Europe is well known, the problem also has another, more complex

---

[5] An evolutionary perspective has also been adopted in Grosfeld (1991a).

dimension, which has not received proper attention. It is common to observe that the incentives of the managers of the so-called socialist enterprises were so distorted that the managers did not maximize those aspects of the enterprises' performance which were the most important from the general societal point view. It is also often observed that some of the enterprises were created to respond to the needs perceived by the planners (or imposed on them by the dynamics of the system), rather than to satisfy genuine demand. Quite independently from all these factors, however, the nature of the planned economy contributed to the creation of certain links among the enterprises which may have made them incapable, or at least much less capable, of functioning within a market economy.

One of the fundamental features of a market economy, when analyzed from an evolutionary perspective, is a considerable amount of duplication among firms in a given branch of production. The fact that the opportunity set for any particular firm is not known *a priori*, but is continually redefined and rediscovered in the process of actually engaging in the firm's activity, means that at any time, but especially when a given industry or technology is in the earlier periods of its development (and flexibility and innovation are still important), different firms will perceive different opportunities in the same area and adopt different strategies for securing the same markets.[6]

This duplication, characteristic of a market economy, not only appeared wasteful and messy to the central planner; it also flew in the face of his desire to structure the industry in a way that would simplify the chain through which the commands of the center would have to travel before they were executed. Moreover, a socialist enterprise never faced the problem of losing the demand for its products because its 'customers' were its captives within the plan. What this means is that, within the context of a socialist economy, there was very little incentive to organize firms as genuinely separate units. Unlike in a market economy, in which vertical integration or other forms of common organization always have their cost in terms of diminished flexibility and the loss of alternative (competitive) sources of supply, the extent of integration in a socialist economy is not limited by any factors beyond

---

[6] Later, when an industry matures and if a 'dominant design' should emerge, the amount of duplication will be reduced and each surviving firm is more likely to have its own niche in the market. We are indebted to Nelson (1991) for the insights concerning duplication of efforts in a market economy. For an earlier comprehensive treatment of these issues see Nelson and Winter (1982).

administrative convenience.[7] In a sense, the planner may really think about the whole economy as one firm, with a number of administrative units, departments and subsidiaries.[8] In this giant 'company' the planner may separate some tasks, but keep others entirely integrated.[9]

The picture presented here is, of course, a stylized one. To the extent to which the planner intended to decentralize the system and avail himself of the benefits of some market-like mechanisms, his tendency to think of the whole economy as one firm had to be modified. Still, the problem that the socialist mode of industrial organization generated transcends the normal concern about the 'monopolies' created by a planned economy. To the extent that large sections of a socialist economy could, up to a point, be thought of as one huge firm, one could expect that each unit of this system would be rather rigidly fitted into the specific place it occupied within the whole. Not only would it be designed without any thought of flexibility, but also, to the extent that the system provided any incentives to produce more efficiently, individual units would develop as many synergies as possible with their immediate suppliers and the recipients of their outputs. In other words, each unit would probably invest heavily in 'niche specific' assets, and this asset specificity would make it very difficult for the firm to function in another environment.

If what we are saying is correct, the cost of transition to a market economy may be quite staggering. In fact, if privatization separates the purely administrative units of the communist economy and forces them to sink or swim on their own, the initial performance of the economy may deteriorate even with respect to the previous low level. That the new companies will be hard put to find new markets for their very specific goods is quite obvious, and they will naturally tend to continue their old associations with their partners in the socialist chain of production. But in addition to resisting genuine transformation, their cooperation with the old partners may now be less smooth and more wasteful than ever.

It may be helpful to look at this problem as a reverse of the process described by Oliver Williamson in his work on institutional integration

---

[7] For an analysis of the theory of the firm in a centrally planned economy, see Zieleniec (1990).

[8] Wiles (1984), p. 39.

[9] An example of a function that remained integrated throughout the whole of the state sector of the communist economy was the choice of the executive personnel, done through a centralized system of so-called '*nomenklatura*' (in essence a central, politically reliable personnel department). Other functions, such as foreign trade, were also highly integrated, this time at the level of a particular industry, rather than of the economy as a whole.

in a market economy.[10] Williamson's theory of the firm postulates that agents who face high transaction costs of operating in a market environment might combine together to lessen these costs. Thus, if a supplier were required to make very 'asset specific' investments in order to provide a better product for the customer (or a customer were able to realize some gains by becoming dependent on a single source of supply), the parties would have serious problems in writing and enforcing a contract to protect themselves adequately against opportunistic (exploitative) behavior by the other party. Similarly, parties may find it difficult to provide each other with important proprietary information that might facilitate their cooperation. In this situation, they may economize on the transaction costs by integrating their operations and reduce the uncertainties they face by becoming two branches of the same firm.

A transition from the socialist system to a market economy reverses this process. While integration under a market system often saves on transaction costs associated with negotiating a satisfactory relation between the parties, disintegration (separation) of the parties accustomed to cooperate with each other in the socialist economy may produce new transaction costs in a market environment. For many years different units in the socialist economy were encouraged (and often forced) to develop such close relationships with each other that they may have become almost totally dependent on their partners for their survival. As long as they were parts of the same 'organization,' the possibilities for opportunistic behavior were severely limited. But when they separate from each other and are made to renegotiate the terms of their new relationship, the transaction costs of their cooperation may increase to the point of becoming a serious obstacle to further development. In their attempts to gain one-sided advantage over their partners in the division of real or imagined rents, the parties may now push each other beyond the point of viability, or they may be locked in a duopoly in which each will be wasting its resources on trying to gain one-sided advantages until they reach an agreement to back into the (perhaps undesirable) *status quo ante*.[11]

---

[10] See Williamson (1975, 1985). For an alternative approach to the same issues, see Grossman and Hart (1986).

[11] The transaction costs of interfirm bargaining can still be increased by the fact that the firms do not face genuine hard budget constraints. While direct subsidies from the state budget have been drastically cut or eliminated by the recent reforms, East European firms can still be subsidized through credits extended by state banks (which are unable to judge the credit worthiness of their clients) or by other enterprises (extending so-called 'interfirm credit'). As a

It is difficult to gauge the extent of such transition problems, but some evidence from the area of so-called 'spontaneous privatization' indicates that they may be serious. 'Spontaneous privatization' refers to privatizations proposed and arranged by state enterprises themselves. In virtually all of these cases, the management, commonly with the support of the workers, is behind the initiative, but their real motives are often unknown. The managers may, of course, intend to liberate the company from the restraints of the old system and attempt a genuine improvement in the company's performance. Or, as is often suspected, they may have in mind appropriating some of the company's assets to themselves, or selling a part of the company in order to prolong the survival of the old ways, or they may be acting under the pressure of workers who want to get out of the system of wage controls imposed on state enterprises.[12] In some cases, however, the aim is clearly to improve the company's position by exploiting its peculiar advantages in the post-communist economy.

Consider, for example, the case (based on real facts in Poland) of a certain 'Design Company' of the kind that the old system commonly attached to a large industrial group or a giant state enterprise. The Design Company, under the old system, was created (often by the consumer of its outputs) to provide, on an exclusive basis, a whole variety of services, such as designing and introducing new engineering solutions or technical improvements, performing complex repairs, etc. The personnel of the company was often trained at the customer's expense and, in its constant cooperation with the recipients of its services, acquired intimate knowledge of the commonly unique, nonstandard technologies used by the customers. (In fact, given the isolation of the communist economies, the nonstandard technologies were often developed by the Design Company itself.) Now, regardless of whether the Design Company has been functioning as a department of a larger unit or as a formally independent enterprise, it wants to be transformed into a self-standing joint-stock company, preferably owned by the employees themselves. Since the company may not have substantial capital assets, the immediate motive behind its privatization proposal may be a desire to escape from the strict system of wage

---

result, the size of the rents available for division is more indeterminate than in an analogous situation in a genuine market economy and the firms may more easily bargain themselves into non-viability.

[12] The last is commonly the case in Poland, where privatized enterprises are not subject to the prohibitive tax imposed on 'excessive' wage increases in the state sector.

controls. At the same time, however, the customer – say, a huge antiquated steel mill, for whom the company produces virtually its whole output – may not be a viable enterprise or may need to cut its costs in order to pull itself out of the red. Nevertheless, as long as the steel mill continues in operation, it is virtually a captive of the Design Company with respect to the provision of its services. It is not surprising, therefore, that in the new situation, the Design Company, even though it may be itself totally dependent on the steel mill, might be able to extract very considerable rents, all the while imposing additional large costs on the steel mill and making it even less able to restructure.[13]

A related aspect of the East European economies is their specialization on the international level, in particular their dependence on the Soviet market for substandard goods, as well as their production geared to the special needs of the Soviet economy. In both of these cases, East European enterprises also made something akin to an asset specific investment, and the consequences of the collapse of the Soviet market may go beyond the usual difficulties faced by a producer whose old customers have disappeared. The problem lies not just in finding new markets, but in a need to change the output and the production process as well.

Information and prices

The possibility that a large part of the capital stock of the East European economies may consist of nonviable enterprises and that many synergies among the existing units may significantly increase the

---

[13] To the extent that privatization is preceded by far-reaching decentralization (as was the case in both Poland and Hungary), the increased transaction costs of negotiating a new relationship among the previously integrated firms should become noticeable earlier. Thus, it may very well be that the unexpectedly high level of inflation following the stabilization reforms in Poland in 1990 has been due in part to this problem. The authors of the *Balcerowicz Plan* had been aware, of course, that the existence of numerous monopolies in the Polish economy could lead to price fixing following decontrol, but they thought they could deal with this problem by lowering tariffs and opening the economy to outside competition. But if what we are saying is correct, the problem is not limited to the absence of competition; it may very well consist in the existence of a large number of local monopolies due to the previously created synergies and asset specific investments. The resulting relations of dependence could then be exploited by particular actors who attempted to extract rents as a result of their specific position within the post-communist chain of production, setting off a chain reaction of inflation. The presence of outside sources of supply may not affect this situation for a while, not only because the firms are bound to each other by the institution of 'interfirm credit,' but also because sunk investment in the synergies surviving from the past make the new entrants noncompetitive.

transaction costs of a transition to a market economy is bad enough. But what makes matters even worse is that prior to initiating the process of reforms *there is no way in which the authorities can learn the extent of these problems*. Again, East Germany, despite all the differences in its situation, provides a potentially chilling example: prior to unification, 20 percent of East German companies were considered nonviable.[14] The estimate increased to 40 percent (with unemployment predicted at 25 percent) shortly afterwards.[15] By April, 1991, industrial output had fallen by 51 per cent since July, 1990, and unemployment (including workers on short schedules) rose to 30 percent. The process is still going on, with unemployment predictions of 51 percent by the end of 1991.[16] In the context of a united Germany, with a deep pocket from which to cover the expenses of unemployment and no real danger of political unrest, the question may be of more limited interest (although even there fiscal consequences of the bailout are becoming serious). In other East European countries, the missing information has crucial policy implications. If, for example, a course of rapid privatization is adopted and no way is found to separate nonviable enterprises from the rest, the introduction of genuine market discipline and hard budget constraints may lead to mass unemployment for which the government will be unable to prepare. If, on the other hand, the state modifies its commitment to a genuine market economy by a policy of aiding the firms that cannot make it in the new environment, the restructuring effort, especially in the situation in which the state cannot know which enterprises are really in danger, is more than likely to be compromised. Quite surprisingly, however, the macroeconomic policy issues have so far been dealt with separately from the privatization question, and no attention has been paid to them in evaluating the alternative privatization proposals.

Another informational barrier posed by the system inherited from the past is the absence of a genuine price system. While this problem is evident throughout the post-communist economies, it is particularly acute in, and of particular relevance to, the question of privatization, in the context of determining the value of an existing enterprise. We have dealt extensively with this problem in Chapter 1, and mention it here only to reemphasize that valuation problems limit the options available to the state in pursuing its privatization strategy, and to repeat that

---

[14] See Blanchard, Dornbusch et al. (1990), p. 84.
[15] See *Washington Post*, July 2, 1990.
[16] See *The Economist*, April 6, 1991.

different privatization schemes must in turn be looked at with respect to how much they can contribute to the solution of these valuation problems.

The absence of financial infrastructure

One of the main obstacles to further development of the postcommunist economies is the absence of a genuine banking system. Similarly missing is an infrastructure of a capital market, and it may be very difficult to create it within a short period of time. Thus, the way in which the development of the postcommunist economies will be financed in the future is a question that needs to be confronted. Moreover, the way in which these economies are privatized is not unrelated to this question.

The banking reform in Eastern Europe, especially in Poland and Czechoslovakia, is still in its infancy. Until recently, banking was completely centralized, with commercial banking being simply a branch of the central bank's activity. The central bank was, in turn, merely an instrument of state planning and control, the importance of which grew as other central planning institutions were relinquishing some of their direct power over the enterprises. In this situation, the central bank, through its local branches, was supposed to assure that the enterprises maintained such balance between investment, wages, and working capital as the state considered desirable.

With Hungary following a somewhat different path, postcommunist reforms in Poland and Czechoslovakia divided the central banks into a number of independent institutions and attempted to introduce some commercial realism into enterprise financing. In practice, however, reforming the banks has not produced a significantly more rational system. First of all, a peculiar East European institution, the so-called 'interfirm credit,' has largely circumvented the banking system altogether. In this arrangement, firms extend credit to their customers and become in turn indebted to their suppliers. Many of the firms show paper profits, but in fact a large portion of their assets consists in the indebtedness of other enterprises, which are in turn linked in this way to others, etc. As a result, the solvency of any particular link in this chain is related to all the others, and no one really knows which are still viable. Second, the banks, with no significantly better knowledge of the real soundness of their clients, developed a system of lending which relies on the entirely unreliable accounting practices still in force, and tend to lend to the larger institutions whose capital assets look like valuable collateral. Together with a centrally controlled interest rate, this system means in practice that large state enterprises of dubious viability can still obtain significant amounts of credit (with which they continue to maintain high levels of employment and postpone radical managerial changes), while the new private sector, with its very thin capitalization, is unable to obtain affordable financing. It seems quite likely that without the entry of a significant foreign component in the banking area, the reform of the financial infrastructure of the East European economies will be seriously retarded.

The limitations of government

The quality of the civil service is another factor limiting the scope of successful reforms. The old bureaucrats had been appointed on the basis of their political reliability and lack of personal independence. The new governments have started to exchange the old personnel, but the process is slow, and the new people are often without much experience (especially when the required expertise involves familiarity with business transactions). Consequently, even in those areas in which government policy in the more stable countries of the West may successfully complement the market, there is serious doubt whether the East European bureaucracies could be trusted to achieve similar results. It will be necessary, therefore, to adopt whenever possible policies that involve minimum reliance on the ability of government officials to make significant decisions. Privatization programs are no exception here. Indeed, they pose some of the most difficult challenges for the government bureaucracy, and different privatization proposals should be evaluated with the idea of economizing on governmental expertise very much in mind.

Evolution or design? The limits of social engineering

In the previous section, we have tried to show how the East European reformers are handicapped in making decisions concerning the appropriate privatization policy by the absence of crucial information about the point of departure of the East European economies. Because this informational barrier stems from the peculiar developmental path of the region, we have characterized the reformers' handicap as their relative inability to 'know the past.'

This, together with the special difficulties the East European reformers have in predicting the future development of their economies,[17] makes planning the transition into an unusually daunting task. Indeed, the East European reformers face a genuine conundrum: they do not really know where they are starting from, where they can or want to arrive, and, last but not least, how to get there. And yet, the transition must, to a considerable extent, be designed, and the reformers cannot afford to rely on spontaneous developments, since the special interests tied to the status quo in Eastern Europe are much stronger than those committed to change.[18] The greatest challenge of the reform program, therefore, is to combine creatively the elements of evolution and design within an appropriately flexible, open-ended institutional framework.

Only a substantive discussion of concrete privatization proposals can bring out the details of this approach. But before proceeding to such a discussion, it will be useful to state two formal features which might be called the basic conditions of institutional innovation.

(1) In order to combine market mechanisms and policy intervention, the reform design must reduce the unacceptably high level of uncertainty at the point of departure. This means that the design must contain mechanisms that reveal as much information as possible in the early stages of the reform process, so that those in authority can use the information to refine and modify government policy and avoid commitments which may have serious unforeseen consequences.

(2) The design must contain self-correcting mechanisms that will allow for a spontaneous evolution of the system instituted by the reform. This feature is made necessary by the fact that no amount of information available at the beginning of the reform process will be sufficient to allow for a fail-proof institutional arrangement. While the reformer cannot foresee everything, he may nevertheless be able to identify the basic types of failure to which the system may be prone. Thus, while the design cannot be made perfect, a number of institutional devices may be inserted into it that can perhaps develop on their own and spontaneously counter some of the most obvious dangers.

[17] See Chapter 2 of this volume.

[18] The special interests' configuration in Eastern Europe is analyzed in Chapter 4. The pitfalls of allowing the economies in the region to develop spontaneously are further analyzed in Chapter 6.

These two formal features distinguish, in our opinion, all successful institutional innovations from conventional planning schemes. Like a system of checks and balances in the constitutional sphere, they allow for an interplay between spontaneity and design, and offer a hope of avoiding the most common pitfalls of 'scientific' attempts to control historical events.

In what follows we shall limit our discussion of the institutional design of the East European transition programs to the most important privatization schemes, namely, those that propose to transfer the beneficial ownership of a large part of state enterprises to the general population (or a large fraction of it), while concentrating control functions in a small number of intermediary institutions. Schemes of this kind have been analyzed in considerable detail in the previous chapters; here, we shall concentrate on those details of their institutional design that may alleviate the problems related to the peculiar condition of the capital stock of the privatized enterprises – the informational gaps concerning their worth or viability, the transaction costs of their breakup, and the lack of a proper regulatory capacity of the government.

The policy implications of the state of capital stock: the speed of privatization

One of the most important differences among the various privatization proposals concerns the way in which they plan to distribute the shares of the privatized enterprises among the intermediary institutions. Some plans[19] envisage a mechanical or administrative allocation, such as giving each intermediary an equal number of shares in each company to be privatized or dividing all of the companies into several groups of 'roughly equal value'[20] and allocating each group (perhaps at random) to one fund. Other plans[21] propose a system of allocation through an auction during which each intermediary would bid, with the help of special vouchers or investment points, for the companies it would like to acquire.

---

[19] For example those proposed by Blanchard and Layard (1990), and Lipton and Sachs (1990).
[20] We put this phrase in quotation marks because we believe that the task of assigning (even rough) values to state enterprises before privatization is truly Herculean (or perhaps rather Sisyphean). The idea that anyone would be able to do that for several hundred companies within a span of a few months appears to us entirely unrealistic.
[21] See Chapter 1 and Frydman and Rapaczynski (1990).

We have explained that the developmental path of the post-communist economies ensures that a certain proportion of state enterprises have negative value and could not survive in a competitive environment. The natural temptation of East European policymakers (and, surprisingly enough, many Western analysts as well) is to want to make sure that the state is not put in a position of having gotten rid of all the valuable enterprises (which constitute a potential source of revenue for the budget) and being left with the worthless scrap of the communist inheritance. Consequently, it is often viewed as an advantage of the plans which envisage a mechanical or administrative system of allocating the shares of the privatized enterprises among the intermediaries that this will also force the intermediaries to accept the weakest enterprises along with the strongest. In fact, however, the effects of such a strategy are likely to be nothing short of disastrous.

The fact that a large part of the country's capital stock may be nonviable carries with it a potential danger that a rapid exposure of the enterprises with negative value to the rigors of hard budget constraints and a competitive environment may result in a string of bankruptcies, leading to a swift fall in production and skyrocketing levels of unemployment. This, in turn, may destabilize the political situation and endanger the whole reform process. One of the main problems with adopting a scheme of rapid privatization, therefore, is that the government may have no way of knowing in advance whether its very effectiveness in moving the country into a market environment will not have the dreaded avalanche effect.

If, indeed, the state of the country's capital stock conforms to the gloomier predictions, the government, having chosen to embark on a privatization scheme with a mechanical or administrative allocation, is soon likely to be faced with extremely unpleasant alternatives. If the intermediaries are free to behave in a way in which an ordinary owner of capital does, they will simply let all the nonviable companies fail. If, on the other hand, as is very likely, the government comes to the conclusion that such a result will not be acceptable to it, it will have to impose on the intermediaries a regime that is well-nigh certain to destroy their effectiveness as agents of genuine restructuring.

It is doubtful whether the government will be able to force the intermediaries to use the proceeds from their restructuring efforts to subsidize the white elephants forced on them by the state. But if it does, it will have basically managed to return to the old communist rule of using proceeds from the more efficient enterprises to subsidize the less efficient ones. The more likely result is that the state will have to provide the subsidies itself. This, in turn, will make it clear to the intermediaries that the safest source of their income lies not in the strenuous job of restructuring but in extracting ever greater amounts of money from the state coffers. This will be particularly true in light of the fact that the state will have no way of knowing how many of the enterprises in the intermediaries' portfolios are indeed nonviable, and will thus open itself to a classic opportunistic strategy by these institutions.[22] Consequently, whether or not the number of nonviable enterprises is in fact large, the outcome might very will be the same.

There exists, however, a relatively simple mechanism which is capable of revealing to the government the approximate extent of the capital stock problems in advance of any irrevocable decisions, thus allowing it to determine the best policy option for controlling the resulting dislocations. This mechanism consists in a standard market mode of allocating the privatized companies to the intermediaries, namely, an *auction* at which the intermediaries bid for the companies they want with the help of an artificial currency, such as vouchers or investment points.[23]

Using an auction as an allocation mechanism has rather obvious advantages to begin with. First of all, various potential managers of the intermediaries might have different skills: some may be specialized in certain types of companies, others may have particular contacts among certain types of businesses abroad and might want to use their help in the restructuring process (perhaps by selling to them a portion of the shares of the privatized companies), still others may be good at liquidating businesses and selling their assets. In all such cases, the prospective managers of the intermediaries would like to be able to influence the choice of the companies in their funds' portfolios, as well the degree of their investment in any particular company – none of which would be possible in a system of random or mechanical allocation.[24] Moreover, the very idea of having to deal with a large number of companies that have potentially negative values may deter good fund managers from entering the field in the first place. But the

---

[22] Incidentally, the fact that this type of outcome is predictable to any potential manager of an intermediary in advance of his entry means that the entrants will self-select for their rent-seeking skills, with the more enterprising managers choosing other business opportunities.

[23] The Appendix at the end of this chapter describes a simple auction of this kind.

[24] In a system of administrative allocation, it might be possible to take managerial preferences into account. But the managers would probably spend more time on lobbying politicians to obtain a few obvious winners among the enterprises scheduled for privatization than on researching most of those enterprises.

most important advantage of an auction is the fact that it would force the managers of the intermediaries to invest seriously in research into the companies to be privatized. (In fact, this would be the only serious initial investment required of the prospective fund managers in exchange for their right to the future streams of income from a local economy.) If a list of the companies to be privatized is announced a few months before the auction to be held, every fund manager will know that his future success depends to a large extent on the wisdom of his initial assessments. He will therefore try to find out as much as possible about the enterprises he might be interested in, and particularly about those with respect to which his special skills may allow him to outbid other buyers. As a result, the necessary precondition of genuine restructuring, the preparation of the plans by which the privatized enterprises may be turned around, will begin in earnest immediately upon the plan's announcement.

In other words, the inclusion of a well-designed auction in a privatization plan will immediately engage the private sector in a competitive process of information gathering, the results of which will become available to the government as well. Unlike the endless valuations commissioned by the East European states in connection with their efforts to sell some of the state enterprises, the research which will be going on here will be done not by consultants, but by businessmen and entrepreneurs who will be backing their estimates with investment decisions.[25] Thus, while no valuations of post-communist enterprises can be fully reliable (because the level of uncertainty is simply too high), these entrepreneurial estimates are probably as good as one can get. And when the auction takes place, all the information gathered in this decentralized market-like fashion will be put together and may be used by all.

From the point of view of the government, probably the most important piece of information to result from the auction will be the number of enterprises that not even one of the fund managers believes has any potential for being turned around.[26] For it is precisely in this

---

[25] Also, as we saw in Chapter 1, the valuations will be simpler, since the prospective fund managers, looking to purchasing the shares of the privatized enterprises with otherwise worthless vouchers, will try to assess the enterprises' *relative* value (i.e. to rank them with respect to one another), rather than determine their monetary worth (which makes it necessary to compare them with all other potential investments).

[26] If there is only one bidder for a given enterprise, a well-designed auction might give it to that bidder for free. Thus, if no one bids for an enterprise, it means everyone thinks it has negative value. See the Appendix for how such an auction might work.

way that the government will quickly obtain a relatively good estimate of the size of the worthless capital stock in the state sector. If the number is not large, so much the better. But if it is large (as might very well be the case), the state may now determine its policy with respect to that part of the state sector, without risking an unexpected shock wave of plant closures or skyrocketing unemployment, and – most importantly – without compromising the restructuring effort with respect to those enterprises that have some potential. The state might at this point assume that the companies transferred to the intermediaries are considered to have some positive value by their new owners. To be sure, the funds might have made some mistakes, and consequently some of the enterprises might still be closed down. Also, some may have been acquired with an idea of liquidation in mind. But by and large, the state can adopt the position that the funds should be given full responsibility for the companies in their portfolios, and take the attitude of firmly refusing to subsidize them in any way. With respect to those left in its possession, on the other hand, the state will be free to adopt a number of policies that will not lead to rapid destabilization or social unrest. It may decide to pay off the debts of some of the enterprises and attempt to auction them again later or give them to the workers. Or it may decide to subsidize them temporarily in some other way, and proceed with a staggered program of closures, so that the newly developing private sector may provide jobs for at least some of the unemployed. The state might even proceed with a privatization of sorts, by putting the white elephants into special liquidation funds, to be auctioned off to those who would undertake to manage them for the lowest amount of subsidies. But in all of these cases, good enterprises would be separated from the bad, so that a continuation of some subsidies would not demoralize the rest of the industry and endanger the restructuring of the whole economy.[27]

One of the consequences of what has been said so far is that much

[27] It should be noted that the proposal offered here also raises serious possibilities of strategic manipulation on the part of the intermediaries. If, for example, the funds know that the state may subsidize the companies they do not acquire during the auction, the funds may attempt to acquire some companies (those that would potentially compete on subsidized terms with the other companies in a given fund's portfolio) just in order to close them down right away and to avoid competition. Or the funds may not bid for companies they consider in fact viable (or at least potentially viable) in the hope that they may acquire them later together with a state subsidy. While problems of this kind are serious, we believe they may be mitigated by a proper design of the subsidy scheme. (We would like to thank Bruce A. Ackerman for turning our attention to the problems of strategic manipulation discussed here.)

of the discussion about the speed with which privatization should proceed in Eastern Europe is basically misguided. Those who say that the state should privatize everything immediately usually have no real appreciation of the political and social problems that may result from a sudden string of bankruptcies of the nonviable state enterprises. On the other hand, those who propose a more gradual process usually underestimate the difficulty that the restructuring process will encounter if the state remains in control for too long and new vested interests develop their hold over the political process of privatization. The answer to the question 'How fast?' needs to be more nuanced than 'fast' or 'slow.' Those enterprises that are capable of being privatized, i.e. those which are either viable in a competitive environment or could be profitably liquidated, should be privatized immediately. Those which are not viable and require a period of transition should be dealt with differently, and not closed down overnight. The problem is how to tell the former from the latter, and the answer is provided by a well-designed auction system as a component of the privatization program. This component will reveal important information at the outset of the reform process and allow for later modifications of its course in light of the knowledge it provides.

Reducing transaction costs

A market allocation of the privatized enterprises to the intermediaries may also provide a partial solution to the problem of opportunistic behavior by the newly privatized firms attempting to exploit the advantages created by their peculiar position within the postcommunist economy. It will be remembered that these advantages could accrue to some firms because the planned economy had fostered a large number of 'niche specific' investments, making many firms too dependent on their suppliers and the recipients of their outputs. In a new situation, in which the firms are free to renegotiate their relations, there may be high transaction costs associated with the transition.

The exact extent to which niche specific investments are capable of slowing down the transition is unknown, and the government has few ways of learning about it. While an auction may reveal the number of nonviable enterprises in the state sector, it is unlikely to provide reliable public information concerning this aspect of postcommunist economies. And yet the macroeconomic risks that asset specificity might create in connection with a policy of rapid privatization may be quite considerable.

There is another way, however, in which the availability of a properly designed auction within a mass privatization plan can reduce the problems associated with the transaction costs resulting from attempts to exploit niche specific investments. This is because an auction, by allowing the intermediaries to choose the companies in their portfolio, will also allow them to acquire interests in companies that have special links to one another and to prevent these companies from exploiting one another.[28] To the extent that synergies created by niche specific investments are genuinely efficient, common ownership, like the Japanese system of *keiretsu*, will protect and improve them, sometimes up to the point of arranging full-fledged mergers. In other cases, in which such synergies have no beneficial long-term effect, the common owner will make sure that the firms are gradually weaned from one another and develop other relations with new customers and competing suppliers. But the weaning will be gradual, and the exploitative opportunities will be diminished in the meantime.[29] In this context, the auction not only serves as an information-revealing mechanism that enables the reformer to adjust his policy, but also as a device that triggers a *self-correcting mechanism* in the reformer's design.

The future of the banking system

One of the most promising, but also possibly controversial, features of mass privatization plans involving intermediaries is their potential to

---

[28] While the simple auction presented in the Appendix does not have any special features allowing the intermediaries to bid for a number of companies as a block or to condition their bids on one company on the success of their bids on others, such features may be built into a more complex design. As it is, however, the auction in the Appendix allows the intermediaries much more freedom in choosing the companies in their portfolio than any mechanical allocation. (We would like to thank Charles Wilson for his insight concerning the importance of this feature of the auction design.)

[29] It may be said that the same common ownership will also foster monopolistic behavior by the funds themselves. Such fears are groundless, however. The funds will have no incentives for continuing inefficient synergies among their own portfolio companies. With respect to companies outside of their portfolios, the market power of the funds acquiring their portfolios through an auction will be no greater (and most likely smaller) than that of the funds which receive their companies according to a random allocation. (This does not mean, of course, that antitrust rules should not be devised to prevent some funds from achieving a high degree of horizontal integration. But most of the phenomena we are now dealing with are vertical, and not horizontal, in nature.)

Some may also argue that an administrative allocation could accomplish similar bunching of companies with potential savings through vertical integration. The idea, however, that any administrator may acquire, within a realistic time frame, a sufficient familiarity with, say, two hundred companies to be able to bunch them correctly is not to be taken seriously.

finesse the existing banking system and provide a germ of a new financial order.

The privatization plans involving intermediaries are often criticized for the high transaction costs they themselves generate. In order to realize this kind of plan, a very large number of individuals (perhaps every citizen) must receive notice of his or her new entitlement, together with an explanation of how the system works and how to exercise any available options. The funds themselves must be set up (and run), and this involves establishing an individual account for every participant. Since the share of each participant may (at least initially) be of small value, administrative costs might eat up a large part of the proceeds.

Arguments of this kind are not devoid of considerable force. The governments considering such plans are therefore looking for ways to cut down on administrative costs and to piggyback their privatization schemes on some existing mechanisms, such as social security registration. Instead of attaching the scheme to various existing channels, however, the initial transaction costs might be viewed as worth incurring in order to provide an important infrastructural element of *future* institutions. It is worth observing, for example, that the initial outlays involved in setting up the intermediaries are in many respects quite similar to those required for setting up an ordinary banking system. Thus, the intermediaries must open individual accounts for a very large number of people, send statements, pay periodic dividends, and be able to receive and execute certain types of instructions (perhaps orders to sell or transfer title to the shares of the fund). Now, it might require only a small additional expense to link these activities with other types of services usually associated with consumer banking: savings and checking accounts, credit lines (perhaps with the shares of the funds serving as collateral), etc.

Similarly, the very idea of the intermediaries' role in restructuring the East European industries suggests close affinities with brokerage, commercial, investment, and merchant banking operations, as well as insurance. The funds may thus be allowed to move monies and personnel among the companies in their portfolio, serve as lenders or agents for the purposes of borrowing (arranging loans or floating commercial paper on foreign financial markets), agents for the sale of stocks or assets, representatives (and perhaps financiers) for the purpose of arranging joint ventures with foreign investors, insurers, and simply pools of capital channeling small savings into the growing economy of a country with a shortage of capital.

Just by looking at this list, a comparison with the institution of 'universal banking' naturally comes to mind. In many ways, such an institution is an attractive prospect for Eastern Europe, given its history of aiding growth in Germany since the nineteenth century. On the other hand, it also raises concerns, historically quite common in Germany itself, about the influence that the newly created financial giants may exercise both in the economic and political domains. The political systems of Eastern Europe are still in their infancy, and the existence of powerful financial institutions may perhaps come to dominate their development. Thus, before a potential danger develops, a decision should be made whether to move in this direction and, if the answer is positive, a system of safeguards should be considered in advance to limit the inappropriate types of influence.[30]

The role of government

There can be no easy substitute for a governmental system of regulation that should provide a clear set of 'rules of the game' within which the intermediaries will have to operate. This task is an extremely demanding one and cannot be dealt with here in detail. What we would like to note, however, is that while there may be no easy substitute for the compulsory rules of the game set up by the state, the very idea of the intermediaries is to remove the state to the maximum extent possible from the area of managerial decision, including, in the first instance, the management of the mass privatization process itself. Thus, instead of the government's getting involved, the intermediaries may be charged with such matters as selling the enterprises the government would like to dispose of for money, liquidating the companies scheduled for closing, managing and disposing of the remaining government holdings, etc.

This idea of 'privatizing privatization', which we have advanced in our previous work,[31] is of particular service in Eastern Europe. There are many things that a French or German bureaucracy could accomplish passably (or even very) well that are likely to be entirely infeasible for the East Europeans. There should be nothing surprising about the fact that governments in Eastern Europe may need as much restructuring and rejuvenation as the postcommunist industry and the service sector. And yet, perhaps because many economists are not accustomed to

---

[30] We would like thank George Soros for his insightful comments about the potential dangers of universal banking in Eastern Europe. [Further discussion of banking reforms can be found in Chapter 4.]

[31] See Frydman and Rapaczynski (1990) and Chapter 1 in this volume.

thinking about political actors in terms as sophisticated as those they use with respect to economic agents, many privatization proposals ignore or minimize the limitations of the available governmental machine.[32]

Still, even when many aspects of the privatization process are themselves privatized, some regulatory scheme must exist under all circumstances, if only to protect shareholders from managerial over-reaching or to control various conflict of interest situations, self-dealing, insider trading, etc. But any regulatory scheme of this kind needs an enforcement mechanism, and this, given the deficiencies of government bureaucracies in Eastern Europe, might put state officials too much in control, so that the intermediaries will attend more to capturing the regulators than to the restructuring process itself. It might thus be a good general policy to rely more on disclosure requirements (calling for divulging all potential conflicts of interests) than on complex approval procedures and outright prohibitions. Also, it might be better to structure the agencies watching over the intermediaries as basically prosecutorial, with the courts serving as the ultimate enforcers, rather than creating powerful rulemaking bodies which could be more intrusive and easier to capture.

Having pointed to the limitations of East European governments in managing the privatization process, we should also note one of their peculiar strengths, often absent in the West. The source of this strength is in fact the same as that of the weaknesses mentioned above: the recent origin of democracy in Eastern Europe.

Mass privatization is a program which may be in the national interest and in the long-term interest of most people. At the same time, in the short run, it has no unambiguous constituency in today's Eastern Europe. The workers are afraid of it, since restructuring is bound to lead to large-scale layoffs and disrupt existing work routines. Managers of existing enterprises are likely to be severely tested by new owners, and many of them are bound to lose their jobs and their influence. Government bureaucrats (including those running the privatization program) are bound to lose much of their power over the economy (including its very privatization). Even the budding private sector has something to fear, since state enterprises are now very weak competitors and highly profitable, easily exploited clients. Those who stand to gain immediately, on the other hand, namely the recipients of

---

[32] Another reason why these limitations are often ignored is that the authors of the proposals may identify *themselves* with the government actors engaged in the reform process, or are reluctant to criticize local governments because of the fear of diminishing their own influence.

the shares of the intermediaries, are diffuse and politically ineffective and often belong to other groups (e.g., workers), who might lose more than the citizens stand to gain from the distribution.[33]

In most well-developed democratic systems, a program of this kind would be likely to fall prey to the hostility of the special interests it affects. The unions, owners' associations, etc. would immediately realize the danger to their membership, and set in motion the usual mechanisms (lobbying, campaign contributions, threats of retaliation, and so forth) by which their objectives are translated into concrete political results. Something similar is much less likely to happen in Eastern Europe, however, since the normal channels of influence in democratic societies have not yet had a chance to crystallize and become firmly established. Even in Poland, where union activity has a considerable tradition, the communication between union leaders and their membership is still imperfect, and it is not clear to what extent the leaders can deliver the votes of the members. Other groups are even less organized. The role of money in political campaigns is still much less than in the West, as is the professionalization of the election machine. In this situation, the role of *political* leaders is much greater in Eastern Europe than in most other democracies. There, leaders may not have a stable political base, and they may often rely on shifting political alliances. At the same time, however, their personal stature and prestige is what matters most at this stage, and they have a far-reaching autonomy in making decisions. If the mass privatization program is successfully executed in the countries of Eastern Europe, it will be largely due to the statesmanship and foresight of the political elite to which the still fresh democracy leaves unusually large room for maneuver. Since this window of opportunity is likely to close in the near future, the speed with which the reform is set in motion and the state precommits to its completion will be of utmost importance.

Appendix: simple auction design for a mass privatization program[34]

The auction presented here was designed to satisfy the following basic

---

[33] The initial value of the distributed property per person will not be large. Estimates in Poland vary between $30 and $200 per person. (A much larger amount will be distributed to workers who will receive 10 percent of the privatized enterprises.)

[34] The idea of a two-stage auction was presented in Chapter 1. Stage I of the auction presented here was designed by Professor Charles Wilson.

conditions: (1) to take into account the preferences of each fund with respect to the portfolio it wishes to acquire (so that the special skills of each fund are used to the best effect possible to restructure and enhance the value of each privatized company); (2) to assure that each privatized enterprise will possess a lead shareholder who will be an active investor; (3) to limit the possibility of strategic manipulation; (4) to be simple and easy to implement.

There are other potential objectives (such as the possibility of taking into account complementarities among some groups of firms) that should be accommodated, but are left out at this stage.

We assume here that there are ten funds and 200 companies at the auction. Each fund receives at the outset an equal number of 'investment points,' which will be the only 'currency' used during the auction. The investment points will have no value outside of the auction.

The design

The auction will have two stages. In Stage I a single block of shares (say, 33 percent) of each company will be allocated. In Stage II the remaining shares of each company will be allocated.

Stage I. (*a*) Each fund submits a sealed bid indicating how many points it is willing to spend on the block of leading shares (33 percent) of each enterprise. Each fund must present all its bids (for all 200 companies) at the same time. Each fund is allowed to bid up to the whole number of its investment points on *each* enterprise (so that the total number of points bid by a given fund during this stage may be greater than the number of points this fund actually possesses); (*b*) the 200 companies are then ranked according to the ratio of the highest to the second highest bid for that company; (*c*) the leading share of the first-ranked company (whose ratio is the highest) is allocated to the highest bidder, but the number of points this bidder must pay is equal to the *second highest bid* on that company.[35] Any bids on the other companies by the winning fund are reduced (if necessary), so that no bid exceeds the

---

[35] Using the second-price auction, in addition to providing incentives for true preference revelation, has the additional effect here of rewarding those bidders who have special skills with respect to restructuring certain companies, since it gives these bidders the companies for which they have such skills at a low price and makes sure that the companies involved (i.e. those whose ratio is high) are auctioned before the funds have spent most of their 'capital.' (At the extreme, the companies for which there is only one bidder are given to that bidder for free at the very outset of the process.)

remaining points held by the winning fund; (*d*) steps (*b*) and (*c*) are repeated until the leading shares of all companies on which anyone bid anything are allocated.[36]

Stage II. (*a*) Each fund submits a sealed bid indicating how many points it is willing to spend on the remaining shares of each company. This time each fund is asked to distribute its remaining points among the companies it wants to acquire; (*b*) the price of the shares of each company is determined by dividing the total number of points bid by all funds for that company by the number of the available shares of that company; (*c*) each fund receives the proportional number of shares of each company for which it bid at the price determined in (*b*).

---

[36] It may be shown that if all the funds bid according to their true preferences, then roughly half of the total number of points available (i.e., half of the total 'money supply') will be spent in Stage I.

4 Corporate Control and Financial Reform*

That enterprises are operated in the interests of the owners, approximately at any rate, is a fundamental assumption in the classic efficiency argument for a market economy. Yet, in actual capitalist economies, the enterprises are seldom owner-operated, the smallest ones aside. These enterprises are owned by shareholders who must rely upon imperfect mechanisms of enterprise control in seeking to select the manager and motivate the manager to act in their interest.[1] Hence the degree to which the classic efficiency argument applies to a country's market system depends on the mechanisms of corporate governance in place, by which owners exercise enterprise control.

* This chapter is a shortened and revised version of a paper which was written with Edmund Phelps and Andrei Shleifer and appeared, under the title 'Needed Mechanisms of Corporate Governance and Finance in Eastern Europe,' in *The Economics of Transition*, 1 (April 1993), pp. 171–207. Helpful advice or comments at various stages were provided by Phillipe Aghion, John Coffee, Jean-Paul Fitoussi, John Flemming, and Henryk Kierzkowski.

[1] There are reasons of efficiency for enterprise investment not to be limited to what is self-financed by owner-operators. The least-cost scale of operation at many enterprises exceeds the wealth of persons willing and able to be owner-operators. Also, there are wealth-owners who could not or would not act as managers. Finally, some owner-operators may prefer to diversify their portfolio by investing in the operations of others. These considerations would not generate shareowning if these owners were willing and able to obtain financing of their desired additional investments from a classically functioning credit market, making available a 100 percent credit solution to their financing problem. But the owners may reject pure debt financing since it would put them too much at risk of bankruptcy and its career costs. Further, since enterprise investments are seldom able to be totally covered by collateral and there are impediments to the exercise of lender control over the operator of an enterprise (the lender cannot monitor and understand everything the manager does), lenders may resist financing all of the investment. They may require the owner to raise matching equity funds, thus necessitating the issue of shares, hence the creation of shareholders, on grounds that the investment will be more carefully managed if the enterprise has a larger stake in the additional investment.

Without arrangements to facilitate owner control, the managers' efforts will to some extent be misdirected; the allocation of investible funds across industries will be distorted by investors' control problems; and the cost of equity finance will be inflated.

The role of debt finance and the corresponding control problems faced by creditors are also important in large enterprises, which are the focus of this chapter, not just in small firms. Since the control that share owners can exert over management is imperfect, owing to the difficulties of obtaining information and of acting cooperatively, the cost of equity finance will in some firms be so high that some debt financing would be advantageous. But suppliers of credit face hazards of their own in entrusting funds to enterprises. Hence the controls that corporate governance provide for creditors are also of considerable importance. Without safeguards for potential creditors, the cost of debt finance will be driven up and the availability of credit contracted, so the credit market will do little to improve the misdirection of enterprises and the misallocation of investible funds across enterprises.

The lesson of this observation for the formerly communist countries in the region of Eastern Europe (including here Central Europe and the former Soviet Union), which has yet to be widely assimilated, is that in their transitions to a market economy they run risks of creating a mutant system that cannot come close to matching the efficiency and dynamism of a normal capitalist system. Instituting a price system, through the decentralization of resource allocation and the deregulation of enterprises, and instituting private enterprise, through legalization of private shareowning and mass privatization, are necessary but far from sufficient to achieve the potential of a capitalist market economy. The step that is so far missing in the privatization plans of most of the East European countries is the creation of an appropriate mechanism of enterprise control. To realize in full the opportunity before them these countries face a double task, that of creating private owners and that of creating arrangements giving owners and creditors some control over the enterprises.

Two strategies now present themselves to the East European countries. One is to create the owners forthwith and to hope that suitable mechanisms of enterprise control will evolve with time. The other is to introduce rudiments of an efficient enterprise control mechanism from the beginning in the process of widespread privatization. It may very well be that without good mechanisms of enterprise control, opting for mass privatization would still be better than the status quo because separating the enterprises from the political sphere would give restructuring a better chance. The main dangers of the first strategy, however, are that privatization without enterprise control will not be good enough to promote desirable restructuring of the enterprises – indeed it may create enterprises too weak to stand independently of the state; and that if a satisfactory control mechanism does arrive, it will come too late to save whatever is salvageable of the state enterprises. Accordingly this chapter will suggest introducing, where politically feasible, some basic corporate governance arrangements – beyond those already touched on in earlier chapters – explicitly into the programs of transition. Yet most of these arrangements could be introduced piecemeal, as they become practicable, and would be no less valuable later on.

Several proposals for enterprise control will be presented and analyzed here. Following a discussion of the limitations of insider ownership (by employees and management), we consider various control arrangements: dependence on the initiative of so-called core (large-scale) investors, outsider ownership of large blocks of shares by financial intermediaries, and large-bank lending along the lines of the German or Japanese models. The prospects for financial markets as the basis for enterprise control in the next few years will also be assessed.

The chapter is in two parts. Part 1 surveys in some detail the variety of organizational forms of enterprises existing at present in the region in order to bring out the changes that would be entailed by alternative proposals for corporate governance arrangements. With this review as background, Part 2 takes up the issues of corporate governance and the various proposals. Some tentative conclusions regarding options for transition policy in the countries of the region conclude the chapter.

1. The existing enterprise system

The creation of the classical command economies involved a wholesale nationalization and unprecedented concentration of the economies in the region, accompanied by the establishment of the highly centralized mechanism of enterprise control. The industrial base of these economies was organized and centrally controlled through what we will call 'socialist enterprises.' Various reforms since the 1950s involved attempts at a partial devolution of control to enterprise insiders, management or workers, leading to claims to entitlements (especially in Hungary and Poland) creating a confusion over the distribution of property rights.[2] Consequently, as the communists fell from power, the countries of the region typically found themselves with unintelligible property arrangements and various mixtures of central and insider control over the various aspects of the socialist enterprises.

In addition to the socialist enterprises, in the 1980s there appeared on the scene two other forms of state or quasi-state enterprises: the limited-liability company and the joint-stock company (both to be defined). These organizational forms are similar to their counterparts in Western Europe. Some of these latter companies have subsequently become privatized.

This initial state of institutional governance forms in the region appears to be one of the important determinants of the policy options for privatization, corporate governance, and reform of the financial system. It necessitates a review of the existing enterprise forms in the region, and requires that their diverse policy consequences be sorted out. Here we begin this exploration with an overview of the main forms of enterprise in four countries: Czechoslovakia, Hungary, Poland, and Russia.[3]

Socialist enterprises

Hungary: the role of the managers. The passage of the Law on Enterprise Councils in 1984 marked the beginning of a major reorganization of enterprise governance in communist Hungary. The law introduced a self-management system into the bulk of the socialist enterprises. The right to appoint the chief executive and to decide on organizational structures, such as mergers, spin-offs and joint ventures, was given to the employees in general meetings, to their representatives, or to enterprise councils (depending on the type of enterprise). The socialist enterprises were divided into the following three legal categories:

- Enterprises (such as public utilities and other strategic units) intended to remain under direct state control and to be supervised by the corresponding sectoral minister.

---

[2] The confusion concerning the assignments of property rights was further compounded in some countries of the region by spontaneous and widespread use of 'socialist property' for private gain. This so-called 'informal' privatization in Hungary is analyzed by Hankiss (1990) and in Poland by Staniszkis (1991).

[3] [For a more detailed description of enterprises in the four countries, see Frydman, Rapaczynski, Earle et al. (1993a and b).]

- Small enterprises employing up to 500 employees. These were to be governed by a body elected by the employees.
- All other medium and large enterprises. In this group, the role of the state in the governance structure was to be taken up by a newly created enterprise council. Half the council were nominated by the workers, one person by the relevant ministry, the rest designated by the managing director and upper management. According to knowledgeable local observers (Mizsei 1990, Voszka 1992), despite the apparently substantial representation of the workers on the enterprise council, employees exerted only a minor influence on key enterprise decisions.

The creation of the self-management system in Hungary has reinforced a longer-term trend toward the replacement of the state on the enterprise level with the enhanced prerogatives of the management. This dominant role of the managers in the governance structure of many large and medium-size enterprises is a distinguishing mark of the Hungarian situation, and stands in sharp contrast to Poland, where the dominant role has been played by labor.

Poland: the role of the workers' councils. Following the explosion of expenditures financed by foreign borrowing between 1973 and 1976, Poland's access to international funds dried up in the late 1970s. As a consequence, by the turn of the decade the economy experienced its deepest downturn since World War II. This significantly decreased the power of the Polish state authorities, which could not block the emergence of the Solidarity union and agreed, in September 1981, to a legal guarantee of worker participation in the management of socialist enterprises. Despite the imposition of martial law (in 1981) and the attendant temporary reassertion of state power through the military, the 1980s marked a significant shift of power within the governance structure of the socialist enterprises from the state administration to the employees. The demise of communism has further reduced the state's powers and left workers' councils and general workers' assemblies as the dominant stakeholders and supervisors of the enterprises' activities. The rights of these bodies resemble those normally held by the board of directors and the general shareholders' meeting in a Western-style joint-stock company.[4]

---

[4] These include the following: the approval of enterprise statutes; the approval of long-term plans and objectives of the enterprise; the annual review of the activities of the enterprise and of

The managing director is usually selected through an open competition. He is responsible for day-to-day management of the enterprise. As noted, his activities are reviewed by the workers' council, which can dismiss him.

Czechoslovakia: the classical governance structure. Although different groups of insiders have played a dominant role in the governance structure of the Hungarian and Polish socialist enterprises, these two countries have been characterized by a significant shift of power from the state to the insiders. In contrast, the state has managed to retain its historically commanding role in the Czechoslovak socialized enterprises.

Although, similarly to Hungary, Czechoslovakia was preparing a large reform package to be introduced at the end of the 1960s, the Soviet invasion of 1968 thwarted the Czechoslovak plans. Subsequently, the state reasserted its administrative powers over the enterprises, effectively preventing the emergence of powerful insiders. This situation persisted throughout the 1970s and 1980s, and consequently at the time of the demise of communist rule, the Czechoslovak socialized enterprises were still a part of the state administrative system, with a governance structure molded during the long period of the command economy.

Each socialist enterprise in Czechoslovakia was headed by the managing director. The director could be nominated by the founding organ (usually the relevant sectoral ministry) or might be elected by the workers' council. However, even in the latter case, the government retained the right to approve or reject the choice of the council. The ministry also approved the compensation of all employees, including top management, and retained the right to interfere with current production decisions. Thus, although workers' councils formally exist in Czechoslovakia, their role in enterprise governance is not important.

Russia. Until Gorbachev's reforms of 1985–88, Russia had a classic central planning system with fewer attempts at reform than its East European neighbors. Beginning in the mid 1980s, the reforms took a great deal of power away from the central ministries and gave it to the managers of the socialist enterprises.[5] While state orders remained

---

the director; the power to decide on the proportion of the profits to be distributed to the workers; the power to review the appointment and dismissal of the managing director and other managerial personnel of the enterprise; the approval of mergers, transformations and the liquidation of the assets of the enterprise.

[5] For an account of the Gorbachev period see Aslund (1991).

important, the managers obtained considerable control over the procurement of inputs, the sale of output, and wage and employment policies. Though some nominal power went to the workers as well, it is fair to say that control remained largely with the managers. Yet the desire by managers to get along with the workers, partly in anticipation of future reforms inviting collusion between managers and workers against the state, has led to a wage explosion (Shleifer and Vishny, 1992).

Though in the late 1980s the ministries retained considerable power over enterprises, by the beginning of the 1990s that power disappeared almost completely. Ministries transformed themselves into associations that received payments from enterprises in exchange for R & D services, coordination of supplies, and other public goods. These associations are trying now to play an active role in the privatization process by effectively transforming themselves into holding companies that will control the assets of, and thus monopolize, individual industries. They have the support of the managers of some enterprises who fear privatization. Whether they will succeed remains to be seen.

State companies and related forms

There also exist in the state sector of the four countries discussed here two more traditional forms of business organization: the limited-liability company, whose shares are not publicly traded, and the joint-stock company, whose shares are so traded. These types of companies have arisen in two ways. The first way, peculiar to Hungary, was driven by the old communist management's desire to solidify its control and independence from the state administration. This was made possible by a peculiar arrangement through which a socialist enterprise might contribute a part of its assets to a newly created company, limited-liability or joint-stock (or both), in exchange for the shares of the new company. In this way, the management of the old enterprises shields the 'socialist' assets in a separate legal entity, often diverting them for private gain and excluding the state from effective control.[6]

The second way in which nonprivate joint-stock and limited-liability companies have arisen in Eastern Europe was driven by the opposite force, namely the state, which has tried in the period following

---

[6] In addition to the management, the participants in the 'second economy' and foreign investors are believed by Hungarian public opinion to have benefited from these arrangements. See Szelenyi (1990).

the demise of the communist regime to assert its legal ownership of the 'socialist enterprises,' and thus to overcome the tangled and obscure entitlements created by the communist decentralization policies. The procedure through which these enterprises arose is often referred to as *corporatization*, meaning here a conversion of a socialist enterprise into a Western-style company – joint-stock or limited-liability – wholly owned by the state. However, the inherited governance structure of the socialist enterprises in Hungary and Poland has made the declaration of the state ownership much more complicated than the process of assigning legal titles to the socialist assets. In fact, this process has proceeded relatively unimpeded only in Czechoslovakia.

Czechoslovakia: state enterprises as transitional forms. After the demise of communism, the dominant role of the state and the weakness of the insiders in the inherited governance structure of the socialist enterprises in Czechoslovakia have facilitated a relatively smooth wholesale switch to the formal state ownership of the industry. However, except for a special group of companies, chosen for a variety of reasons to remain under state control, the state is supposed to retain its ownership rights in the new joint-stock companies for a strictly limited period of time. Thus, for most industrial enterprises, corporatization is only the first legal step before privatization.

It is worth noting that the assertion by the state of its property rights over the socialist enterprises in Czechoslovakia results in a very centralized structure of ownership. Upon selection for the mass privatization program, the assets of the selected enterprises are transferred to one of the three newly created Funds of National Property (one federal, and two republican). These funds are then responsible for transforming the socialist enterprises into joint-stock companies, wholly owned by the state. The shares of these companies are then to be sold to the Czechoslovak public (mostly in exchange for vouchers), domestic and foreign institutions, and private investors.

There are a number of other features of the Czechoslovak mass privatization program that testify to the dominant role of the state in the privatization process. The most significant of them is the limited role of insiders. In preparation for the privatization process, each enterprise prepares a so-called privatization project, often with the help of outside consultants. This, to be sure, gives the managers a significant role in the process. However, any other party of outsiders is also entitled to prepare a 'competing' project. The decision as to which project is implemented is then made by the Federal Ministry of Finance or an agency of one of the republican administrations.[7] Moreover, once the project is approved by the designated state organ, the Privatization Law stipulates that the enterprise will merely '*inform* the competent trade-union authority about the privatization proposal' (Lindsay 1992, emphasis added). This stands in sharp contrast to the situation in Poland, where the workers' representatives have played a dominant role in the socialist enterprises and were ultimately able to retain significant decisionmaking powers in the process of ownership transformation initiated by the first post-communist government.

Poland. After several months of intense discussions, the Polish privatization law was enacted in the summer of 1990. In most cases, the law ceded to the enterprise employees the virtual veto power over the corporatization decision. The transformation of a socialist enterprise into a state company is carried out by the Minister of Privatization, at the request of the founding body[8] or at the joint request of the managing director and the workers' council.[9] Even in the former case, however, the consent of both the managing director and the workers' council is required.[10] While the law also gives the prime minister the right unilaterally to order the corporatization of an enterprise, the framers expected that this prerogative would be exercised only in unusual circumstances.[11]

In order to make corporatization more attractive to insiders, exemptions from the special tax on enterprise capital (*dywidenda*) were granted to the transformed enterprises, and they were also relieved from a portion of the excess wage tax. Thus, contrary to the spirit of corporatization, which should in principle result in greater protection of an enterprise's assets, the transformation of the Polish socialist enterprises into state companies has been linked with the softening of the

[7] See Mladek (1993) for some additional details on the Czechoslovak mass (also called large-scale) privatization program, and Lindsay (1992) for a text of the privatization law.

[8] The founding body is the office of state administration (usually the relevant ministry), under which the enterprise falls.

[9] The general meeting of the work force's delegates and the founding body are also asked for an opinion.

[10] The law also requires that in this case the general meeting of the work force or its delegates be asked for an opinion.

[11] This expectation turned out not to have been entirely correct, since the government used the threat of prime-ministerial prerogative to prod the enterprises into action. However, the Privatization Ministry, swamped by other tasks and incapable of asserting its authority over the converted enterprises, has not pursued corporatization, except in those cases in which conversion was seen as a necessary step preceding imminent privatization. This left the majority of the Polish enterprises in their old (labor-dominated) form.

budget constraint and the formation of unrealistic expectations of wage increases at the expense of other factors of production.

With corporatization, the supervisory and management boards of the new company are appointed. By law, two-thirds of the supervisory board is nominated by the Minister of Privatization, and one-third is comprised of the representatives of the workers. In addition, the minister can decide to take over a part or all of the company's debt and issue new shares to increase the share capital. The minister is also formally in charge of the activities leading to privatization.

Only limited information is available on the actual governance practice of the newly transformed enterprises. However, systematic research (e.g., Chelminski et al. 1992) and anecdotal evidence indicate that the insiders, especially the management, have preserved their privileged status. As a rule, there are no significant changes in the key management positions in the new companies.[12] Also, although workers' councils cease to exist upon corporatization, workers' representatives on the supervisory board often continue the activist Solidarity tradition and play an important role in enterprise decisions.[13] Other informal reports indicate that the supervisory boards are either passive or simply ignored by the insiders. It thus appears that in most cases corporatization has not yielded the hoped for changes in the corporate governance structure and behavior of the state enterprises.

Hungary: 'cross-ownership' of state companies by socialist enterprises. In Hungary, the Company Law of 1988 permitted a peculiar hybrid between company and socialist forms of economic organization. As mentioned earlier, the law gave the enterprise council of a self-managed enterprise the right to create a new economic entity and exchange enterprise assets for the shares of the newly created joint-stock or limited-liability company. This mechanism has led to a widespread trans-formation of socialist enterprises into mere holding companies, 'owning' the shares of new companies created out of their assets.[14] In this way, the

---

[12] It should be noted that commonly cited reasons for the continuation of the role of former management is that it can help assure the continuation of the *former* links of the enterprise with other enterprises. The preservation of the connections between the state companies and state banks is one of the major obstacles in the implementation of the banking reform in Eastern Europe. We will return to this issue in Part 2.

[13] For example, the current abnormal employment policy of no layoffs in the face of sharply declining sales is consistent with the strength of labor in the newly created state companies. Apparently, the maintenance of employment has often been demanded by the workers' council as a condition of their agreement to corporatization.

[14] This 'spontaneous reorganization' of the socialized assets in Hungary has crucially shaped the progress of the Hungarian privatization to date.

state lost control over a large portion of the socialist assets (indeed, often the best portion) and, despite later attempts in March 1990 to reassert its rights through a specially created State Property Agency (SPA), has never succeeded in fully restoring it.[15]

In addition to this hybrid of a Western-style company owned by a socialist enterprise, a number of other socialist enterprises in Hungary have been converted to a corporate form in accordance with the Transformation Law of 1989. This law, enacted toward the end of the communist regime, allowed a reorganization of whole socialist enterprises (rather than of a portion of their assets) into joint-stock or limited-liability companies, with most of the shares formally owned by the state. However, as in the case of the corporate forms created on the basis of the earlier Company Law, the corporatization of the whole enterprise was often driven by the management's desire to gain an ownership stake in the new company and to insulate it further from state control.[16]

A public outcry against the abuses of the corporatization process prompted the last communist government to take some steps to assert state ownership rights over the remaining socialist property, although no genuine enforcement occurred until the first postcommunist coalition. This effort involved, above all, the creation of the SPA,[17] which was made the formal owner of certain types of state property (Lindsay 1992, pp. 115–16).[18]

Under the new structure, insiders of the self-managing enterprises (as opposed to the state-managed enterprises) have still retained a right to initiate and prepare the transformation of their enterprises, but the SPA can veto the proposed transformation. The SPA also can, and occasionally does, place enterprises reluctant to undergo transformation under direct state supervision.

---

[15] An important feature of the Company Law was that it made the registration of new companies formally independent of the government. It is decided upon by a special Court of Registration, which can decline the application only in the case of an infringement of the law.

[16] The main benefit to insiders from corporatization under the Transformation Law of 1989 (as well as a powerful inducement to an undervaluation of the assets of the enterprise to be transformed) resulted from the provision that 20 percent of the shares of the new company should be set aside and made available for purchase by the insiders at a discount of up to 90 percent.

[17] Some observers believe that the Hungarian laws creating the SPA and regulating the management of state property 'try to *maintain* spontaneous privatization with an appropriate dose of central interference' (Mizsei 1990, p. 30; emphasis added).

[18] Three types of state property were covered: all shares of state companies transformed according to the Transformation Law and not sold or given to other parties; capital of state-managed enterprises; and assets of liquidated socialist enterprises.

Despite all these efforts, the insiders continue to play a crucial role in the corporatization and privatization processes. To begin with, the SPA cannot properly process all the transactions within its jurisdiction, leaving much of the actual work to the insiders, with negotiations settling the more controversial cases. Most importantly, a loophole in the law left the companies created on the basis of the 1988 Company Law outside SPA's jurisdiction (Mizsei 1990). Finally, in the case of new transformations under the Company Law of 1988, the SPA supervises only the larger transactions, involving amounts in excess of $400,000.[19]

The Company Law and the Transformation Law have resulted in a further complication of the governance relations of the Hungarian companies: spreading cross-ownership. Under the Company Law, ownership of the newly created companies is limited to institutions, and new companies are often owned by several institutions (banks and other companies). Under the Transformation Law, management has a clear incentive to diversify the ownership of the shares in order to dilute the influence of the state. This has led to extremely tangled property relations that may, in the long run, have significant implications for the effectiveness of the corporate governance of the Hungarian economy. Often the ownership is sufficiently diffuse to leave management in control.

The system of insider control developing in Hungary is also evolving a number of mechanisms that prevent outsiders from gaining control of the companies created in the process of corporatization. Thus, for example, new issues of shares on the Budapest stock exchange are primarily used to augment the share capital of the state companies, without ceding ownership or control to outside private investors. Not even foreign investors have managed to overcome this barrier to the ownership of publicly traded companies, with only one company traded on the Budapest stock exchange having a foreign majority stakeholder.[20]

Among the other important emerging institutional players in the Hungarian corporate governance regime are the state commercial banks established as a result of the break-up of the former unitary banking

---

[19] In practice this amount is much larger, with the SPA granting routine approval in the cases involving an amount below some threshold. Also, the restriction on the value of the newly created 'subsidiaries' may be relatively easily avoided by setting up a number of smaller units, until all the units exceed 50 percent of the value of the enterprise's assets (Stark 1990, pp. 369–70).

[20] The company, Novotrade, has been publicly traded since 1984. The current proportion of foreign ownership is about 80 percent. Foreign investors also hold an option for a majority ownership of another company, Scala.

system. In the process, the banks have inherited nonperforming enterprise loans as part of their assets, and some of these loans have since been converted into equity.[21] These banks, with their long-standing links to the state enterprise sector, are an integral part of the insider-controlled institutional cross-ownership network of the Hungarian economy. On the other hand, the Hungarian banks, unlike their counterparts in the other countries of the region, have had several years of experience with more market-oriented policies, and the recent measures undertaken by the Hungarian government to tighten their capital adequacy requirements and to discipline the enterprises in the state sector raise some possibility that the banks could play a more constructive role in the future evolution of the Hungarian corporate governance structure.

Russia: emergence of spontaneous share societies. In Russia many socialist enterprises have taken the initiative to transform themselves into share societies. The stock issued has tended to be placed with other socialist enterprises (in exchange for services, supplies, etc.), with banks and other state institutions. In many cases, the shareowners include various state bodies: municipal governments, state wholesalers, research institutes, and so forth.

At these stock companies, control over the selection of personnel and the direction of the company are in the hands of the insiders, not outside shareholders. This is supposed to be changed by the Corporatization Decree of July 1992, though the extent to which this decree will be obeyed by the managers is not clear at this time.

Many enterprises in Russia have in recent years formed leasing arrangements with the ministries or with their parent firms. These leased enterprises often occupy the premises of the parent firms and divert human resources and materials and other capital as well from the state sector. Nevertheless, the leased firms may become very important in the privatization process as they have accumulated substantial financial resources and in some cases market know-how to make them potential leaders in privatization.

---

[21] The most famous debt–equity swap involved the Tungsram company and one of the largest Hungarian banks. The Hungarian Credit Bank exchanged Tungsram's outstanding debt of Ft 6.42 billion for 91 percent of its equity. A controlling stake (50 percent plus one share) was ultimately sold to General Electric, but the bank has remained the second largest stakeholder (Radio Free Europe 1992, p. 35).

Foreign investment in joint ventures

The participation of foreign investors in the ownership of companies in Eastern Europe gives rise to both a separate type of legal form – the joint venture[22] – and to a whole host of special issues related to their role in the corporate governance structure.

Hungary. Hungary has a liberal climate for foreign investors, including the possibility of full repatriation of profits and 100 percent foreign ownership, except in the banking sector where governmental permission for foreign participation is required. Foreign investment typically takes the form of joint ventures with domestic state or socialist enterprises.[23] According to Csaki (1992), Hungary has attracted as much as 50 percent of total foreign investment in Eastern Europe.[24]

Apart from the sheer size, the most remarkable feature of the pattern of foreign investment in Hungary is that foreign investors seem quite willing to acquire minority stakes in the Hungarian companies. In particular, the average foreign ownership share in joint ventures of companies established under the 1988 Company Law has been under 50 percent. To be sure, a foreign investor may acquire *de facto* control without owning a majority of the shares.[25] Nevertheless, the fact that the foreigners are in many cases willing to trust their investments to domestic management is quite remarkable. One explanation for this may be that the Hungarian managers are viewed as significantly superior to their counterparts elsewhere in the region. While this is certainly the case, other reasons may also play a decisive role. The most important among them is the possibility that the Hungarian managers cause their companies to contribute their most valuable assets to the joint ventures, and that the foreign investor is offered a particularly attractive 'deal' in exchange for accepting the continued control of the other parent's insiders. The position of these insiders is significantly strengthened by their ability to attract foreign capital, and they may often derive significant

---

[22] Joint ventures, which are the earliest forms of foreign participation, dating well into the communist period, can be formed with domestic state companies or socialized enterprises. More recently foreign investors can also acquire the shares of a corporatized enterprise.

[23] Some of the smaller joint ventures are often created in order to gain tax preferences granted to ventures with foreign participation. Typically, a domestic investor invests his own foreign currency through a foreign 'front' company.

[24] Foreign investment in Hungary in 1991 amounted to $1.9 billion.

[25] Evidence that the foreign partner usually maintains strong managerial presence can be found in Csaki (1992), p. 14.

pecuniary benefits as well.[26] Some indirect evidence for this proposition comes from the fact that foreign partners are most willing to accept minority positions in the cases in which the new entities are created out of the parts of a parent state company (or socialist enterprise) in accordance with the Company Law of 1988. As we have seen, these transactions are the least scrutinized ones, and it is plausible that the most valuable assets of the domestic parent are included (at a low valuation) in the joint venture.[27] It may also be significant that out of the total of $1.9 billion foreign investment in 1991, only $350 million was spent by foreign investors on trade sales processed by the SPA.[28] Thus, about 80 percent of foreign investment consisted of 'greenfield' projects or 'deals' between foreign investors and domestic companies, banks, or socialist enterprises outside the domain of the SPA.[29]

Czechoslovakia and Poland. Similarly to Hungary, Czechoslovakia and Poland also have liberal foreign investment laws. The foreign investment record to date in both countries is weak in comparison with Hungary.[30] Therefore, the effect, if any, of foreign participation on corporate governance is naturally even less pronounced in Czechoslovakia and Poland than in Hungary. Furthermore, a few larger transactions which have been concluded have often involved either the option on or an actual initial majority purchased by the foreign investor. The domestic party to the transaction has been the state and not the self-managed enterprises, as is often the case in Hungarian joint ventures.

As for other transactions involving foreign participation, few in Poland involved sale of shares to foreign investors and the Polish general public through initial public offerings, and it is expected that in the ongoing Czechoslovak large-scale privatization program, foreign investors will participate in the privatization of only forty-nine

---

[26] These benefits include participation in the highly paid management positions of the newly created joint venture (Csaki 1992), or a potential increase in the value of the shares acquired by the insiders of the domestic institutions when foreign investors enter into joint ventures with these companies.

[27] Faur (1993), p. 16.

[28] These estimates were supplied by Laszlo Urban, a director at the SPA.

[29] Similar conclusions are suggested by the observation of Mizsei (1992) that among the most important factors contributing to the Hungarian success in attracting foreign investment is the drive by domestic insiders to find and conclude transactions involving foreign investors.

[30] Foreign investment in 1991 was about $600 million in Czechoslovakia and $700 million in Poland. The Polish figure comes from unofficial estimates by the Central Statistical Office.

enterprises or their parts out of the total of 1,491 units in the first wave of the program (Havel 1992, p. 4). Although the expected increase in foreign investment in the Czech Republic may modify the picture, to date (early 1993), foreign investors have not played a significant economy-wide role in the corporate governance system in either of the two countries.

Privatized companies

Although there has been a substantial foreign investment in Hungary and there is an expectation of its sizeable increase in the Czech Republic, domestic investment by the general public in the privatized companies has been minimal.[31] So far, the participation of domestic residents in the process of privatization has been primarily confined to insiders. However, this situation will soon change in the Czech Republic, where the ongoing large-scale voucher privatization program will transfer ownership of socialist enterprises to a large part of the Czech population and vest an as yet unknown measure of control over the newly created companies in the financial intermediaries.[32] Furthermore, insiders have not been granted special preferences in the Czech program.

In contrast, the only programs that have yielded any results in Poland and Hungary have involved the insiders, and various sales programs aimed at general citizenry of both countries have yielded disappointing outcomes. In Hungary, domestic residents have not acquired any shares of large and medium-size companies in the first groups of sales attempted by the SPA. In Poland five companies were put up on sale through the initial public offering in November, 1990.[33] Because demand was deficient, the subscription period had to be extended and the five companies were finally sold for a total of $31

---

[31] This is primarily due to the lack of domestic capital. For a more extensive discussion of this and other problems with privatization through sales in Eastern Europe, see Chapters 1 and 5 of this volume.

[32] Under the Czechoslovak plan, the citizens can deposit their vouchers with spontaneously arising intermediaries. In turn, the intermediaries and the remaining citizens will bid for the shares of the privatized companies at the special auction. Although the resulting structure of ownership and control is not yet known at that time, intermediaries may end up holding significant stakes in the companies privatized with the use of vouchers.

[33] According to the Polish Privatization Law, employees can purchase up to 20 percent of their enterprise at half the selling price. The total value of discounts given to employees cannot exceed the product of the average pay per employee in the state company during the preceding twelve-month period and the number of employees purchasing shares.

million.[34] According to a report published by the Polish Ministry of Privatization, sixteen months after the first initial public offerings (as of February 29, 1992), thirty state companies had been privatized 'individually', eight had been fully privatized through initial public offerings, two by employee 'buyouts', twelve through negotiated trade sales, five using a mixture of initial public offerings and trade sales, and three through auctions. The total sale proceeds were about $190 million which amounts to about 5 percent of the estimated book value of all state enterprises. Meanwhile, many more enterprises in Poland were privatized through a process involving a form of installment sale, usually to insiders, called 'liquidation.'

This form of privatization can be initiated by the founding body or the workers' council, but, in nearly all cases the initiative came from the workers' councils. Moreover, privatization through liquidation is usually closed to domestic and foreign capital. Out of 353 privatizations through liquidation up to the end of 1991, in 283 cases insiders leased the newly created company: only in twenty cases did outsiders buy a controlling stake in the company (Szomburg 1993).[35]

Russia has a reasonable foreign investment law as well as liberal rules for foreign investment in the initial privatization of enterprises. In fact, hundreds of joint ventures have formed in Russia in recent years. Unfortunately, many government agencies are fighting bitterly about jurisdiction over foreign investment, which imposes extremely high bureaucratic costs on investors. The absence of clear rules and authority is probably the single most important deterrent to foreign investment in Russia as well as an important obstacle to investment in general (Arrow and Phelps 1991).

Summing up

The thrust of what has been learned from this survey can be briefly stated. In the East European region in general, the state is not the sole effective owner of the socialist enterprises and free to distribute shares in them as it wishes. The managers and workers also claim effective ownership rights and take economic and political action to defend these

---

[34] Moreover, to avoid undersubscription of some issues, state institutions acquired the remaining shares (Berg 1992).

[35] There are indications, however, that many fewer deals are actually closed than the Ministry approves (Berg 1992). [For more up to date information, see Frydman, Rapaczynski, Earle et al. (1993a), pp. 181–203.]

rights. In Russia the local governments and branch ministries are also claimants. These various 'stakeholders' exercise a degree of *de facto* ownership in the sense of being able to exert some influence over enterprise assets in their own interests. But these claims are conflicting, or overlapping, and often vague, hence not comprising a well-defined pattern of property rights.

This combination of extensive insider autonomy with extremely ill-defined property rights and expectations in the East European region yields a set of incentives that is seriously detrimental to the prospects of the region's economies. The situation varies somewhat among the countries involved, but the incentives of the people in control of the larger economic units are clearly at odds with the interest of the state enterprises and the health of the economy as a whole. This state of affairs leads to all kinds of attempts at wild appropriation, the diversion of enterprise resources to private uses (even if such uses are not efficient), attempts to maximize present wages and employment, a decapitalization of enterprises through lack of reinvestment and modernization, increase in future indebtedness to cover present expenses, and so forth. Where the old state subsidies to these enterprises have become less plentiful, a system of interfirm credit has arisen by which the enterprises are able to support each other in their desire to continue in this fashion.

2. Alternatives in corporate governance and corporate finance

Corporate control, as that term is used by economists, refers to the corporate-governance arrangements by which shareholders hire and fire managers and monitor and reward them in order that they serve optimally the shareholders' interests. Every system of corporate governance is a structure of control rights, and the owners of enterprises want the system that is best for the price of their shares and thus best for them. In analyses of these arrangements, the shareholders are said to be the principals and the problem is to choose and to motivate a manager, called the agent, to pursue their interests to a cost-effective extent.[36]

Of the control difficulties, the one more frequently discussed is the

---

[36] The idea of agency problems goes back at least to Hume and Smith though it is not part of classical (and neoclassical) theory. Formal study of agency problems, which began with Arrow, Ross, Stiglitz, Grossman and Hart, and others, is one of the highlights of modern, or postclassical, economic theory.

task of monitoring and motivating the manager so as to restrain his self-interested behavior. The manager has objectives, such as survival of the firm, its growth and diversification, managerial salaries and perquisites, and so forth, while the objective of shareholders, in contrast, is typically value maximization – the highest possible price for their shares. The agency problem is compounded in situations where all the shareholders have small holdings. There it is too costly for any one of them to engage in the monitoring and analysis that would be required to ensure that the manager acts in their interest; each shareholder finds it advantageous to be a free rider. Corporate governance mechanisms have evolved in Western market economies that serve to alleviate this control problem.

It could be asked how severe the agency problem is in Western corporations. It is true that, in most cases, the manager would not want to set so high an annual salary and expand the scale and prestige of the firm so much as to jeopardize severely the prospects for the firm's survival and thus the manager's own job.[37] But, short of crippling the firm, there can be a *wide discrepancy* between the optimum for the manager and the optimum for the shareholders. Since the balance of benefits and costs truly attributable to actions is typically estimable only with some error, if calculable at all, the manager is able in various cases to portray actions taken as profitable and actions not taken as unprofitable or too risky for the owners, where the latent function (in Merton's terminology) of these policies is simply to serve the manager's self-interest; the shareholder cannot sort out legitimate cases of tacit knowledge from cases of misrepresentation. Another source of such a discrepancy is the difference in time horizon between manager and shareholder. The shareholder knows that his shares, being alienable, will have a market value when he sells or makes a gift of them, and how valuable they will be depends on the (expected) subsequent profitability of the enterprise. As a shareholder, therefore, he will care about the profitability of the enterprise far beyond the duration of his own shareholding. The manager, in contrast, cannot sell or donate the rights to his managerial post, so he has no direct stake in the profitability of the firm beyond his own tenure.[38] The effects of this

[37] Plainly this statement does not apply to managers nearing the end of their managerial lifespan.

[38] If it were the case that the managers faced a perfect labor market and this market paid sole attention to the performance of the share price under a manager's previous tenure, the agency problem would be very different, to say the least. However, since the movements of share prices

discrepancy could persist since the replacement of a manager is costly for the shareholders or creditors instituting the action. Moreover, the pursuit of these self-interests by all managers may largely remove the risk to each.[39]

The problem of changing managers for reasons of their lack of capacity or qualifications is the central question of enterprise control. It is of great importance that the owners have a mechanism by which to replace the manager, and also important that, if the existing owners are unwilling or incapable, the market should have a way of changing the owners if other would-be owners place a high enough value on doing so. Bankruptcy provisions whereby creditors can change the manager in the event of default serve to ensure low-interest credit and also to assure owners of effective control in this contingency.[40]

This dimension of enterprise control will be especially important in Eastern Europe. In the West, managers have arrived at their positions through a process of suitable training and subsequent evaluation. In Eastern Europe, in marked contrast, the background of the extant managers, for all their talents and experience, is surely less suited to running capitalist enterprises. Worse, many enterprises in Eastern Europe now require for their survival a major restructuring for which many of their managers will be poorly equipped. Finding the right managers for restructuring and subsequent operations is going to be extremely important. Many managers will need to be replaced by new blood. The cost or indeed the very feasibility of meeting this problem appears to hinge on the mechanisms of enterprise control that are going to arise in the privatization process.[41] For this reason especially, consideration of the appropriate governance structures for the newly privatized firms is crucial for the success of the market-economy in the region.

We shall now present and analyze what seem to be the major

---

do not reflect only the decisions of managers, the managerial labor market will never be solely based on the share price criterion. Also, the manager may see that some decisions of his that would be costly to the shareowners might go undetected by those who might otherwise attempt to unseat the manager.

[39] These remarks offer a foundation for the view that corporations in Western economies suffer from what has been dubbed 'short-termism' – though the source is not the myopia of the stock market but the inability of the market to curb the inherent present-mindedness of managers. Similar reasons produce present-mindedness in politicians and short-termism in government (Phelps 1991).

[40] An article by Aghion and Bolton (1992) provides the appropriate control perspective.

[41] The reference here is to privatized firms since this book is not primarily dealing with the issues of the governance of corporatized enterprises remaining in state hands.

corporate governance arrangements being considered in the region, leaving for later the possible role of financial institutions and paying special (but not exclusive) attention to the potential effects of these alternative arrangements on restructuring. The discussion will be confined to large and medium-size enterprises owned or to be owned by a number of shareholders.

Ownership and control by insiders

The crucial issue in corporate governance of large and medium-size units in Eastern Europe concerns the establishment of an appropriate distribution of property rights that will radically reduce the existing agency problems of enterprises, privatized or to be privatized. As discussed in Part 1, the insiders (management and/or labor) have *de facto* unsupervised control over most decisions concerning socialist enterprises (except in the Czech Republic) and this inherited structure is not favorable to the massive restructuring required by the East European economies. The key issue now is which new governance mechanism will be most conducive to the necessary restructuring, recognizing that existing interests may force adoption of some less favorable governance arrangements.

Non-managerial employee ownership. It is possible in Russia and some other countries in the region that non-managerial employees (henceforth employees) will be major recipients of the shares of enterprises distributed in large-scale privatization.[42] In the privatization program enacted in Russia, enterprises might elect Variant 1, giving the employees 25 percent of the shares free of charge, or Variant 2, a closed subscription to insiders, in which they would be able to purchase for cash or vouchers up to 51 percent of shares at a low multiple of book value.[43] If the sale of shares to the public proceeds slowly, which would not be surprising, then in many companies the employees together with the management and the government will be the only shareholders, at least over the near term.

---

[42] Indeed, there are many people in Russia, including many members of Parliament and the head of the Moscow City privatization, Larisa Pyasheva, who are ardent advocates of giveaways of state firms to the workers. These advocates in fact criticize the Russian privatization program for giving insufficient recognition to the workers.

[43] The multiple was 1.7. In Variant 3 open to small firms, the manager and the other employees can each buy up to 20 percent at book value. [For a more detailed discussion of the Russian program, see also Chapter 6 below, and Frydman, Rapaczynski, Earle et al. (1993b).]

This prospect raises the issue of governance of enterprises with a substantial worker ownership share. The prevailing view among Western economists has long been that worker ownership is a bad idea. Nevertheless, it must be noted that there is a distinction to be made between employee ownership of a claim to a portion of the cash flows of their enterprise and employee control of the enterprise. In the United States, a country where employee stock ownership is unusually common, of the one thousand public corporations with the largest employee stock ownership, only four had a worker representative on the corporate board, according to a recent survey.[44] Even in those cases, board representation by no means entailed substantial control rights. In the majority of the other firms in the survey, the governance arrangements specifically ceded the employees' vote to the management. In general, worker ownership in the United States is widely regarded as a mechanism for entrenching the control rights of the managers against those of outside shareholders, particularly the takeover practitioners. In the rest of the world as well, there is evidence that where we see employee ownership we see virtually no employee control or even significant participation in control.[45]

There are several reasons for expecting this to be so. Hansmann has argued that employees differing in age, the part of the plant they work in, and their value to the company have different objectives, which makes worker control problematic. Unable to govern the firm effectively, the workers are usually willing to vest the control of the firm with another agent, the manager.[46] Another point is suggested by Polanyi's notion of tacit knowledge: the adequate justification of the decisions which must be taken in enterprises to all the interested parties would be so expensive to communicate to them and for them to master that a collective decision process would not be cost-effective.

On the other hand, one wonders how independent from the employees a manager would be willing to be if employee ownership were so substantial that they could often influence heavily the terms and the tenure of the manager. To the extent that the manager would then cater to the employees, several ill-effects could be expected to result. The managers of the enterprises would tend to raise wages and, although a small increase might be repaid with improvements in

---

[44] Blasi and Kruse (1992).
[45] An extensive survey and analysis of worker ownership around the world has been provided by Hansmann (1990).
[46] Hansmann (1990).

absenteeism or alcoholism, the economy would suffer side-effects in the form of reduced hiring of young workers.[47] Also, the managers in enterprises that are over-expanded or overmanned will postpone the necessary adjustments, causing such misallocations in the economy to be prolonged. In the East European region such misallocations are massive, so the need for adjustment is acute. We conclude that if employee ownership impinges on what would otherwise be full or near-full managerial control, the resulting behavior of the enterprises is likely to be a further bias away from concern with future profitability.

The strategy adopted in the Russian privatization program is to offer the employees the substantial ownership described above but in such a way as to make the employee influence over enterprise control weak and of short duration. A measure embedded in Variant 1 of the plan makes the employees' shares nonvoting, although it is increasingly expected that the enterprises choosing the privatization course will opt instead for Variant 2 in which all insiders' shares may be voted. These shares are alienable, however, and it is hoped that employees will sell them on an informal market. As they sell their shares to outsiders, they will lose whatever influence came from their power as shareholders to vote their interests as employees.[48] If – notwithstanding the grounds for worry on this score – the employees sell as hoped, the privatized companies will begin to look more like companies with managers and outside shareholders. But even then the further question is whether the outside shareholders will be able and willing, in view of the governance structure set up by the Privatization Plan, to exert important influence over the control of the enterprises. The risk is that the managers will be entrenched, and the lack of qualifications and capacity of many of them will impede the restructuring badly needed to revitalize the enterprises.

---

[47] The reason the employees are present-minded, preferring to see the firm's cash flow go to higher wages than to increased investment, is the same reason that the managers are present-minded: the employees cannot sell their job rights in the future. The employees' short-termism is even more pronounced in many enterprises in Eastern Europe now because overmanning on a grand scale has created intense job insecurity. Of course, the employees' ownership of alienable shares tempers a little this short-termism but cannot offset it appreciably, since only a fraction of the shares are owned by the employees and only a fraction of each employee's income derives from share ownership.

[48] The Privatization Plan in Russia will either give away the employee shares or sell them at a low multiple of book values unadjusted for recent inflation. It is thus hoped that the workers will want to cash in quickly on rapid increases in the value of their shares.

Ownership and control by outsiders

If, with privatization, the worst problems of insider control are to be removed, additional arrangements must be made empowering and motivating outsiders of one kind or another to engage in enterprise control.

Students of economics and of corporate governance have identified a number of forces and instruments that operate in varying degrees to give outsiders influence over the management of the enterprise. They are listed below with a citation for each:

Incentive devices

- Giving managers an equity stake or other incentive pay. (Jensen and Meckling (1976); Jensen and Murphy (1991).)
- Firing the manager if he performs poorly. (Morck, Shleifer and Vishny (1988); Jensen and Murphy (1991).)
- Not hiring the manager to a new job if his reputation is bad.

Product-market forces

- Product-market competition leading to bankruptcy.

Shareholder mechanisms

- Takeover or proxy fight. (Jensen and Ruback (1983).)
- Interference by active block investors, through the board or not. (Shleifer and Vishny (1986).)

'Debt' mechanisms

- Public debt with the threat of bankruptcy and liquidation. (Jensen (1986); Hart and Moore (1989, 1991).)
- Private bank debt with the threat of bank control or liquidation. (Jensen (1986); Hoshi, Kashyap, and Scharfstein (1991).)

Consider, first, the incentive devices. Each of these devices is obviously a tool to encourage efficiency and something that can be used with almost any system of corporate governance, not a governance mechanism itself.

Of these incentive devices, the view in the technical literature is that the second and third are not as strong as one would like. Of course it is true that managers earn large rents and have considerable firm-specific human capital, so being fired is certainly not costless to them. One reason for the view in the literature is that the market for managers is extensive in the United States and other large economies, and the threat of firing or reduced pay may impart less discipline than might be expected. However, in the East European countries, the mobility of managers is a great deal more constricted, so the risk of dismissal would undoubtedly be more effective than the literature in the West would suggest. The more important reason is that, as managers are naturally influential with the board of directors, they are seldom fired except for extremely poor performance. On the other hand, in Eastern Europe, where managers will typically face a difficult time, they may come under more than the usual scrutiny and criticism.

There is no doubt, however, that an equity stake or other incentive pay (as in the first incentive device) can be efficacious. Jensen and Murphy (1991) found that direct ownership of shares is by far the most effective *incentive device* for manager motivation. It appears from this research that giving managers some small though significant stake in the enterprise, say a 5 percent stake as provided in the Russian program, is a good idea. Yet, at some point further increases in the manager's holdings are actually detrimental to his managerial performance, according to empirical evidence from the American economy presented by Morck, Shleifer and Vishny (1988).

It must be stressed, however, that, even with optimal incentive packages for managers throughout the economy, there still have to be control mechanisms enabling *outsider principals*, first, to monitor the performance of the manager and, second, to fire the manager and to choose his replacement. These two control functions have special urgency in the region of Eastern Europe, as emphasized earlier. The shareholder and debt mechanisms listed above are control mechanisms of this sort.

Before turning to these governance mechanisms, though, let us discuss the idea of product-market competition as a disciplinary force. The matter of industrial concentration is obviously highly relevant for the countries in Eastern Europe which contain, to varying degrees, highly concentrated industries created by the central-planning system. A long tradition in Western economies is the thesis that monopoly is the enemy of efficiency and dynamism.[49] Although dissonant voices are sometimes heard, for example Schumpeter and most recently Hart

---

[49] The view that the monopolist prefers the quiet life was put forth by Hicks, and an analysis showing that the monopolist is less interested in innovation than a firm in pure competition would be was produced by Arrow.

(1983), the weight of opinion continues to regard competition as an important spur to improved performance.

The stronger position has sometimes been espoused that competition could serve as an adequate substitute for effective mechanisms of outsider control over enterprises. This position has its roots in the earlier 'Chicago' argument about the 'evolutionary' effects of competition in driving out firms failing to meet some standard level of performance in keeping up profits.[50] The hypothetical firms in that argument, however, were capitalist firms, perhaps even owner-managed firms. In the radical extension now sometimes heard, the same argument is said to apply even to economies in which the firms (at least the great majority) are effectively controlled by insiders or are state-owned. The claim is that the managers cannot afford to do anything other than to maximize the value of their respective enterprises if they are faced with the pressures of a competitive product-market environment.

The more persuasive view is this: more competition is better than less, up to a point at any rate. In Eastern Europe more competition would be a major improvement. Even a small amount of competition might shake up some companies there. But competition is *not sufficient*. If all enterprises are saddled with managers that are incapable or entrenched, the product-market competition among them, however intense, will not succeed in weeding out any of these managers and correcting their common ill-effects. In our estimation, the same objection can be sustained if such managers are merely the norm, not universal. One argument is based on a view of product-market competition as beset by informational frictions and difficulties of inference.[51] Another argument is that bankruptcy of most enterprises might bring a bail-out from the state – too numerous (if not too big) to fail.[52] Hence our view is that competition is in no way a substitute for a system in which outsiders have governance mechanisms by which they can exercise effective control over the managers.

However, even if a persuasive view to the contrary should be developed, there is the further problem with reliance upon competition in that government policy in Eastern Europe is unlikely to foster a great deal of competition. Continuing pressures on the governments there to

---

[50] The classic statement is by Alchian, a counterstatement by Winter.

[51] This is the approach taken by Winter.

[52] By this second line of argument, the East European economies are going to face serious trouble, as some already have, when they open their doors to foreign competition, unless these countries turn out to exhibit little real-wage resistance (which they have not done so far).

offer soft budgets, protectionism, and market segmentation can be expected. Hence, again, appropriate and effective mechanisms of corporate governance appear to be especially necessary for good economic performance in Eastern Europe.

We will review now the mechanisms of outsider control over enterprises, beginning with a discussion of the shareholder mechanisms.

Many East Europeans favor an early development of stock markets in their countries both because they view them as inherently non-bureaucratic and because of the symbolic importance of capital markets in post-communist society. In the West, takeover and other aggressive corporate control mechanisms such as proxy fights are extremely important in the United States and perhaps Britain, but not anywhere else in the world. There is a vast literature on hostile takeovers.[53] The consensus of this literature is that hostile takeovers indeed serve to discipline managers in some cases: most importantly, in the American experience, to reverse wasteful diversification. However, takeovers are an extremely costly control device and one that requires very liquid and effective capital markets. It is for this reason that they are uncommon elsewhere in the world. For the same reason it is inconceivable that they would be able to play an important role in the East European region for many years to come.[54]

As we noted earlier,[55] even if there existed a realistic possibility of instituting liquid stock markets in Eastern Europe, some people have argued that the resulting increase in the liquidity of investments would have certain deleterious effects on shareholder activism, since the availability of 'exit' decreases the attractiveness of 'voice.' Also, reliance on takeovers for external monitoring increases the job uncertainty of company managers and may be responsible for a tendency toward short-termism: the managers who fear being dismissed in the wake of a takeover may lose incentives to postpone a part of their compensation in exchange for greater security and may be reluctant to develop firm-specific skills that can become useless if they are not retained by the new owners.[56]

An important shareholder mechanism throughout Europe is that of the core investor – generally an investor who amasses a sufficiently

[53] See the summaries in Jensen and Ruback (1983) and in Shleifer and Vishny (1991).

[54] Proxy fights for the control of the board of directors might appear, but this too is an extremely expensive control device and hence should not be counted on in any but the most extreme circumstances.

[55] See Chapter 2 in this volume.

[56] See Franks and Mayer (1990).

large holding of shares in an enterprise to make it possible and worthwhile to participate actively in the control of management. These core investors, whether or not on the board of directors, try to use persuasion with the board to get their way, but sometimes work to fire the managers, replace the board, or even mount a takeover. How effective these investors are is not yet a point of consensus. Skeptics suggest they are often captured by the managers or bribed to exit through so-called greenmail and targeted share repurchases.

In Eastern Europe the question arises, where will core investors come from? As long as there is no prospect of an extensive stock market, core investors will not arise through placements in the bourse by wealthy individuals. With regard to direct investments, there are very few East Europeans who could afford to buy a significant block of shares in a large company. Further, there are not many people in Eastern Europe with sufficient expertise to facilitate and supervise the introduction of modern production and management techniques, and only a foreign investor could facilitate contacts with potential foreign joint-venture partners or an entry into foreign markets. Foreign investors can play this role in some cases but certainly not in the majority of enterprises.

The main way open now to the establishment of holders of large blocks of shares – blockholders – is to create them artificially as part of the distribution of shares in mass privatization. These large blockholders are often envisaged to be foreign or domestic financial institutions. Since we have discussed extensively in the previous chapters the role that financial intermediaries may play as equity owners in the privatization plans of a number of countries in Eastern Europe, we would like to focus in what follows mainly on their role as potential creditors, as well as the role of other financial institutions, such as banks, pension funds, and international lenders, which may become potentially important large-scale investors, both in the equity and debt of East European enterprises.

The debt mechanisms listed above are extremely important around the world. Fear of bankruptcy and consequent loss of their jobs, with or without liquidation, does evidently motivate managers. Fear of aggressive interference from bank lenders, even without liquidation of the firm, also motivates managers.[57] Of special interest, however, may be a combination of equity and debt holdings in the hands of the same

---

[57] While these ideas have been in the air for some time, formal economic analysis has just begun to focus on the 'agency' role of debt. See Jensen (1986), and Hart and Moore (1989, 1991).

institutional investors, such as the German or Japanese banks, whose monitoring of enterprises is often credited with the exceptional performance of the German and Japanese economies today. A similar claim is sometimes made about the beneficial influence of the Morgan Bank on the performance of the American economy at the turn of the century. Under the bank system, banks have close relationships with the enterprises to which they supply debt finance (and sometimes equity finance), and thus they have access to inside information not normally available to securities markets, so that the enterprises may not need to retain a substantial portion of their earnings to signal their own evaluation of their investment prospects and thus encourage a supply of credit or equity finance. In fact, Hoshi, Kashyap and Scharfstein (1990) found that bank-affiliated firms in Japan exhibit smaller sensitivity of investment to internal cash flow. DeLong (1992) found similar evidence for J.P. Morgan-affiliated companies. All this evidence suggests that bank relationships improve efficiency. At the same time there is no clear evidence as yet on the relationship between bank affiliation and management turnover. Evidence such as this has stimulated interest in importing merchant banking to the East European region.[58] Nevertheless, as will be obvious from the following discussion, the existing state banks in Eastern Europe (including Russia) are not remotely equipped to play such a role as now constituted.

The drag of the existing state banks. Pointing to the apparently beneficial role of banks in Germany and Japan, some analysts draw the conclusion that a principal aim of reforms in Eastern Europe should be to strengthen the existing banks and look to them as engines of restructuring and subsequent growth. Their proposals usually take two forms: that privatization in Eastern Europe should make the banks into serious equity holders of the privatized state enterprises, and that these banks be enabled and encouraged to use their leverage as creditors to initiate and supervise a program of restructuring the state sector.[59] The first objective could be accomplished through large-scale debt–equity swaps (by which banks would convert their mounting bad debts into voting stock of the present state companies)[60] or through the inclusion of the existing banks

---

[58] 'Asian-style banks eyed for Eastern Europe,' *Wall Street Journal*, European Edition, July 22, 1992, p. 1.
[59] Corbett and Mayer (1991).
[60] As indicated in the previous section, this is already happening in Hungary.

as beneficiaries in the proposed mass giveaway privatization programs.[61] The second objective could be accomplished, according to its proponents, through a program of recapitalization of the existing banks, followed by their privatization and restructuring.

Unfortunately, the idea that the existing offshoots of the communist banking systems in Eastern Europe could be rapidly transformed into the future analogs of the Deutsche Bank seems to slide over the tremendous obstacles that lie in the way of reforming the existing banking institutions.

In the later stages of the communist regime, the state banks did indeed play a role in the governance of state enterprises. This was due to the fact that in the process of decentralization, the planning authorities had relinquished some of their rights to make managerial decisions for the enterprises, and gave more autonomy to the managers who had to work within certain specified parameters. At this point, a number of monitoring functions devolved to the state 'monobank', which acted as an accounting unit for the central authorities and enforced the adherence by the enterprises to the financial parameters set by the planners, especially in the area of investment and the use of working capital. It is obvious that in exercising this role the bank did not act as the owner of the enterprises. More to the point, neither did it act like a creditor in the capitalist system, since its decisions were based on a system of centralized resource allocation, not an assessment of the firms' profitability and future prospects. Finally, the budget constraint faced by the bank itself was even 'softer' than that of the enterprises: the function of central banking and the control of the money supply were not separated from commercial banking, with deficits in enterprise financing simply covered through the printing of money. The branches of the monobank were thus not run as business entities, even as compared with industrial enterprises, but rather served as a conduit of governmental policy and an extension of the central apparatus of economic control. In this sense, few, if any, of these banks' practices and routines could be used for disciplining the enterprises following the transition to a more market-oriented economy.

The transition from the communist regime to the present system of bank financing entailed a separation of central banking from commercial banking operations and the creation of a number of commercial banks out of the single state bank. A certain number of independent

---

[61] Lipton and Sachs (1990).

banks (some of them with a serious foreign component) were also allowed to come into being, but they do not as yet play an important role. And since the break-up of the old monobank was accomplished along the old territorial branch lines, there is relatively little competition among the existing financial institutions.

But the most important obstacle to transforming the existing banks into genuine banking institutions is that, despite the superficial reforms, the existing banks have inherited the *modus operandi* of their communist predecessors and quickly become entangled in a process of spontaneous evolution that, far from enabling them to function as genuine monitors of corporate performance, made them into the main tool in the state enterprises' strategy of resistance to significant departures from the status quo.

The starting point of this evolution was determined by the following factors:

- The 'new' commercial banks, being in fact the old regional branches of the state monobank, had over the years developed a symbiotic relation with the large enterprises which they had been financing under the old regime, and were expected to continue financing under the new. This meant not only that they tended to follow the old lending patterns, but also that their managers viewed their interests as analogous with those of the *nomenklatura* managers of the industrial firms. They felt equally threatened by the new regime, and they looked with sympathy on (and often personal interest in) the industrial managers' desire to translate their temporary control over state assets into a permanent slice of personal wealth.
- The new banks lacked any expertise in credit evaluation under market conditions, and thus, when they were not guided by some special reasons (or interests) in their lending policies, tended to favor those borrowers who had large fixed assets that could serve as collateral. This, in turn, tended to favor the same large enterprises and starve the new businesses, regardless of their genuine long-term creditworthiness.
- Even if the banks were to try to move toward a more rational system of evaluating their borrowers, the absence of a modern market accounting system, the lack of any reliable historical track record of the old enterprises (since they had functioned in a regime of chronic shortages, artificial prices and a maze of subsidies and rationing), and the rapidly changing domestic and international conditions (the collapse of CMEA trade) meant that reliable evaluation of the worth

and performance of the state enterprises was a task transcending the abilities of even the most seasoned analysts or accountants. As time proceeded, the difficulty of evaluating the company books was further compounded by the fact that the companies have become mutually indebted to each other. Much of this interfirm debt was involuntary: customers would simply not pay for deliveries, and the supplier, too dependent on the customer for its survival, simply could not afford to demand payment. Instead, it continued production and kept the unpaid debts on the asset side of the ledger, relying on its own ability to obtain supplies in the same fashion. Since these intercompany debts came to constitute a substantial portion of the assets of most state enterprises, they linked the solvency of the enterprises together, and made any evaluation of an individual company very difficult (not only because its solvency may have been illusory, but also because the customers might not be able or willing to take its products if they were to be forced to pay for them in cash).

- Perhaps most importantly, as part of their inherited relationships with the large industrial enterprises, the banks inherited the accounts of their old customers, together with a growing mountain of bad debt. Under the old conditions, such debt did not have great significance, since the banks had been following central directives in their lending policies, and both they and the enterprises they were lending to were ultimately protected by the state's readiness to cover the resulting deficits. But under the new conditions, the enterprises' inability to pay threatened the solvency of the banks themselves. In the absence of any strong regulations concerning write-offs on the banks' own books, the banks had every incentive to continue rolling over the bad debts and refinancing their old customers, regardless of their ultimate ability to repay.

- In some countries (Hungary, Russia), the new banks were partially owned by the enterprises to which they had been lending. This of course created additional commonality of interest and additional pressures to finance regardless of profitability.

Given this starting point, and the fact that the large state enterprises needed to receive continued financing to function (a complete moratorium on credit would have been both impossible and inadvisable), the state banks were inevitably drawn into a process in which they became the main substitute for the previous budgetary subsidies provided by the state. To be sure, credit did become tighter and interest rates were sufficiently high (even though, given inflation, they turned out to be negative in many countries) to make the state enterprises look elsewhere for sources of additional support. This they found in the rapidly mushrooming institution of interfirm credit, but the bank credits continued to provide an important way of postponing unpopular moves, such as cutting production even further or laying off workers. The further the process continued, the more dependent the banks became on the survival of their clients, and the more unable to refuse further rolling over of clearly bad debts. The fact that some of the banks were also partially owned by the enterprises they were lending to contributed to further deterioration.

With time, the banks' incentives to continue throwing good money after bad only grows stronger. For the longer the process continues, the more inconceivable it becomes that the state could allow the enterprises (and the banks) to go under. The web of mutual dependence among the banks and the large enterprises (with the enterprises also tied among themselves through the institution of interfirm credit and abnormal dependence as mutual customers and suppliers in a very concentrated economy) means that any attempt to cut off the lifeline of further credit might cause a chain reaction of bankruptcies, pulling down good companies together with the bad ones. It is then perfectly rational for the banks to play along, until the state decides to bail them all out.

It is necessary to grasp fully the depth of these problems inherent in the present banking system to see the danger of any attempts to make the existing banks into the fulcrum of a future corporate governance structure in Eastern Europe. First, recapitalizing the banks with the equity of the state enterprises might create more problems, not solve them. If the banks acquire their equity *in addition* to their debt claims (as they would if they were to be included in a giveaway program), their status of equity holders would only strengthen their interest in keeping the companies afloat, since their common stock would likely be wiped out in any bankruptcy proceeding. If they acquire equity through swaps for bad debt, the situation might simply remain unchanged in this respect (since their books would still suffer if the value of their equity were to be wiped out),[62] but worsen in others:

---

[62] Unlike debt, which may retain some value in the case of bankruptcy, equity is likely to be wiped out in any liquidation (or even reorganization) proceeding. This may make banks much more risk prone than if they were to continue holding debt positions.

the chances of a genuine change to be brought about by new owners in an effective scheme of privatization of the state enterprises would be diminished.[63]

Any other form of recapitalization, unless done within the context of an effective transformation of the whole governance structure of both the banks and the state enterprises, is likely to be equally problematic.[64] For the underlying problem is that the state enterprises have a strong interest in continuing the present system (many, if not most of them, may go under without it), and they constitute a tremendous pressure group for some form of subsidization. This is a pressure that the existing banks are unlikely to be able (or, for that matter, willing) to resist, even if their books are cleaned up at the expense of the budget. The very act of the clean-up would in fact create a reasonable expectation of future bailouts, and it would not be easy to embed it in a program that would credibly precommit the state to no repetitions. A program of this kind would have to modify in one fell swoop the whole incentive and decisionmaking structure of the economic units in the present state sector, and this type of wholesale reform is difficult to conceive. At the very least, it would have to bring in some entirely new players, free of the old ties and interests, and powerful enough to make a difference.

The answer usually given at this point is that the recapitalization of the banks (whether through a state takeover of bad debts or with the equity of the state enterprises) should be accompanied by a privatization of the banks themselves.[65] This, it is claimed, would change the incentive structure of the bank managers, and give them a fresh start. The problem, however, is that an effective privatization of the existing state banks is not an easy matter, and it is not clear that it is worth the trouble and expense. As they are, the banks are likely to have negative value, if their liabilities to depositors are taken into account. The amounts it would take for the state to pay off their liabilities are so

---

[63] In those cases in which the banks themselves are owned by the enterprises to be privatized, their becoming equity holders of the enterprises would only create a legal form of protection of self-dealing and the absence of any external accountability.

[64] The technical problems of any recapitalization scheme would be quite daunting. The nub, roughly, is that any wiping off of debts is likely to constitute a potentially enormous one-time redistributive transfer to enterprises that are not worth saving. The more the scheme tries to differentiate between bad and good debts, the more it leaves potentially viable enterprises burdened with the past, while it gives a new start to those that are considered unable to recover sufficiently to be able to pay. In economies that are starved for capital and in which the state budget is chronically in deficit, this may be a tremendous misallocation of scarce resources.

[65] Begg and Portes (1992).

enormous[66] that the state could probably capitalize an entirely new banking system with these funds, *and this course ought to be seriously considered.*

The assets of value at the state banks are the performing loans on their books, their good will, and whatever expertise and special knowledge they may have of the enterprises with which they have been dealing. It would be wrong to ignore these factors if they could be sold independently of the intangible liabilities attached to them: the personnel that is not only incompetent but opposed to radical changes in the *modus operandi*, the bad habits and routines, and so forth. In what follows, we shall consider some means by which this could be accomplished, though it should be realized that these intangible liabilities are likely to be extremely difficult to neutralize, and may cripple the existing banks for a long time to come.

To be sure, in a general transformation of the financial institutions of Eastern Europe, during which new institutions will be appearing, the state enterprises will be privatized, and competition among financial institutions will increase, the existing state banks may slowly evolve in a desirable direction and remain a part of the new economic landscape. But for now, their symbiosis with the existing state enterprises is among the most important obstacles to change and will naturally require a comprehensive solution.

Creating new banks and shrinking the state banks. The entry of new banks in Eastern Europe has been slow. The reasons for this are not hard to fathom: there is little domestic capital available, and foreign banks are deterred from entry by the existing state of the financial sector and the difficulty of dealing in an unfamiliar economic and regulatory environment. Although the number of cooperative and other private banks is quite impressive in some countries, and there is also a sprinkling of foreign entrants (most notably in Hungary), the new banks are usually small and the total size of the new banking sector is rather insignificant.

With time this situation may change, but there is an obvious chicken and egg problem here: the banks are likely to enter when the economy is seen as reviving, but the presence of a viable banking sector is probably indispensable for a genuine revival. This does not mean that the problem is insoluble – after all, the world is full of both chickens and eggs, difficult though this may be to explain. An evolutionary

---

[66] A very optimistic estimate by Begg and Portes (1992) is that they amount to 5 percent of GNP in Czechoslovakia.

development may take place under certain circumstances, and countries like Hungary may be well on the way there. But in most post-communist economies, the development of a viable banking system is likely to require some encouragement from governments and perhaps international financial agencies.

The solution of the bad enterprise debt problem may be an occasion to foster the creation of new banking institutions. Most recapitalization schemes presume that the funds injected by the state into the system would have to go to the existing banks. Instead, as we have indicated already, they might be used to capitalize new banks. The standard recapitalization proposals suggest that the state should issue its own paper (treasury bills or bonds) in lieu of the nonperforming enterprise debt.[67] Under this scenario, the state banks would receive the state obligations in exchange for the writing off of the bad loans. But this clearly is not the only possibility.

A better plan might be to eliminate the same bad debts from the asset column of the existing banks, and in exchange to relieve them of a corresponding amount of their own liabilities. This would mean that the state, in exchange for the banks' writing off some bad enterprise debts, would remove some deposit accounts from the banks and transfer them to a new institution, together with a sufficient amount of its own treasury bills to cover these liabilities. The owners of the new bank would have to put down a certain amount of equity and pay for the infrastructure of the new institution, but the equity contribution would be leveraged by its new deposits transferred from the old state banks.[68]

A scheme of this kind would not eliminate the existing state banks altogether. Instead, it would 'shrink' them and allow for the creation of new large banks that would provide healthy competition to the old institutions. A move of this kind would also make the state's pre-commitment to not repeating the bailout more credible: the new banks would not operate according to the old rules, and their existence might make future failures of the old banks conceivable.[69] In the long run, the state banks would have to adjust (and be privatized) or perish.

---

[67] How to identify nonperforming debt is a serious problem in itself.

[68] The scheme here leaves it open whether the new deposits migrating from the old banks are accompanied by the bad loans.

[69] The scheme's chances of working would be much improved if the timing of the recapitalization were to coincide with a large-scale privatization program for the state enterprises. This would not only make it more likely that the enterprises would not easily fall back into their old dependence, but might also provide an opportunity for a realistic estimate of their own viability (and of their ability to repay their debts), described in Chapter 3.

It should go without saying that this scheme is only an example intended to open up discussion of ways to create a well-functioning banking system, while neither resurrecting the old system through recapitalization nor utterly bankrupting it.

Other lending institutions.[70] Banks are no longer the primary source of commercial debt financing in the developed capitalist economies, even in those countries, like Germany, where banks continue to play an important role in corporate governance. Many other forms of credit are less expensive and easier to obtain. The bond market provides possibilities of long-term financing, while the rapidly growing commercial paper market is a source of cheap short-term funds. Is there any possibility that East European companies might gain access to this form of financing, and what would be the effect of this with respect to their corporate governance structure?

Debt holders in the international markets, unlike banks, do not exercise serious supervision over the issuers. Exit and diversification are their primary methods of protection against loss due to insolvency of individual borrowers. Extensive use of diversification means that even quite risky ventures may obtain financing (*vide* the quality of some junk bonds in the recent past), so long as the degree of risk is known within certain parameters, and an appropriate premium is paid for the risk. Moreover, the desire of large funds to diversify their holdings geographically, so as to minimize country risks, means that the East European companies might in a not too distant future obtain access to some fraction of this enormous pool of capital.

The way in which access to international financial markets relates to the issue of corporate governance is through a special kind of intermediary institution. The key to being able to issue debt in the international markets is an appropriate *rating*. These ratings are provided by specialized institutions, such as Moody's and Standard & Poor's in America and their counterparts in Europe, and to obtain them companies must satisfy all kinds of requirements.

Efforts by East European companies, perhaps with some degree of government encouragement and coordination, to achieve ratings, even of low non-investment grades, by internationally recognized agencies might have an extremely positive influence on the way business is conducted in the region. Ratings would imply not only a modern

---

[70] The main idea of this section was suggested by John Coffee.

method of bookkeeping and a degree of transparency currently absent, but also create pressure to maintain a high degree of responsibility and regularity in meeting corporate obligations, and a system of independent monitoring of management and company performance. While initially only a few companies may be able to obtain internationally recognized ratings, they might become models for others and a conduit for further investment. Moreover, even before internationally recognized ratings become available, efforts by governments and international institutions may establish a reliable local rating system that would in time smooth the flow of debt financing in the region.

Privatization intermediaries. East European countries are either putting into effect or planning mass privatization programs using special financial intermediaries charged with exercising monitoring and control functions on behalf of a large number of dispersed shareholders. A program of this kind is being realized in Czechoslovakia, and is in an advanced stage of preparation in Poland. Russia and other countries in the region are also contemplating a role for intermediaries.

As we have indicated earlier,[71] setting up the privatization intermediaries involves many standard transaction costs associated with the creation of a consumer and commercial banking system: the intermediaries must set up and service individual accounts for their shareholders and their role as monitors of the performance of the companies in their portfolios would make it much easier for them to engage in lending operations. They would also be obviously well positioned to provide investment banking services, and perhaps even insurance. In addition to saving on transaction costs, adding banking activities to the intermediaries' scope of operations would also significantly alter the intermediaries' incentives in dealing with the companies in their portfolios. The intermediaries would now be likely to hold both debt and equity of the privatized enterprises, and they would have a much greater incentive to become more active investors, closely monitoring the companies' performance and controlling their management. They could also leverage their equity holdings through their lending operations, thus assuring quick growth and greater diversification.[72]

---

[71] See Chapter 1 and Chapter 2.
[72] The relation between the strategies of 'exit' and 'voice' has been brought to light by Hirschman (1970). For a recent discussion of these issues in connection with the active governance role of institutional investors, see Coffee (1991).

If allowed to develop in this direction, the intermediaries would naturally come to resemble the universal banks known from the German model. In view of its potential to accelerate the much needed growth of a modern banking sector in the region and the dim prospects of the existing banks' fulfilling this role, such a development seems attractive. Moreover, the history of universal banking in Germany over more than half a century confirms its potential for becoming a powerful and constructive element in the new corporate governance structure of the region. But universal banks may use their financial muscle for good or ill in both economic and political fields. With weak political systems in Eastern Europe such powerful financial institutions may become overbearing. Moreover, the absence of other centers of economic power may give the new banks a near monopoly status and contribute to their degeneration. These dangers mean that a system of safeguards should be considered.

The privatization intermediaries might also be encouraged to form joint ventures with the existing state banks, especially if the latter were to be privatized at the same time. In this way, the old banks could provide some of their useful infrastructure, such as branch offices, and information concerning the enterprises to be privatized, while the new entrants would bring in modern banking expertise and their foreign connections.

Pension funds. The countries of Eastern Europe have inherited from their communist predecessors an extremely heavy burden of welfare obligations toward their citizens. Moreover, benefits have usually been linked to the amount of average salary, so that they are likely to grow. Quite simple calculations show that, unless cut, their size will outpace the state's ability to pay.

In order to prevent a future crisis, a number of East European governments are contemplating changing their pay-as-you-go systems and capitalizing a portion of their pension funds with a part of the equity of the state enterprises included in the mass privatization programs. While this seems to be a good idea, capitalized pension funds might also be created independently of the mass privatization programs, either by the state (which may decide to fund them with its debt instruments) or by private institutions responding to individuals' desire to supplement their reduced state pensions with private savings (for which the state may create special tax incentives).

The potential of such a development for the strengthening of the corporate governance system in Eastern Europe is quite considerable. To realize it, attention should be paid to how the pension system is reformed and to the direction in which it evolves.

There are two basic considerations related to the potential of the pension funds for the monitoring and supervision of corporate performance. The first is that pension funds are usually quite conservative and not particularly active investors. Their conservatism is, of course, a function of their responsibility, and a substantial portion of their investments must remain in very secure obligations. But inactivity is not an inherent or necessary feature of pension funds; on the contrary, their very size (a depository of a large portion of the savings of the whole population) makes exit progressively less effective as a means of preserving the value of their portfolios. A number of pension funds in the United States have responded to this problem by 'indexing' their investments, and their trading is limited to a few adjustments. Some of these funds, such as Calpers, have consequently begun to be more active, seeking information from the enterprises and trying to raise the value of their investments through the exercise of 'voice' rather than exit. While the American experiences are not easily transferable to Eastern Europe, the potential size of the pension funds and the thinness of financial markets in the region also makes it likely that the funds might have somewhat restricted exit from their positions. In this context, they might similarly turn to voice.

The forms which pension plans' activism may take are quite varied, and many of them might have a beneficial influence on the corporate governance system in the region. One way, besides the direct involvement in the affairs of the companies in their portfolios, is to follow the practice of some American funds and require the presence of independent, professional directors on the boards of the companies in which the pension funds hold significant investments. This may create a demand for high quality monitors, set new standards for boards of directors and generally raise the quality of performance supervision. Another way in which the funds might get involved would be to support a reliable investment rating system for the region in connection with their purchasing of corporate bonds and other debt securities.

In addition to the problem of the pension funds' potential passivity, their future in Eastern Europe also raises other concerns, similar to those discussed in connection with the privatization intermediaries: whether the pension funds will be truly independent institutions, interested in maximizing the value of their portfolios, or whether they will become politicized and subject to special interest pressures. This phenomenon is not unknown in the United States, of course, where pension fund investments have often been used by the management to shore up their failing enterprises or by the unions to preserve employment. The additional danger in Eastern Europe relates to the role that the state is likely to play in the creation and regulation of the new pension funds. The funds might provide a rich source of political patronage, and the potentially enormous sums involved might create an irresistible temptation for politically motivated subsidization of a variety of special interests.

Again, there may be no foolproof method of dealing with this problem, but there are some steps that may make the pension funds more independent. The most important among them is to stimulate competition among a large number of separate funds by allowing a relatively free entry and providing each beneficiary with an individual account and the freedom to choose how it is invested.

5 Insiders and the State*

The meaning of privatization in Eastern Europe

To understand the process of privatization in Eastern Europe it is critical to appreciate its special significance in the historical context in which it is played out. Unlike in the West, where providing revenues for the state budget was of paramount significance, privatization in Eastern Europe, despite the unrealistic initial expectations of revenues from the sale of state enterprises, has only negligible influence on the budget.[1] As we shall see presently, the political context of privatization is also very different: while privatizations in the West were frequently motivated by the desire to win political support for the parties favoring more free-market economic policies, the reformers in the East often have no discernible constituency supporting large-scale privatization, and the interests ranged in opposition to most radical privatization programs are usually much stronger and better organized than in the West.

There are two basic purposes defining the meaning of privatization in the East: the need to depoliticize most economic decisions by separating the economically dominant enterprise sector from the state,

---

* This chapter is a slightly revised version of a paper which appeared under the title 'Insiders and the State: Overview of Responses to Agency Problems in East European Privatizations' in *The Economics of Transition*, 1 (January 1993), pp. 39–59.

[1] In Hungary, which has been the most successful in implementing privatization sales programs in the region, the total proceeds from privatization collected by the State Property Agency in 1991 were Ft 39.18 billion (approx. $500 million). This represented about 2 percent of the consolidated state budget.

and the need to create a new institutional structure of corporate governance, favorable to the process of rapid revitalization and reorientation of the East European economies.

The objective of depoliticization

The purpose of separating the economy from the state is an easily understandable one, but also more complex than usually realized. Two evils flowing from state ownership are usually mentioned in this context. The first is the excessive political power of the state arising in situations in which, in addition to its control of the normal apparatus of coercion, the state is also able to influence directly the economic well-being of every individual within its jurisdiction. This kind of danger has often been stressed by the libertarians in the West,[2] and it was a problem often experienced by the dissident intellectuals and academics under communism, who spent much of their lives as night-watchmen and cleaning persons. Not surprisingly, in the country in which the communist state was, until the very last moment, most actively using its economic power in this way, i.e. in Czechoslovakia, the new authorities, in which the former dissidents played a prominent role, considered the speediest possible elimination of this power of the state to be the main initial objective of their privatization program, even if they had to pay for their rush with a less than perfect preparation of the other aspects of the very complex ownership transformation.[3]

The second of the oft-cited evils flowing from the politicization of the economy is the inefficiency resulting from the rent-seeking behavior of politicians, which dominates the decisions of state-owned enterprises. The usual story is one of officials using the state sector as a source of patronage, the inability of the state to resist demands for never-ending subsidies to the enterprises owned by the state, and the readiness of state bureaucrats to support regulations protecting the state sector. While privatization is often seen as a remedy for these evils, it is not clear that such a remedy will always be effective. The assumption underlying the claim about the effectiveness of privatization as an instrument of depoliticization is that it is somehow more

---

[2] See Friedman (1962).
[3] This view is based on interviews with several of the authors of the Czechoslovak mass privatization program.

difficult for the state to use its political power on behalf of special interests that cannot achieve their objectives through the market, if the state does not own the enterprises to which these special interests raise their claims. Insofar as certain forms of rent-seeking are concerned, such as patronage appointments, for example, this assumption is warranted. In general, however, the ordinary regulatory powers of the state provide more than sufficient means for the state bureaucrats to dispense their largess to any special constituency, such as management, labor, or party affiliates, without the additional power deriving from state ownership. Under special political and economic conditions, subsidies to private enterprises are in fact not necessarily more difficult or infrequent than those to state companies, and the economic cost of tariffs, trade quotas, price supports and tax exemptions for special interests in many European or South American economies is much greater than that of the privileges granted to state enterprises. What assures a degree of protection against the rent-seeking behavior of special interests, and gives credibility to the state's withdrawal from a range of ordinary economic decisions, is not so much the absence of direct state ownership as the presence of a powerful constituency in the economic sphere, which perceives its own interests as incompatible with an excessive level of state intervention and which protects these interests through the use of its political and economic power.

Privatization and corporate governance

This consideration brings us to the second purpose of privatization we have mentioned – the creation of a new institutional structure of corporate governance which would not favor a policy of massive state support, but rather give rise to powerful new interests opposed to state intervention.

It is clear that not every form of privatization must lead in this direction. Indeed, the danger of an opposite development is very much alive in Eastern Europe, where the present insiders – above all the management and labor – have a vested interest in preserving their privileged position under the new circumstances. Thus, if the state withdraws from its ownership position and leaves in its place a structure in which the insiders remain in effective control of the formally privatized enterprises, while at the same time their incentives are not radically altered, it is likely that they will continue to pursue policies and strategies designed to force the government into a new system of *political* enterprise governance, with all the attendant evils of state intervention. Instead of genuine restructuring, the effect might very well turn out to be a crystallization of the now still inchoate entitlements of the insiders into formal ownership, and the consequent strengthening of their hold on the East European economies, which may make future corrections even more difficult.

The corporate governance arrangements instituted by the privatization program may be characterized from the point of view of two separate objectives. The first concerns the agency problems endemic to the state sector in Eastern Europe. The second is the need to attract external sources of capital and expertise necessary for the purpose of economic restructuring.

Agency problems

The role of corporate governance is usually framed in terms of aligning the incentives of the managers and other decisionmakers inside a modern corporation with the interests of the owners, which are considered to be a proxy for the social interest in the efficient use of the resources at the disposal of the corporation. In the absence of special arrangements that assure a degree of incentive compatibility and a substantial amount of monitoring of managerial behavior, the managers have a tendency to act opportunistically, to the detriment of their principals. This phenomenon takes a number of forms. One of them is so-called 'shirking,'[4] i.e. the slackening of effort by the agents who cannot appropriate a sufficient portion of the benefits they produce. Another is an attempt at an illicit appropriation of some of these benefits through a variety of perquisites, empire building, or outright stealing. Perhaps the most important consequences of the misalignment of incentives, however, are the agents' unwillingness to take justifiable risks, because of their very high firm-specific invest-ment,[5] and their tendency to 'short-termism,' due to their limited tenure at the firm and their inability to appropriate the remote returns of their actions.[6]

---

[4] The term 'shirking' is used by Alchian and Demsetz (1972). Others focus on the idea of monitoring.

[5] The manager's main asset is his human capital, which he invests in his firm with very little ability to diversify: while he can, to some extent, try to preserve his future employability, his dismissal or the firm's failure cannot fail to affect him significantly.

[6] For a discussion of this point in the context of East European privatization, see Phelps (1991).

Agency problems are of great importance in every economic system, and a number of different complex institutions have developed over time in different market societies to mitigate their effects.[7] For several reasons, these problems are especially acute in the post-communist economies, making the reform of corporate governance arrangements of particular urgency in the region.

First, monitoring is far more difficult under the conditions prevailing in the region. In the West, monitoring is greatly facilitated by a number of factors, such as well-established accounting procedures, the long record of corporate performance against which to measure the present actions of the management, the existence of robust capital markets and specialized financial institutions engaged in decentralized evaluation and assessment of corporate performance, the presence of the market for managerial talent which makes the agents mindful of their ability to secure future employment if their performance falls below acceptable levels, and a number of other institutions. In Eastern Europe, by contrast, accounting methods are not reliable, past performance, given the environment of the command economy and controlled prices, is meaningless, and the long history of communist administration has trained the managers in the art of avoidance to a degree undreamt of by their Western counterparts.[8] Moreover, the insiders who have for decades learned to consider shirking and illicit appropriation of state property their God- (or Party-) given right, are quite demoralized by the new system, and often perceive the state's attempts to reassert its ownership rights and convey them to new parties as violating the insiders' pre-existing entitlements. Consequently, they are apt to resist any attempts to monitor their behavior and sabotage efforts to set up an institutional structure that would subject them to external control.

The second reason why agency problems are more severe in Eastern Europe than in the West is that the role of external intervention in corporate decisionmaking is of particular importance during times of rapid change, when old routines must be discarded in favor of a new *modus operandi*. We have mentioned already that even in normal times, managers are more risk-averse than the owners, due to their heavy firm-specific investments. During normal times, however, routine

---

[7] The study of these issues owes much to Jensen and Meckling (1976), and Fama and Jensen (1983a, b). For a discussion of corporate governance, agency problems, and the supply of finance in different economies, see Helwig (1991).

[8] For recent analyses of the classical command economies, see Kornai (1992).

behavior can safeguard most of the firm's interests, and risky innovation is only occasionally important. When the pace of change becomes very rapid, however, and particularly when the firm gets into trouble (as most East European firms are likely to do in the difficult period of transition), the spirit of entrepreneurship becomes particularly important. Experience in the West shows that these are also the periods when the external intervention of the owners or their representatives is most common. In corporate governance systems based on monitoring by financial institutions, such as in Germany or Japan, the monitoring institutions, which tend to be quite passive and supportive of management during normal times, become active when the firm gets into trouble or when a basic reorientation is viewed as necessary. Similarly, in systems based on monitoring by financial markets, the times of managerial ineptitude or inability to adjust to changing circumstances are the most likely occasions for a takeover and external intervention. It is quite likely, therefore, that in the absence of an effective governance structure enabling the assertion of the interests of the owners, the East European firms might be particularly prone to fall victim to managerial ineptitude or outright dishonesty.

A further reason why agency problems are particularly sharp in Eastern Europe is that the time horizon of the East European managers is particularly strongly distorted, as compared with their Western counterparts. Quite apart from the fact that it may be especially difficult to reward managers for their long-term decisions in the East European environment, in which the measurement of their long-term future performance is even more unreliable than in more stable societies, the very fact of approaching privatization and other potentially radical changes to be brought about by the economic and political reforms makes the managers more likely to concentrate on their short-term returns, regardless of the bright prospects that may be in sight for the firms they control. In an atmosphere in which the managers, who were mostly selected for their old political loyalties or because of their popularity with the labor force,[9] expect that the reforms will lead to their dismissal, they have an obvious incentive to make the greatest possible amount of resources available for disbursement as long as they are still in control, even at the cost of

---

[9] This last is particularly common in Poland, where the reforms of the 1980s gave the workers' councils the right to elect the managers of state enterprises. To some extent, the same mechanism operated in Russia as well.

neglecting the maintenance of the plant and decapitalizing the firm in the long run. If, on the other hand, the managers expect to be offered an opportunity to acquire significant ownership stakes in the firm, they may be tempted to reduce the short-term value of the enterprise in order to lower the price at which they will be able to purchase their stakes.[10]

Finally, the agency problems in Eastern Europe are made more severe by the heavy influence of labor in the governance structure of the enterprises. This problem is particularly acute in Poland, where communist reforms of the 1980s gave extraordinary powers to workers' councils, but it is also severe in a number of other countries of the region. While the interests of the managers may be aligned more closely with those of the owners by a number of compensation arrangements, the alignment of the workers' incentives is much more difficult to achieve, since even if they are offered a participation in the firm's profits or a degree of co-ownership, the maintenance of their employment and salary levels still remain the workers' most important stakes in the enterprise, and dominate any other interests they may be granted. At the same time, one of the fundamental facts of life in Eastern Europe is the over-staffing of most firms, and the need to improve their productivity through rather drastic reductions in the levels of employment. Consequently, the influence of labor on the corporate decision-making process creates a very powerful conflict with the goals of postcommunist restructuring.[11]

Access to capital and expertise

Ownership and corporate governance arrangements are also extremely important for the satisfaction of the capital requirements of the economy, as well as the diffusion of technology and expertise necessary for the running of modern enterprises. The problem is, again, especially acute in Eastern Europe, where the existing capital stock is misallocated and obsolete, where the sources of domestic capital are scarce, where the banking system often resembles that in

[10] Considerations of this kind may in part explain why Hungarian enterprises, in which the managers have a rather confident expectation of the continuation of the status quo, perform better than those in the countries in which the future is more uncertain.

[11] While, for example, the Russian system of self-governance has been modified in favor of more managerial controls, it is very significant that the recent reforms have not so far led to any significant unemployment. The situation is similar in this respect in all the countries of the former Soviet Union.

the West no more than in name, and where the influx of foreign capital and expertise is obstructed by political and economic uncertainty and the high transaction costs of foreign investment. In these respects, the different privatization programs have very different consequences. While the situation is by no means identical in all the countries of the region, the enfranchisement of the present corporate insiders is likely to lead, in all of the East European countries (with the possible exception of Hungary), to a situation in which the people in charge of the enterprises have few contacts abroad and do not inspire the confidence of Western investors. Similarly, efforts to import foreign financial expertise may be delayed by the strengthening of the power of the existing banking system (through swaps of equity for the extensive bad debts of state enterprises, for example), while the creation of new financial institutions (perhaps owned or managed by foreign parties) may provide a desired link to Western sources of capital.[12]

Monitoring arrangements with the participation of agents whose judgment and financial expertise is familiar to Western investors might make portfolio investment in Eastern Europe feasible in the not too distant future, while many other ownership arrangements are likely to foreclose that option and force continued reliance on trade sales involving rather substantial transaction costs, such as individual monitoring by each investor or the necessity of accompanying investment with managerial control.

New ownership arrangements

Our discussions so far indicate that the choice of the privatization path will have a potentially long-lasting effect on the success or failure of the restructuring efforts in Eastern Europe. But the impact of the considerations raised here is not the same in all areas because the same or similar objectives can be accomplished by different means in the different types of enterprises and institutions. Thus, for example, in the area of small enterprises, shops and service establishments, the best way of dealing with the agency problems we have pointed out is to make

---

[12] The importance of facilitating access to foreign expertise and capital in mass privatization programs is stressed in Chapter 1 of this volume. Its role in banking reform is discussed in Chapter 4. For an alternative proposal emphasizing the reform of the existing banks in the region, see Begg and Portes (1992).

sure that the owner and the manager are indeed the same person. In large enterprises, on the other hand, the creation of individual or family ownership is not feasible,[13] and probably not desirable (see Fama and Jensen, 1983a and b), so that more complex governance arrangements must be instituted. In the context of Eastern Europe, these arrangements always raise the question of the relative power of corporate insiders and outside investors. This consideration is, in turn, related to the speed with which privatization proceeds, the general rule being that conferring special privileges on corporate insiders makes speedy privatization much easier, but also impedes the institution of corporate governance arrangements required for a rapid implementation of badly needed economic restructuring.

Thus, in the case of so-called 'small privatization,' where secondary markets can be relied on to develop rather quickly and the danger of blocking new entrants does not seem grave, a transfer of ownership to the present insiders may be both easier and more efficient than bringing in outside investors. The same, however, is not likely to be true in the case of large enterprises, where it is not likely that the secondary markets can quickly correct an already-established ownership structure. Similarly, while product competition may be quite effective as a disciplining force in such areas as services and retail trade, it is much less likely to be as effective in controlling managerial behavior in large enterprises (thus making external control even more important). And the situation is different again with respect to medium-sized enterprises, where a number of special solutions have been tried throughout the region.

Privatization of trade and service establishments

Privatization of small economic units, such as shops and service outlets, is frequently lumped together with the sale and leasing of somewhat larger production units under the common rubric of 'small privatization.' In the context of Eastern Europe, however, where production is very concentrated, some of the 'small units' include enterprises with as many as 200 employees. Since ownership transformation with respect to these enterprises gives rise to a quite different set of issues, we will

---

[13] The lack of concentrated wealth in Eastern Europe makes such arrangements unlikely to arise through sales. Giveaways, on the other hand, cannot be legitimized if enormous amounts (the assets of large companies can run into hundreds of millions of dollars) were to go to a few individuals.

discuss them separately in the section devoted to the privatization of medium-sized state enterprises.[14]

Although rapid privatization and liberalization of retail trade and services can quickly lead to dramatic improvements in the satisfaction of the long-neglected needs of the population, it has not been pursued with the same vigor by all the governments in the region. Moreover, even when appropriate legislation was put in place, its implementation has often been subject to intense political controversies and was hampered by the inherited organizational and administrative structure of the retail and service sectors, restrictive regulation, and other policies effectively impeding the entry of new units and the restructuring of the existing ones. Yet whenever state policy created appropriately favorable conditions, nearly instantaneous improvements could be felt, and the expected blossoming of private initiative soon followed in its wake.

The most important objective of the privatization of small trade and service establishment is a speedy introduction of owner-managed businesses. Such individual or family-run units can quickly adapt to changing circumstances and reallocate the existing stock of consumer goods, as well as make room for action by relatively numerous entrepreneurial individuals and create an important middle-class constituency for the new regime. Interestingly enough, however, a speedy transition to owner-manager arrangements has often been impeded by concerns about the justice of the process and the commitment to the use of market mechanisms in the course of privatization.

The fairness and efficiency issues were frequently intermingled. The ownership of a corner grocery store was often seen as a most desirable thing, and the ownership arrangements in the retail sector are highly visible to an average person. The prime candidates for ownership were the employees of the small establishments, who felt that their status should give them close to absolute priority. Ranged against them were the proponents of free markets, who believed that only a competitive allocation through a public auction could assure both fairness and efficiency. The often heard counter-argument in favour of a more administrative solution was that the people most likely to win such auctions would be rapacious foreigners, black marketeers, and the

---

[14] The overview of privatization programs presented below is, of necessity, limited to the general features related to the solution of the problems discussed in the preceding sections. For a comprehensive summary of all privatization programs in Bulgaria, Czechoslovakia, Estonia, Hungary, Latvia, Lithuania, Poland, Romania, Russia, and Ukraine, see Frydman, Rapaczynski, Earle et al. (1993a and b). [For a recent study of small privatization in Poland, the Czech Republic and Hungary, see Frydman, Rapaczynski, et al. (1994).]

cronies of the old regime. A special argument in the Baltic countries was that the people who had money would most likely be the neighboring Russians, who had control of the printing presses flooding the market with ever more worthless rubles. Compromise solutions, in the form of auctions with restrictive access or preferential treatment for the insiders, were also proposed.

Perhaps the most disruptive among these special arrangements has been the mandatory use of vouchers (in a fixed proportion to cash) in any purchase of a store or other small establishment. While programs of this kind (in Lithuania, for example) were primarily designed to keep out the Russians, when combined with limitations on the transferability of vouchers, they often resulted in complicated schemes clouding property titles, or in multiple owners of a business best suited for a single proprietor.

In most countries, the privatized units do not include real estate. Typically, the buyer purchases inventory and equipment, and acquires the right to lease the premises from the owner, usually the state or a municipality. While this type of arrangement is, of course, normal around the world (and real estate might be privatized separately), it might create disincentives for new owners if the term of the lease is too short or inflexible. The restricted transferability of leases, which is often a consequence of the preferential terms on which it has been granted, might also impede the optimal use of the property.

The governments in the region often announced their intention to rely on open auctions as the preferred or exclusive mode of privatization, but strong pressures from the insiders usually resulted in a series of special preferences, either in the form of price reductions or entry restrictions. Resisting insider pressures was particularly difficult for the municipal and local governments, which frequently own the real estate; these governments also favored the use of administrative allocations, since they gave them the ability to favor their political clients and offered attractive opportunities for corruption. One study of the allocation procedures in Poland shows that only 9.3 percent of the over 10,000 municipally-owned shops rented in the first half of 1990 were allocated by auction, despite the fact that prices set at auctions were often thirty to forty times higher than the bureaucratically-set rents.[15]

---

[15] Tamowicz (1993) explains that even when auctions were conducted, bidding was often limited to insiders, or the insiders received preferential rent 'givebacks.' The argument commonly used in favor of insider preferences was that high rents would result in higher retail prices and slow down the privatization process.

While an open auction procedure is likely to lead to a better initial allocation of resources (as well as net more proceeds for the state), there is a clear trade-off between the speed of the process and the degree of its openness. The preparation of the auctions is time-consuming, since the authorities must properly disseminate information and carefully set the opening price and the contract conditions, but the biggest delays are caused by the rule, followed in a number of countries, that in order to prevent rigged procedures, there must be at least two bidders for every object. Also, to prevent what is perceived as a threat of foreign domination, only citizens can usually take part in the first round of sales. As a consequence of high initial prices set by officials eager to avoid suspicions of irregularities, the scarcity of capital, and restrictive lease conditions, properties often remain unsold and have to be included in another round. Thus, despite the corruption bred by administrative allocations, an informal process is likely to result in a speedier withdrawal of the state. Although the initial allocation may not be optimal, it is usually sufficient to lead to significant improvements (if other conditions are favorable) and, if secondary markets are allowed to function,[16] they quickly lead to further ownership changes.

The results from Poland and Czechoslovakia illustrate this point rather nicely. Czechoslovakia, as usual, was the most uncompromising in its adherence to market methods of allocation[17] and opposition to preferential treatment for insiders. But of the planned 100,000 establishments (including some small businesses, in addition to shops and service outlets), only 25,584, or about 25 percent, were sold as of March, 1992.[18] By contrast, in 1990 alone, some 80,000 small stores are said to have been sold in Poland, where most transactions did not involve competitive procedures.[19] From all other indications as well, private activity in the retail and service sector in Poland seems the most vibrant in Eastern Europe.

It should be stressed that improvements in efficiency of the privatized units depend on a number of other important factors, in addition to the speed with which they are privatized. Price controls and

---

[16] This condition is not likely to be satisfied if the terms on which the insiders acquire their title are openly preferential. But if the pretense of sales at full prices is maintained, the restrictions may be avoided.

[17] The only exception was the exclusion of foreigners from the first round of auctions. But if a unit was put up for sale for the second time, anyone could participate.

[18] The Czech privatization approach envisages transferring the assets remaining unsold in the 'small privatization' program to the 'large privatization' program.

[19] See Bandyk (1991).

other restrictions clearly impede both the progress and the effectiveness of small privatization, since they greatly add to the uncertainty concerning returns on the initial investments. Furthermore, unrealistic controlled prices necessitate further restrictions on the use of the acquired property. As long as the price of bread, for example, is held at ridiculously low levels, any attempt to release bakeries from state control would immediately result in their conversion into other types of shops where the returns are greater or prices are not as strictly controlled.

In addition to price controls, the inherited structure of the retail trade can seriously impede the privatization of individual units. There are two aspects of this problem that deserve particular mention: the integration of small units into large, monopolistic trade enterprises and organizations, and the market power of state-owned monopolistic distribution networks.

The need to break up the large enterprises can seriously delay the privatization of smaller units. In Hungary, for example, where the State Property Agency (SPA) attempted to privatize 10,000 retail outlets within the so-called 'pre-privatization program,' the not surprising lack of enthusiasm on the part of the parent enterprises slowed down the whole process and, when combined with unduly high starting prices, resulted in the sale of only 3,000 units by the end of April, 1992.[20] In Poland, by contrast, where the break-up of large retail organizations was accomplished mostly indirectly, by a simple device of giving the municipalities the right to find a new tenant for the premises in which particular stores were located, privatization proceeded with much greater speed.

Market power of the state distribution networks in Eastern Europe is also recognized as particularly detrimental to the reform efforts. Even after the privatization of retail outlets, the emergence of alternative distribution channels and sources of supply is crucial for the revitalization of retail trade. Where the power of the distributors was not broken (as in Russia, for example), they continue to function as a cartelizing agent for the retailers, leading to price inflation and output restrictions. Where, however, foreign trade has been liberalized and the government encouraged the emergence of independent, entrepreneurial distributors (as happened in Poland, where many small trucks were sold to private

---

[20] The SPA's reaction to complaints that the prices were initially set too low led to a situation in which there were no bidders in nearly half the auctions in the program.

individuals by cash-starved state enterprises), there followed an explosion of retail activity, fueled in large part by consumer imports.[21]

Large-scale privatization

Given the tremendous concentration of East European industry, large enterprises, often with over 500 or 1,000 employees, constitute the core of the economies of the region. Without privatizing this sector, the states are certain to continue to dominate the economic life of Eastern Europe. Moreover, even if a significant number of new private industrial companies were to appear in the near future,[22] the very presence of a dominant state sector is likely to make their activities parasitic on the inefficiencies of the remaining state enterprises, which are likely to remain among the most important customers and suppliers of private-sector firms. Thus, the privatization of large state enterprises is necessary for a healthy economic development, but it also presents the greatest technical and political difficulties. The firms themselves are often white elephants epitomizing the communist misallocation of resources, with obsolete physical plant and technologies, bloated labor-force, and no clear markets for their products. Their book values are nearly always enormous and the real worth often negative. The countries of Eastern Europe lack capital markets that could absorb the huge amount of assets that need to be privatized, and the levels of domestic savings are far too low to create an effective domestic demand. The interest of foreign investors is also relatively limited, given the risks associated with entry, difficulties of valuation, and the level of monitoring and managerial involvement necessary for protecting their investments. Consequently, the levels of foreign investment outside of Hungary and Czechoslovakia have been quite negligible in comparison with the scale of the required ownership transformation.

The political obstacles to the privatization of large enterprises are no less serious than the technical problems. It is quite clear that the restructuring process, if undertaken in earnest, will lead to the closing of a substantial portion of the large enterprises,[23] as well as to significant

---

[21] According to sources in the Ministry of Privatization, a total of 300,000 private stores operated in Poland at the end of 1990 (this number includes new, and not only privatized, stores).

[22] This has not happened anywhere so far, with most of the private sector development occurring in the trade and service sector.

[23] One of the problems in this context is that it is in fact impossible to estimate *ex ante* the proportion of large enterprises that are simply not viable in a market environment. For a discussion of this issue and some suggestions on how it may be dealt with, see Chapter 3.

employment reductions in the remaining ones. This fact alone would be enough to give rise to a powerful labor lobby inimical to speedy privatization. But perhaps the most fundamental political obstacle to privatization in many East European countries is that even prior to the beginning of this process, the state had ceased to be perceived as the real owner of the nominally 'state' enterprises. In countries such as Hungary and Poland, and even in Russia, the economic reforms of the late communist period devolved a significant amount of power from the planning authorities to enterprise insiders, such as managers, workers' councils or labor collectives. In a rather characteristic communist confusion, this decentralization, intended to confer on the insiders a degree of managerial autonomy, has been conflated with a devolution of pseudo-ownership rights as well: the managers and workers who took effective control of the enterprises quickly came to view their position as an entitlement, assuring them, in the wake of the communist demise, ordinary property rights in their enterprises.

The process of the delegitimation of state ownership was not uniform in all the countries of Eastern Europe. In fact, the hardline communist regimes, such as those in Czechoslovakia and Romania, have maintained their centralized control over the enterprises, and their successors, with the undiminished power of the state, may now enjoy some 'advantages of backwardness.'[24] But the heirs of the more 'reformed' communist regimes had to begin the process of privatization by asserting their ownership rights over the nominally state enterprises. The new authorities in these countries quickly created special institutions, such as the Hungarian State Property Agency or the Polish Ministry of Privatization, charged with representing the interests of the state as the owner of the enterprises, and converting them into standard forms of corporate organization, such as joint-stock and limited-liability companies, which would give a clear legal form to the concept of state ownership.[25]

Public offerings and trade sales. In the earliest period of the postcommunist history, the new governments partly underestimated the strength of the special interests unleashed by the decentralizing communist reforms and

[24] The phrase is due to Gershenkron (1962).
[25] In Hungary the process of corporatization had in fact preceded the state's attempts at asserting its ownership rights over the nationalized industry; the reason for this was that even before their fall, the communist managers realized that the corporate forms could also be used to isolate them from future attempts at ownership reforms. For further discussion see Chapter 4 and Voszka (1993).

partly benefited from a short honeymoon that may have created a genuine window of opportunity for radical ownership transformations. The pioneering governments in Poland and Hungary felt compelled, to be sure, to offer some concessions to the enterprise insiders who could attempt to block new privatization efforts, but they also proceeded with design and implementation of privatization measures that emphatically denied the right of the insiders to control the process of transformation. Unfortunately, the methods chosen by them were intended to copy the experience of Western privatizations, without realizing their utter impracticability in the context of the East European situation.

The most fatuous was the experience of early privatization in Poland, the only postcommunist country to embark on a significant program of privatization through traditional sales of shares to the public (IPOs). Ignoring the absence of the financial-market infrastructure necessary for IPOs in the West, the government's confident intention in 1990 was to begin by selling twenty 'good' firms. Foreign investment bankers were hired to prepare the issues by analyzing and valuing each company, with Polish consulting firms serving as trainees, but – significantly – no firm would agree actually to underwrite the issue. Legislation was adopted to open the stock exchange in Warsaw (based on the French model of the Lyons bourse), symbolically located in the building formerly housing the Central Committee of the Communist Party. Groups of targeted buyers included foreign investors, domestic private investors, institutional investors, and employees of the enterprises to be privatized.

The result was not encouraging. Only five companies were privatized by IPOs in 1990, raising some Zl 300 billion ($21.6 million at the time) in revenue, of which nearly a quarter was spent on administrative costs. The final receipts were lower than the initial asset valuation of Zl 500 billion and, in order to avert embarrassment, some of the shares reportedly had to be purchased by state banks. In addition, despite very significant inflation during the 1990–92 period,[26] all but one of the companies involved were still trading significantly below their issuing price in 1992.[27] Perhaps significantly, the only exception was a company in which the management had purchased a significant block of shares.

---

[26] The overall Polish GDP deflator increased by 538 per cent in 1990, and by an additional 48 per cent in 1991.

[27] The same companies traded, on the average, at 26 percent of their book value. See Frydman, Rapaczynski, Earle, et al. (1993a). [The prices on the Warsaw stock exchange have since risen dramatically, and one can even speak of a speculative boom.]

This last observation points to the corporate governance issues neglected in the original IPOs, which dispersed the ownership of the privatized enterprises, and provided little in the way of the disciplining effect that private ownership was expected to bring to the managerial practices of the Polish economy. Since this fact may have contributed to the lack of public confidence in the success of the program, the authorities realized the importance of securing the participation of a 'core' or 'strategic' investor, who would be willing to acquire a substantial block of shares, bring in more capital and expertise, and monitor the insiders' performance. Such an investor, however, is not likely to appear in the process of ordinary sales through the securities markets and must instead be actively pursued by other means. Consequently, the next public offerings in Poland were combined with another method, such as a trade sale to interested foreign parties, and six more companies were floated in this way in 1991. On the whole, however, the program of public sales was found to be a slow, costly and ineffective method of privatization: no other country in the region has followed the Polish example, and Poland itself has just about abandoned the program.

Given the failure of the Polish IPOs, trade sales, either through public tenders, auctions, or negotiated private placements, became the other early favorite of the postcommunist governments. Since such sales require capital outlays far exceeding the means of most domestic investors, the purchasers have mostly been foreign companies, which results in the additional benefits of improving the balance of payments and bringing in foreign expertise. In terms of corporate governance, most trade sales are also beneficial, since the foreign buyer usually has its own investment goals and is ready to take over the management, or at least monitor closely the performance, of the company. But precisely because trade sales involve large outlays of capital and are costly from the point of view of monitoring and managerial involvement, they can provide a solution to at most a small fraction of cherry-picked companies in Eastern Europe. They also have a potential for breeding resentment in the xenophobic atmosphere of Eastern Europe, and this fact makes politicians extremely careful to avoid any accusation of selling out too cheaply. As a result, most sales are mired in long bureaucratic delays, and the price demanded is often unrealistically high.

Problems of this kind are especially acute when the negotiations are conducted by the central authorities, intent on retaining full control over the process. This was the case in Hungary, for example, when the SPA announced with great fanfare its so-called 'first active privatization program,' which was supposed to have provided an alternative to the perceived abuses of 'spontaneous' privatization by enterprise insiders. The SPA solicited the help of international consultants with substantial privatization-related experience, and selected a number of prestigious auditing firms and investment banks from England, France, and Japan. The twenty companies chosen for the program were picked for their good business prospects, but the effort has been an almost complete failure, with no genuine privatizations and only a few shares sold to private investors.

When the initiative for particular trade sales comes from prospective investors (as is usually the case in Poland and Czechoslovakia) and when insiders are given a greater role in the process (as is the case in most actual sales in Hungary), success is more likely to result. But numbers are still quite small, and they are not really significant outside of Hungary and Czechoslovakia.[28]

Giveaways and insider control: the politics of mass privatization. Given the gradual transition to the new regime in Hungary and the strength of the managerial interests nourished by decades of communist reforms, it is likely that the more ambitious attempts to reassert the ownership rights of the state over the Hungarian enterprises were doomed from the very beginning. The most that could be achieved was a certain degree of monitoring and control over the actions of the managers, and the curtailment of the worst abuses of the early spontaneous privatization. As time went by, therefore, the SPA abandoned its plans for centrally-managed privatizations and began to cooperate with the management in the decentralized process of ownership transformation. This process, characterized by negotiations among enterprise insiders, potential investors, and the SPA, has led to a relatively high level of foreign investment,[29] but also to the creation of complicated and confusing property relations. On the one hand, Hungary has been held up as the most successful economy of the region; on the other hand, the progress of

---

[28] Both of these countries can boast of some large transactions, such as the sale of the Czech automobile maker, Skoda, or the Hungarian electric bulb maker, Tungsram. A few larger transactions have also occurred in Poland, where seventeen firms have been privatized through trade sales before the end of February, 1992.

[29] The total amount of foreign investment in Hungary in 1991 has been estimated at $1.9 billion. Significantly, only $350 million was spent by foreign investors on trade sales processed by the SPA. About 80 percent of foreign investment consisted of greenfield projects and deals between foreign investors and domestic companies, banks, or socialized enterprises outside the domain of the SPA.

privatization has been quite slow (see Voszka, 1992), and the degree to which privatization translates into new corporate governance arrangements is rather unclear. Hungarian companies have developed a number of cross-holdings, in which groups of state companies and banks hold shares in each other, with even the foreign investors usually managing to acquire only minority positions (see Faur, 1993). As a result, the grip of the managers over the enterprises is as strong as ever, and the role of outside ownership appears negligible. To be sure, with the system's rather strong commitment to the hardening of the budget constraint and the economy's heavy involvement in international trade, the Hungarian enterprises are so far doing relatively better than their counterparts in the other countries of the region. But production is still falling, and the viability of the Hungarian model, heavily rooted in the special Hungarian conditions, for the other countries appears questionable.

This was clearly the view of a number of governments in the region, which began to search for a suitable alternative to spontaneous privatization and the resulting insider control over large state enterprises. Since the sales programs quickly came to be seen as incapable of providing a solution applicable to more than a few enterprises, the attention of the reformers shifted to a range of giveaway proposals, which offered the hope of a speedy transfer of ownership to private hands, with the additional potential of achieving a measure of social justice and building some political support for privatization among the broad masses of the population.

Plans of this kind had been proposed in Poland very early in the reform process, but the authorities took a long time to act. As we have noted, from the beginning Poland took a strong position against the perpetuation of insider control. This was partly due to the fact that, unlike in Hungary, where the insiders in charge were the rather experienced managers, the Polish enterprises were dominated by labor, and the potential danger from insider control was correspondingly greater. But the window of opportunity during which the new government could perhaps have overridden the insider opposition was spent unproductively promoting large-scale sales. By the time the government realized its mistake, its ability to put new ideas into practice was dramatically reduced. Still, the new authorities did not give in to pressures from corporate insiders, and embarked on a program of mass privatization designed to bring outside control to at least a section of the Polish enterprises. The program encountered significant resistance and its parliamentary approval was delayed, but it is still on the agenda.

While the Polish program languished in committees, Czecho-slovakia had also prepared and partially implemented a much more ambitious program of mass privatization with the use of vouchers and financial intermediaries. Another mass privatization program is being implemented in Romania, and more recently in Russia. What unites all these often quite different plans is their common reliance on free or nearly free (direct or indirect) distribution of shares of the privatized enterprises to wide sectors of the population, with varying degrees of attention paid to the problems of corporate governance. But where the plans differ quite considerably is in the degree of their reliance on market mechanisms in the very process of privatizing the large state sector: while some programs attempt to disengage the state as much as possible from the running of the privatization process, others refuse to 'privatize the privatization' and assign to the state the task of managing in detail the transition itself.

The presupposition of all the mass programs is that effective privatization must be based on a free or nearly free distribution of the privatized assets, since only in this way can the scarcity of capital and valuation problems be overcome. But free distribution, which must involve an extremely large number of recipients, each of whom will hold only a very small stake, immediately raises the problem of ownership dispersion, which threatens to negate any corporate governance improvements that do not arise from the very fact of the state's withdrawal. Since secondary markets usually cannot be relied on to correct this situation with sufficient speed (for all practical purposes, such markets do not even exist in Eastern Europe), all mass privatiz-ation programs foresee the creation of some intermediary institutions that could concentrate the dispersed citizen holdings, and exercise monitoring and supervisory powers on behalf of the small stakeholders. Among the other potential advantages of such intermediaries is their ability to provide the means of diversification for small investors and, under certain conditions (primarily if the intermediaries involve a significant component of foreign ownership or management), facilitate the enterprises' access to foreign sources of capital and expertise.

Within these parameters, the several plans differ considerably along a whole set of distinct dimensions.[30] The most important of these differences relate to the degree of continued involvement of the state in the structure set up by the program, and to the political trade-offs

---

[30] For a systematic analysis of these dimensions and a comprehensive taxonomy of free distribution plans, see Chapters 1 and 2, also Earle, Frydman, and Rapaczynski (1993b).

necessary for the plans' realization. In this respect, the Czech and the Russian programs fall on the side of state noninvolvement, allowing unlimited consumer choice (individual citizens receive special vouchers which they can use to purchase directly the shares of the privatized companies or place them with an intermediary of their choice), free entry of intermediaries, and a more (in the case of Czechoslovakia) or less (in the case of Russia) credible state precommitment to nonintervention.

In the Polish programme, on the other hand, the state will license a limited number of intermediaries, allocate the shares of the companies to be privatized among their portfolios (with the shares of each company divided into blocks of predetermined size, ensuring that effective control of each company will be exercised by one 'lead' intermediary), and retain a supervisory role in the intermediaries' governance (with foreign managers working on a contractual basis). Only when the structure is, for all practical purposes, fully in place will the Polish citizens receive, for a small fee, the shares of the intermediaries themselves, unable to invest directly in the privatized companies or to choose between the intermediaries.[31]

The Romanian plan involves an even more rigid design, with one state-controlled fund retaining 70 percent of the shares of each company in the program. In any plan with such heavy state involvement, the government is likely to be held responsible for the success or failure of each intermediary. This, in turn, gives the intermediaries a tremendous hold over governmental policies, with the consequent likelihood of subsidies and other forms of state intervention.

The differences among the various mass privatization programs are not just a question of design – the basic variations can be seen as flowing from differences in political situation.[32] The primary factor is, again, the relation between the state and the corporate insiders. In this perspective, the Czechoslovak programme can be seen as reflecting both the strength of the state vis-à-vis special interests and a successful political maneuver. On the one hand, the Czechoslovak plan, unique in Eastern Europe in this respect, did not give any automatic privileges to the insiders, and forced them into a speedy and dramatic transformation of the ownership relations. On the other hand, consciously or

---

[31] The citizens will be able to exercise some choice through transactions in the secondary markets, and their decisions may have some influence on the intermediaries' incentives, since the compensation of the intermediaries' managers will be partly in the stock of their funds.

[32] See Stark (1992).

unconsciously, by stressing nearly exclusively the political aspects of the withdrawal of the state from the position of ownership, and leaving entirely open the question of the governance structure expected to emerge from the process, the Czechoslovak authorities gained a surprising measure of support for the program from the managers themselves. These managers, to whom the law gave a choice between the voucher program and other methods of privatization (such as trade or asset sales),[33] overwhelmingly chose very significant levels of participation in the voucher program, apparently in the hope that it would result in dispersed ownership and allow them to retain control. In fact, however, the numerous intermediaries acquired over 70 percent of all vouchers, and are likely to play a significant role in the governance of the privatized Czechoslovak companies in the future.

But as the Romanian plan shows, the strength of the state can also result in quintessentially 'statist' solutions;[34] indeed, such an outcome is the most natural, unless the politicians in power have a strong ideological commitment to a free market economy or perceive their chance of electoral success to lie in their ability to build a large citizen constituency against the hostile interests of the insiders (both of which seems to have been the case in Czechoslovakia). The Romanian authorities, by contrast, did not anticipate opposition from special interests at enterprise level, and followed their natural bureaucratic inclinations.

We have already explained that the Polish government embarked on its mass privatization program as the only chance of continuing the privatization process without capitulating to the demands of enterprise insiders. For this reason, the program was consciously designed to assure strong outside control over the privatized enterprises, with each board of directors dominated by foreign-managed funds. But this explicitly announced goal resulted in an intensification of the opposition to the program from both labor and managerial interests, with the result that it had to be confined to a small number of largely self-selected enterprises, and the government felt under great pressure to anticipate

[33] Each enterprise in Czechoslovakia had to prepare its own 'privatization project,' but any other person could propose an alternative, with the choice among the competing projects made by the republican Ministry of Privatization. There were 2,884 basic or obligatory projects and 8,065 competing projects submitted to the Czech Ministry of Privatization. Among the basic projects, conversion to joint-stock form (leading to share sales, meaning mostly voucher privatization) predominated; among the competing projects, direct sales predominated. While the managerial projects were chosen more often than the competing ones, the procedure ensured a degree of control over managerial abuses.

[34] For an extensive discussion of the Romanian approach, see Earle and Sapatoru (1993).

and avoid all possible abuses that could expose it to further criticism. In this way, the program probably became 'over-managed' and over-protective of the new institutions.

Political imprints are also visible on the face of the Russian mass privatization program, which uses vouchers as an artificial form of capital, to be combined (somewhat unusually) with the use of money. The Russian plan contains a number of very pro-market features, such as the immediate and unlimited transferability of all shares and vouchers, and the ability of each recipient to use vouchers either to purchase the shares of a company of his choice or to invest them in any one of the spontaneously created special investment funds. While these features are clearly designed to facilitate the outsiders' ability to invest in the privatized enterprises, the program at the same time offers the insiders unprecedentedly preferential terms, allowing them to purchase up to 51 percent of their companies at 1.7 times book value unadjusted for inflation.[35] Also, since Russian vouchers are denominated in rubles, their value to insiders is many times greater than to everyone else. Finally, a provision limiting the investment funds to the ownership of no more than 10 percent of the shares of any one company confines the funds, at least initially, to a subsidiary role in the governance of the privatized enterprises, Thus, as a price of being able to push through their program, the authorities evidently felt compelled to grant the insiders an initial right to maintain and sometimes even strengthen their hold on the enterprises, in the hope that the acquisition of serious ownership stakes would sufficiently modify the incentives of the insiders to wean them away from the state and allow for badly needed restructuring. The authors of the program also evidently hope that secondary markets will develop quickly enough to permit subsequent corrections in the initial distribution of ownership rights, with the workers in particular cashing in early on their very substantial capital gains.[36]

Privatization of small and medium-sized enterprises

While much of the attention has been focused on the plans to privatize large East European enterprises characteristic of the communist economies, the most active privatization efforts, outside the area of very

---

[35] Given the sky-rocketing inflation rates in Russia, the right to purchase at book-value-related prices makes most of the assets in fact close to cost free.

[36] [For further reflections on the Russian program, see Chapter 6.]

small establishments, have taken place in the sector of smaller state enterprises. Although the exact definition of businesses in this category varies from country to country, the enterprises in question usually employ between 50 and 500 persons. As we have indicated earlier, the privatization of some of these units has been lumped together with the sales of retail stores and service establishments, but they actually raise different issues and are often dealt with in separate programs. As a rule, the enterprises have been considered too small to be converted into joint-stock companies with the purpose of selling their shares to a number of separate investors. Instead, the preferred privatization method is to sell the whole business as a unit or to liquidate the original enterprise in order to sell its assets. A range of intermediate arrangements has also been tried, such as leasing, management contracts, or installment sales.

Although some small and medium-size enterprises have been sold to outside, sometimes foreign, investors, the bulk of transactions in this area involves some form of compromise between the desire of the insiders to gain the ownership of their enterprises and the state's interest in controlling the process, both in order to assure the efficient use of the property and to obtain some revenues for the budget. In many countries, the process of privatization of enterprises in this category started even before the new regime took over; it is here that most of the well-publicized excesses of 'spontaneous privatization' took place. The form of these illicit or semi-legal transactions differed from country to country, but they shared the same basic features: through a series of transformations, a state enterprise would be converted into some form of commercial company or its assets would be siphoned into a new entity, which would in turn be wholly or partly owned by the *nomenklatura* insiders, who managed in this way to turn their *de facto* control into legal ownership.

With the advent of the new postcommunist authorities, the state imposed a series of restrictions on the 'spontaneous' transactions, but did not stop them altogether. Indeed, some of the most successful privatization programs in Poland and Hungary have involved insider-initiated transformations, resulting in a large measure of insider ownership, and it is evidently hoped that the same process will occur in Russia. Only in Czechoslovakia has the privatization of enterprises in this category proceeded in a centrally-orchestrated and fully public fashion. But even there, the insiders were able to propose, as part of their privatization projects, their own acquisition of a portion of their enterprises.

The involvement of insiders in the privatization of small and medium-sized enterprises seems, on the whole, a desirable feature, since it provides a relatively effective way of mitigating some of the agency problems we have discussed earlier. In the case of the large enterprises, individual or family ownership is not a realistic or efficient answer to the problems of incentive compatibility, and more elaborate corporate governance arrangements must be found to ensure the satisfaction of the capital requirements of such units and their access to the needed managerial talent, technology and expertise. In the case of the smaller units, however, significant managerial involvement of the owners is not only feasible, but quite common in most developed economies. The task of the privatization authorities has been therefore to find the appropriate legal and technical arrangements through which the partial enfranchisement of the insiders could be combined with some access to external sources of finance and expertise, and provide assurance of a sufficiently vigorous restructuring effort.

The vehicles of small privatization have been quite diverse so far, and some solutions are rather innovative. It would go beyond our scope to discuss them in detail, but a brief mention of the most important techniques may be in order.

Management and employee buy-outs. Given its popularity in the West, this method was originally expected to be very common. In fact, however, the experiences of the West once again turned out to be of limited use. Management and employee buy-outs require the buyers to be able to obtain credit to leverage their transaction. In the conditions of Eastern Europe, sources of genuine investment credit are, for all practical purposes, nonexistent, and even if they were available, the enterprises involved cannot easily be evaluated by the potential creditors. True insider buy-outs are therefore rare; in Poland, for example, there were only two partial employee buy-outs up to the end of February 1992, with a combined value of under $700,000.

Leasing arrangements. This is a popular technique, with some special local characteristics. A form of leasing was used in the Soviet Union prior to its dissolution, and all the former republics still have many of the 'lease enterprises' created in this process. The Soviet form of leasing, however, was often little more than a profit-sharing arrangement for the management and the employees, with the lease specifying so many conditions concerning the operation of the enterprise, its relations with customers and suppliers, and so on, that little restructuring could be expected. Consequently, the present Russian privatization program foresees the liquidation of all lease enterprises. The state has decided, however, to honor the buy-out provisions contained in the old leases, so that they may affect the future of the enterprises involved.

A much more effective program has been implemented in a large number of Polish enterprises (385 up to the end of the first quarter of 1992). The Polish lease is a rather interesting vehicle, which requires the creation of a new commercial company with the participation of a substantial portion of the employees of the old state enterprise. The new company then leases the assets of the state enterprise, which is then liquidated. The 'rent' on the lease is calculated in such a way that the payments are at the same time installments on the purchase of the assets, which become the property of the lessees at the end of the term. In order to make the required initial down payment, the employees often find another shareholder for their company, who acts as a 'core investor.'

Sales of assets. Many smaller companies, both viable and insolvent, are liquidated and their assets sold, usually at reduced prices payable in installments, to the enterprise insiders who set up a new business. Again, the insiders often bring in another investor who puts up the required deposit. In a variant of this arrangement, sometimes involving foreign investors, the assets of the old company are contributed by the state to the new company (a 'joint venture'), and the state retains a stake which is then sold to the insiders.

Management contracts. Again, management contracts, perhaps involving foreign management teams, were expected to be popular arrangements, permitting the importation of foreign expertise without the political and other risks associated with outright sales. In fact, however, arrangements of this type, involving genuine outsiders, are extremely rare. Instead, management contracts have been used to give the existing managers a stake in the enterprise, and they usually involve a commitment by the managers to privatize the enterprise by the end of the contract. An interesting program of this kind has been introduced in Poland, and another is being contemplated in Russia.

Auctions and tenders. Nearly all the countries of the region envisage sales of whole enterprises through the use of auctions (where price alone decides who can purchase) or competitive tenders (where the purchaser must satisfy a number of other conditions). While these types of transaction with respect to most East European enterprises are more easily decreed in a law than realized in practice, the important feature of most of them is a series of preferential terms for the insiders. When these reductions are sufficiently big, and when additional capital is provided to the insiders in the form of vouchers (Russia) or cheap credit, auctions may be an effective way of permitting management and employees to convert their insider status into ownership.

Finally, an interesting procedural device has come into use in Hungary since June, 1991, which combines the spontaneous nature of much of the insider privatization with a decentralized delegation of the role of the state in the privatization process. In this program, called 'self-privatization,' the (voluntarily) participating enterprises must employ an independent consulting and property evaluating company from a list compiled by the SPA. The enterprise in question may, of course, propose its plan, but the consulting company is ultimately responsible for the actual sale, for which it receives a percentage of the price plus a bonus tied to the speed with which the transaction is processed. The most interesting aspect of the program is that, in accordance with its commitment to 'privatizing privatization,' the SPA must accept the resulting sale, although it may impose sanctions on, or exclude from future transactions, any consulting firms which violate legal regulations.

6 Ambiguity of Privatization and the Paths of Transition to a Private Property Regime*

Privatization in Eastern Europe is about three years old. While this is by no means a long time, and the process is still in full swing, it is also a sufficiently long period to take stock of what happened and what lessons may lie ahead.

What we mean by 'taking stock' is not one more summary of the programs adopted in each country and an assessment of their achievements.[1] Rather, we have in mind an intellectual reflection concerning the very meaning of the process that came to be known as 'privatization,' and a reappraisal of the 'background knowledge' with which the process of transition to a market economy should be approached.

When 'privatization' became the word of the day in Eastern Europe, most policymakers and external observers made a number of rather simplistic assumptions which have since become increasingly hard to maintain. To be sure, those assumptions were most often not clearly articulated; sometimes their very articulation would probably have been enough to make them problematic. But only the experience of the reality of East European privatizations forced their reconsideration.

In the early days of East European transition, the very concept of

* This chapter was written in collaboration with John S. Earle. Comments by Steven Brams, Richard Ericson, John Nellis, and Edmund Phelps are gratefully acknowledged. Research on this chapter was supported by a grant from the National Council for Soviet and East European Research.
[1] We have provided such a general assessment in Frydman, Rapaczynski, Earle, et al. (1993a and b).

privatization was taken over from Western experiences and taken to refer to a transfer from the state to private parties of a legal title to ownership of productive assets. The effect of this move was expected to be a transition from one idealized state of affairs to another: from the 'command' to a 'market' economy. The two states were idealized because neither existed anywhere in the world, at least not at the time when the transition began. Eastern Europe was no longer (if it ever had been) a pure command economy. Rather, many years of reformist tinkering, especially in such countries as Hungary and Poland, produced a significantly decentralized system, with a myriad of special interests fighting for access to scarce resources in a process over which the central planners had long lost most of their control.[2] The market economy, in the direction of which the countries of Eastern Europe were supposed to move, was also thought about in rather anachronistic terms as a system in which most owners directly operate and manage the assets under their control, and the state limits itself to only minor forms of intervention. It was known, of course, that no Western economy was of this type, but it was also (mostly tacitly) assumed that Eastern Europe, with its backward economy and clumsy state apparatus, should not aspire to the most modern versions of Western capitalism. Instead a dose of nineteenth century *laissez-faire* seemed what the doctor ordered for the next decade or so.

The concept of a 'private property regime'

As time went by, however, the simplistic assumptions underlying the initial approach became increasingly inadequate, and the experience of privatization began to reveal its bewildering complexity. The reason for this was that privatization was not an intra-systemic move, in which assets changed hands, while the concept of ownership remained constant. In the context of Eastern Europe, privatization was inherently tied to a *systemic* transition and the creation of what may be called a 'private property regime,' i.e. a social and economic order defining a new set of expectations that individuals may have with respect to their ability to dispose of the assets recognized as 'theirs' by the legal system. What this order involves is a complex network of institutions

---

[2] The post-reform political arrangements in Eastern Europe and some of their consequences for the choice and feasibility of privatization policies are discussed in Stark (1990), and Chapters 4 and 5.

and social relations far transcending the merely legal aspects of property arrangements.

The concept of a private property regime is designed to reflect the delicate balance, struck by each economically successful society, between private action and state administration. While it is customary in both legal and economic circles to think of the distinction between individual and state action as something self-evident, in fact individuals always act against a very thick background of expectations engendered by historically arisen practices and institutions, among which the role of the state has always been of paramount importance.

Understanding the role played by the state in a system of property relations begins, of course, with the legal system. Whether property is a creature of law and derives from the state, as Bentham claimed,[3] or the law merely enforces some more fundamental principles,[4] without legal recognition no entitlement to the exclusive use of valuable resources is fully defined. To be sure, most people most of the time respect other people's rights without being threatened by the sheriff, but the state's willingness to enforce the privileges of ownership is always in the background. Still more importantly, the legal system plays the extremely important role of *clarifying* the exact scope of various entitlements and laying down the rules according to which property rights can be exercised.

It is often said that one of the preconditions of successful economic development is that the state should lay down the relevant entitlements with precision and enforce them in an impartial and speedy manner. (Even if the state gets some of the entitlements wrong, it is often added, the parties, if free to contract, will correct this by appropriate private agreements.)[5] Unfortunately, these things (usually said by economists unfamiliar with the workings of the law) are easier said than done. Indeed, history knows no society of any complexity with a legal system that could be genuinely said to satisfy this condition, and the literature concerning the perplexities of the law is as old as the stories of love and war.

What every lawyer knows is that even the most elementary legal rules are never really 'simple,' although under some circumstances they may yield relatively unproblematic applications. Routine cases may be settled rather easily, but at the borders of every legal rule there are

---

[3] Bentham (1931 edition).
[4] See Locke (1963 edition).
[5] The classic presentation of this argument is to be found in Coase (1960).

'hard' cases, where disputes will arise and not be resolved in a clear way. Moreover, it is no comfort that the hard cases are idiosyncratic or unusual, because the most important function of private property is precisely to allow for those idiosyncratic and unusual cases in which the owner makes a nonstandard, unpredictable use of his assets. Where uses are predictable and routine, they may be performed by a bureaucrat acting in accordance with a manual; where this is impossible, and more flexible, decentralized arrangements involving private property become indispensable, hard cases also begin to come up with unwelcome frequency.

The role of the state is much more extensive than just enforcing correlative rights of the owners. The state also claims a right to restrict private uses of resources, even though preexisting and recognized rights are at issue, when it acts for the public good. In this context, the state is no longer an arbiter of private conflicts, but attempts to reallocate certain resources and redesign the rules of the game in order to improve overall welfare. The most common type of this intervention has the purpose of correcting real or alleged market failures, due to existing externalities, transaction costs, informational disparities, monopolies, and other impediments to the proper functioning of the market. Not only does this activity generate hundreds of volumes of laws and regulations, but also each of the rules contained in these volumes generates a penumbra of hard cases that cloud the owner's title and his right to use his property without accountability. It is fashionable nowadays to inveigh against much of this intervention, but it is also well-nigh indisputable that the complexity of a modern economy demands the ever more complex legal framework of its operation. The modern corporation and the stock market could hardly function without laws determining the fiduciary obligations of corporate managers and directors, securities laws protecting the investor, or labor laws assuring peaceful relations between the employers and the employees. We may always hope for better and simpler legislative solutions, but the idea that the regulatory function of the modern state could be very significantly restricted is both unrealistic and probably misguided.

Finally, the modern state has not renounced its time-sanctioned right to enact and enforce a whole panoply of rules designed to give political expression to a moral outlook or social ideals which do not rest on economic considerations at all. Thus, most states redistribute incomes through taxation and other means, in order to alleviate poverty, make certain goods (such as medicine or culture) available to a wider circle of consumers, or to support certain lifestyles (such as home ownership or independent farming), even though economic efficiency suffers as a result.

All of these rules limit some people's right to use their resources in a number of ways, force them to share the benefits of their property with others, as well as modify the expectations they may have with respect to their ability to use their property in an unrestricted way in the future. To be sure, most Western governments are committed to the idea that there are some limits beyond which the state cannot go in modifying preexisting property rights for the benefit of the community (or whatever other social reason) without compensating the owners of those rights. But in just about every country, these limits are themselves quite unclear, generating a plethora of further rules and hard cases. Thus, while most states, with the help of the takings clauses (as well as a number of other provisions) in their constitutions, attempt to provide something in the nature of a 'hard' constraint on their discretion, these protections are, by themselves, of limited value. The constitutional provisions usually guard at most only against the crudest form of expropriation, leaving intact the enormous powers of taxation and regulation to modify and diminish most entitlements. More importantly, even the flexible constitutional protections do not derive their force from the paper on which they are written, but from an extremely delicate and complex mechanism by which political and economic power is distributed in a modern society. If therefore the owner has some kind of realistic expectation of continued control over the resources at his disposal, the boundaries of that expectation are in practice quite vague, and its scope depends on a number of factors that escape any simple enumeration.

What few economists thus genuinely appreciate in connection with the functioning of the market economy is that *political governance* is no more a planned or rational structure than corporate governance or the price system itself, and that its effect on the economy, far from being one of occasional intervention, provides an ever present element of the regime within which property operates. While it may be useful for some purposes to think of the state as merely providing a background support for the rules of the market, in every actual situation government presence is as pervasive as that of transaction costs. Moreover, the regulatory activity of the government does not follow some abstract and predetermined rules, but is basically reactive to the situation in the market, both in terms of the content of the regulation and the process by which they are promulgated. The market determines the strength of the various interest groups which formulate their plans for governmental intervention, and that intervention in turn modifies the forces of the market and the relative strength of the interest groups. The development of the regulatory system, much as the development of other economic institutions, is therefore not an outcome of a fully rational choice of 'optimal' solutions, but a gradual, incremental, *path dependent*, and to a large extent *contingent* historical process. Consequently we do not, and probably cannot, have a purely theoretical account that would permit us to understand fully the workings of these complex institutions. Property, we would like to say, is a much vaguer and complicated concept than is usually imagined and, as such, it is more a subject of inherently 'unscientific' historical and political inquiry than an object of theoretical economic analysis.

The consequence of all this with respect to the transition in Eastern Europe is that the reform process there is a much more uncertain undertaking than it initially appeared to most economists, who were inclined to believe that economic theory was able to provide a reliable guide for policy decisions. In the case of some measures, such as anti-inflationary steps, a sound economic policy can, under favorable political conditions, be firmly implemented by the state and produce more or less expected results. Microeconomic restructuring, however, especially on the scale necessary to infuse Eastern Europe with genuinely market-oriented practices and behavior, involves tampering with extremely complex and delicate institutions, the success or failure of which depends not only on the correctness of an abstract design, but also on a number of contingent circumstances which decisively influence individual and group behavior, and which no design can fully control.[6] Privatization, understood not as a mere ownership transfer, but as a comprehensive reform intended to liberate the productive forces of a society, is a prototype of a microeconomic restructuring process, in which the elements of design must work in tandem with unpredictable, spontaneous evolution of economic institutions.

The ambiguity of privatization

Despite the largely intangible nature of the balance between the private and the public, economically successful societies have nevertheless

---

[6] The peculiar microstructure of the East European economies may also be responsible for some unexpected consequences of standard anti-inflationary measures. For example, see Calvo and Coricelli (1991), and Frydman and Wellisz (1991).

managed to establish a type of equilibrium between government action and private entrepreneurship that allows for a relatively stable set of expectations affecting incentives of agents to dispose of their assets. These expectations affect such matters as the extent of the agents' entrepreneurship, the temporal horizon of their actions, the extent of their consumption and investment, the degree of their reliance on governmental support, etc. By contrast, Eastern Europe entered the period of transition with a balance so far shifted in the direction of state administrative involvement that a mere transfer of title to various kinds of assets would not be of much significance, unless accompanied by a radical transformation of the agents' expectations with respect to their ability to make all kinds of uses of the assets officially designed as 'theirs'. The problem with a transition of such magnitude, however, is that *neither the agents themselves nor the government can know with a sufficient degree of precision the consequences of the programs and policies adopted as a part of the privatization efforts.* In the absence of a historical background of property rights, the future balance between private action and the state is much more indeterminate than in the established market economies, and all the parties involved are to some extent aware that it rests largely on a set of unarticulated social practices and tacit assumptions beyond the control of any individual actors, including the government and its policymakers. In this context, the government may not only have significant difficulties in making credible its commitment to the explicit policies it announces, but also face the problem of unintended consequences of its actions, which may complicate the very meaning of it efforts. In particular, three separate factors may be responsible for introducing three largely unexamined levels of complexity into the concept of privatization in Eastern Europe.

- In the absence of an established system of property rights, which constituted the background of conventional privatizations in the West, privatization policies in Eastern Europe may fail to convey effectively the vested type of entitlements they are intended to transfer. This may be due to two types of problems. First, while we have seen that the government is always both a player and a rulemaker on the economic scene, the borderline between these two roles is significantly more fluid in a society without a stable private property regime. Moreover, when a government has a near-monopoly on certain assets indispensable for the private sector, it is much more able to dictate the conditions of transfer than when it has to compete with other providers of similar assets. As a result, the government may have difficulties in committing itself to relinquishing its control over the privatized assets and its representatives may be unable to resist the temptation of limiting the nature and the scope of the transferred rights, so that the recipients of the privatized assets remain unduly insecure in their entitlements. Second, the rooting of property rights in a whole set of institutional arrangements means that, in ordinary times, most of such rights are only marginally enforced by the legal system, while the core of the institution of ownership is a matter of unquestioned and largely unreflected social and economic practices created through a long evolutionary development. This does not just mean that a 'culture' of respect for property must exist in a society in which property rights are effective, but also that most property-related arrangements in an advanced economy involve various *self-enforcing mechanisms* ingrained in the incentive systems of spontaneous economic behavior, and that the legal system is only able to police a thin layer of aberrational occurrences. But this background of self-enforcement may be absent from the privatization policies in the period of transition, with the result of precluding an effective establishment of the property rights intended by the policymakers.

• While the nefarious role of the state as a nearly exclusive owner of productive assets was stressed in the initial arguments in favor of privatization, it was most often not observed that the state does not cease its intervention with the relinquishing of title. Indeed, the very same noxious behavior of officials, who subsidize inefficient firms and otherwise use their political power to reallocate scarce resources to those who cannot obtain them through the market may be practiced in favor of private parties as much as in favor of state-owned firms, and there is no *a priori* argument that a mere transfer of title should lessen, rather than increase, this type of official behavior. Privatization is a transfer of valuable resources from the control of some parties (state bureaucrats) to others, and one of the primary effects of this transfer is to enfranchise the new owners and make them more powerful, not merely in the economic, but also in the political sense. This in turn means that the new owners are as likely to make a political use of their new resources as they are to use them in a more conventional, economic fashion. Privatization must, therefore, be understood as a political phenomenon as much as an economic one, and this not just in terms of the *ex ante* configuration of political forces that might make some programs politically more palatable than others, but also in terms of the *ex post* effects of the transfer of the privatized resources that might create new and ever more successful forms of rent-seeking behavior. Rather than an unquestioned boon, privatization thus becomes an ambiguous, open-ended process that might lead to bad as well as good consequences.

- The economies of Eastern Europe are not a 'virgin territory,' like a new American continent that is to be built up from scratch. Instead, the region is populated by very large, although extremely dysfunctional, industrial organizations, and, as far as possible, privatization is supposed to transform these into viable business institutions. This means, however, that when the state withdraws from the position of ownership, something must take its place, and, given the size of the entities involved, the new arrangements are not likely to involve an owner-managed form of organization, but something resembling the systems of governance characteristic of the advanced industrialized economies, where ownership and managerial control are largely separated and the monitoring of corporate performance takes place through a host of various complex mechanisms. In other words, privatization of large enterprises is, again, not just a transfer of title, but a complex operation designed to establish for the first time the institutional meaning of ownership in a new and nonstandard economic environment. The choices of privatization strategies facing East European policymakers are further complicated by the fact that the advanced economies, to which the region would naturally aspire, reveal a significant variety of institutional corporate governance arrangements, which decisively affect both the internal corporate structure of individual firms and the way in which resources are allocated among the various branches of the national economy. More-over, our understanding of these historically and largely contingently arisen institutions is not sufficient to allow for a simple transplantation from one environment to another. The economic effect of the transfer of ownership accomplished through privatization, therefore, is not at all clear in advance of the whole process. Instead, the creation of new ownership arrangements must proceed largely in the dark and its ultimate consequences may not become evident until well into the future, when their potential dangers may turn out to be at least partly irreversible.

Here we confine our attention to the first two factors: the difficulties of establishing property rights and the political and economic arrangements which are capable of supporting a private property regime. Although a number of our arguments are also applicable to the difficulties of establishing a privately-based system of corporate governance in Eastern Europe, these problems will largely remain in the background of our discussions.[7]

The difficulty of establishing property rights: the ambiguous role of the state

It has been pointed out earlier that, in an important sense, the old communist order of Eastern Europe did not have any genuine property rights in productive assets, since decisions concerning economic resource allocation used to be made in a political-administrative mode, attempting to control directly the behavior of each individual, while the essence of property-based arrangements involves reliance on the self-interest of individual owners acting under the constraints of a market.[8] In this sense, privatization in Eastern Europe is not a mere transfer of assets from the state to private parties, but rather an attempt to establish a system of genuine property rights in the first place. Unfortunately, the task faced by the state in this attempt is quite daunting and the outcome is often less than satisfactory.

Of the many difficulties encountered by the state on the way to establishing secure property rights, there are two that have not been widely noted and deserve to be elaborated. The first is related to the dual role played by the state as both the rulemaker and a player in the emerging property market. The second stems from a failure to create sufficiently self-enforcing mechanisms of property rights to enable private parties to rely on their ability to enforce them against other private parties.

The state as a rulemaker and a party to property transactions

When the state privatizes in a Western economy, it engages in a transaction that may sometimes be of greater magnitude than ordinary market transactions,[9] but is not otherwise significantly distinct from those that take place among private parties. With the exception of those instances in which the state conveys property rights to a monopoly (in

[7] A discussion of corporate governance in the context of Eastern European privatizations can be found in Chapters 2 and 4 in this volume.

[8] See Chapter 1 in this volume.

[9] For example, the market value of the assets of British Telecom at the time the British government announced its privatization, in 1982, was estimated at about $10 billion. See Vickers and Yarrow (1986).

which case significant restrictions may attach to the entitlements conveyed after the transfer),[10] the nature of the rights conveyed from the state to private parties cannot diverge too far from those that a private party may acquire from another. Privatization takes place against the background of certain standard expectations that a new owner has with respect to his or her acquisitions, and if the rights in the privatized property are too different from this standard, potential buyers will not take up the offer, but look instead to other opportunities in the private sector.

The situation is very different in Eastern Europe, especially in the early stages of the transition. Here the state is not just one seller among many, but a player with close to a monopoly on some of the most important assets, without which the private sector could not operate. As a consequence, the state has often been able to make special rules, while also playing the game: instead of conveying a simple and secure interest in the property, it has tried to tailor the entitlement in such a way as to maximize a host of its own ideological or bureaucratic objectives. A good example of this can be seen in what has otherwise been the most successful privatization effort to date, namely the so-called 'small privatization' of retail trade and consumer service units in the countries of Eastern Europe.

Given the sorry state of the capital stock in the consumer sector under communism (dilapidated and neglected stores), the nonexistent or nearly worthless inventory (since most desirable goods were in chronically short supply), and the absence of any intangible values, such as goodwill, the only genuinely valuable asset of most state-controlled stores in the wake of the fall of the old regime was the premises on which they were located. Privatization was thus not a matter of conveying a going concern of an existing store or a restaurant, but simply a transfer of real estate on which an essentially new business could be established. Looked at from this perspective, privatization of an existing store was thus not significantly different from establishing an ostensibly new, 'startup' business: in both cases, access to scarce real estate, largely controlled by the state, was a key to the whole transaction. The only difference between 'privatized' and new ('startup') businesses was the irrelevant distinction between replacing an old unit in the same sector or establishing a business on premises that had been used for some other purpose.

---

[10] For a discussion of the privatization of monopolies, see Baumol (1993).

The paradox of small privatization is that, in most cases, it has involved no privatization at all, since the conveyance of the only desirable asset in the whole transaction, i.e. real estate, most often stopped far short of a transfer of genuine property rights. Instead, the state most often made the premises available on the basis of a short lease (often less than two years) and restricted the user's already limited rights with a whole host of other stipulations, such as prohibitions on changes in the line of business, restrictions on subletting and other forms of alienation, limitations on the ability to fire employees, etc. Moreover, instead of charging market rents for the property, the state often transferred the premises to previous insiders (management and employees of the privatized units) on preferential terms that made the insiders only more insecure of their continued tenure. While the businesses run by the new owners are clearly private and have shown a considerable level of dynamism, the continued dominance of the state over the real estate market makes the new property rights insecure. As a result, most shopkeepers in Eastern Europe have an unusually negative reaction to leasing arrangements, and the average investment in units occupying leased premises is dramatically smaller than in those in which the premises are purchased.[11] The reason for this is clearly related to the fact that the 'privatization' of premises is tenuous and incomplete: the attempt at creating genuine property rights has clearly not advanced sufficiently far and the new businessmen anticipate that the state might use its market position to extract all kinds of unexpected future concessions.

The elusiveness of property rights in an insider-dominated system of privatization: the Russian mass privatization program

Even when the state unquestionably intends to precommit itself to the establishment of clear property rights and makes significant attempts to part decisively with its former control over the privatized assets, it may fail, for a number of reasons, to put in place a sufficient institutional framework to ensure the effectiveness of ownership. A few examples from Russia may provide a good illustration.

The Russian privatization program was very consciously designed with political considerations in mind. The architects of the elaborate

---

[11] For recent evidence on the post-transfer behavior of units in small privatization programs in the Czech Republic, Hungary, and Poland, see Frydman, Rapaczynski, et al. (1994).

scheme of employee preferences specifically intended to overcome the tremendous resistance to privatization coming from a coalition of forces within the government and the elites of the industrial *nomenklatura* by enlisting the insiders on the enterprise level on the side of the government program. At the same time, the government did not believe that a purely insider privatization was desirable, and attempted to ensure that outsiders – either ordinary citizens or domestic and foreign investors – gain an ownership stake in Russian enterprises. For this reason, the Russian program combined a set of insider preferences with a voucher program designed to allow ordinary citizens (and even foreigners) to participate in the privatization process.

According to the Russian plan, every citizen received, free of charge, vouchers with the nominal value of 10,000 rubles, with further tranches of voucher distribution to come in the future. While the plan contains a number of features, such as immediate and unlimited transferability of all shares and vouchers, which are designed to facilitate the acquisition of control by enterprise outsiders, the program allows the insiders to acquire up to 51 percent of their companies at no charge or extremely discounted prices.[12]

The insiders have a choice among three so-called 'variants' of preferences for themselves. Under Variant I, the workers receive, without payment, up to 25 percent of the shares of their enterprise (if their value does not exceed twenty times the minimum wage per worker) in the form of preferred, nonvoting stock, and they are entitled to purchase up to an additional 10 percent of the shares (with full voting rights) at a 30 percent discount from the nominal price. In addition, high administrative officials of the enterprise (the manager, his deputy, the head engineer, and the treasurer) are also granted an option to purchase at the nominal price up to 5 percent of the shares (but not more than 2,000 times the minimum wage per person). Under Variant II, the insiders receive no formal discounts, but they may purchase up to 51 percent of the shares at 1.7 times the nominal price, with no additional restrictions. Finally, under Variant III, available only to enterprises with more than 200 employees and fixed assets with a book value between Rb 1 million and Rb 50 million, the employees are entitled to purchase up to 20 percent of the shares at a discount of 30 percent from the nominal price (provided the total does not exceed

---

[12] For a description and early analysis of the Russian program, see Shleifer and Vishny (1992) and Frydman, Rapaczynski, Earle, et al. (1993b).

twenty times the minimum wage per person), and a smaller group of insiders, who gain the approval of the whole collective and undertake special responsibilities for the future of the enterprise, may obtain, for one year, the voting rights to 20 percent of the shares, which, if they fulfill their commitments, they can purchase at their nominal price (without any further restrictions) at the expiration of the one-year period.

In addition to these advantages, the insiders can use their vouchers to pay for their preferentially acquired shares, and they may acquire additional shares with funds from so-called 'personal privatization accounts,' into which their enterprises can transfer a portion of their after-tax profits. Most importantly, the nominal price of the shares purchased by the insiders is determined in relation to the book value of the enterprise, which has not been adjusted for inflation. As a result, all the other discount features are of no great importance, since the shares are nearly free anyway. Indeed, to quote just one example given by the head of the State Property Committee, Anatoly Chubais, the residual value of a Volga car on the books of a Moscow taxi cab company would be between Rb 2,000 and Rb 3,000 i.e. between $2 and $3 at September 1993 exchange rate. Not surprisingly, therefore, the Russian insiders overwhelmingly chose Variant II, which gave them the greatest proportion of shares, and the proportion of enterprises choosing this variant has grown over time, as inflation progressively eroded their book value.[13]

The incentives and rights of the insiders. As a result of the system of insider preferences, the overwhelming majority of Russian privatized enterprises will end up under insiders' control. There is some reason to doubt, however, that the form of control rights conferred on the holders of Russian securities, as long as they are overwhelmingly linked with insider status, amounts to real ownership, comparable to that which exists in the context of a genuine private property regime.

To see this, let us look more closely at what is meant by the 'privatization' of large enterprises in the recent Russian experience. In the Russian political game, the government's policy of conferring legal entitlements on the insiders on the level of individual enterprises clearly

---

[13] The price of vouchers fell to barely over Rb 4,000 in May 1993. It rose afterwards, but at a rate slower than inflation. By purchasing vouchers on the open market (which could be used as a means of payment for shares at the nominal value of Rb 10,000), the insiders could still lower the real price of their preferentially acquired shares.

meant some relaxation of bureaucratic control by the old branch ministries, with their roots in the planning system and the bureaucratic *nomenklatura*. But while the greater autonomy of the enterprise insiders is now formalized under the name of 'ownership,' the real question is to what extent their rights and interests in the enterprise have really changed.

To begin with, it is relatively safe to say that, in a great majority of cases, the *incentives* of the new insider 'owner' to engage in significant restructuring are rather minimal. The workers, to whom the Russian program gives significant portions of ownership, are still more interested in their wages and employment than in shareholders' profits, since dividends are not likely to constitute more than a fraction of their income. In most enterprises, especially the less viable ones, managers may also find subsidies a safer business strategy than restructuring, which is not only socially costly, but also far from certain to be successful.[14] Thus, the 'normalcy' established as a background of insider control is likely to consist in the preservation of the status quo. As in every system, this background of 'normalcy' is bound to be an important factor when one moves from incentives to rights: To what extent can a person endowed with a formal ownership title deviate from the standard established by the background practices of a given system? What uses of property, in other words, are self-evidently legitimate, so that their enforcement by the legal system is not required, except for a margin of aberrational cases? If a managerial group in control of a Russian enterprise decides on significant layoffs or even the closing of the enterprise and a sale of its assets, will they be able to assert their effective control just because they have the votes of a majority of directors representing the shareholders of the corporation?

The answer to this question is far from clear, and on it rides the question of whether effective property rights have been transferred to the new owners of the Russian firms. If the change in the behavior of the control groups in Russian enterprises is very gradual, the state may back a few owners who want to break from the old mold, and a small number of enterprises might be successfully restructured. The problem with such gradual changes is that they might take longer than the Russian economy can afford. What is more interesting, therefore, is whether the hold of 'normalcy' could be broken and whether a large

---

[14] It is to be hoped, of course, that managers of enterprises with better capital stock will show more interest in genuine restructuring. For a discussion of a related point, see Boycko, Shleifer and Vishny (1992).

number of enterprises could simultaneously enter a restructuring process in the near future. This could come either through a state policy designed to change the incentives of the insiders (mostly by tightening budgetary constraints, so that enterprises would have to restructure to survive) or through a large number of outsiders acquiring control rights from the insiders and attempting to institute significant changes (how likely that is to happen, we shall consider in a moment).

There are good reasons to doubt that a critical mass of restructuring would be feasible under present Russian conditions. Given the enormous misallocation of resources in the Russian economy, and the tremendous hypertrophy of both the heavy industry and very large and ineffective institutional structures (huge state enterprises), large-scale restructuring is likely to lead, at least in the short run, to widespread unemployment and social dislocations. These, in turn, are likely to lead to political unrest and pressure on the state to go back on macro-economic reforms or to intervene directly in favor of a number of special interests at the enterprise level. Faced with this pressure, the state might well step in to curtail, or perhaps even revoke, the control rights of the people whom it now designates as 'owners'.

The point of what we are saying is not to make a prediction of how strong the insiders' pressure may actually be or how the Russian government will behave in the future. Nor is it even that the government *should* maintain a tough stand in the face of political pressure: the social cost of too rapid changes may perhaps be too high to permit such resoluteness. The point is rather that to the extent that doubts persist concerning the government's likely response to a clamor for protection of special interests, the very system of property rights the authorities are trying to set up through the present privatization program is in doubt as well.[15]

The future of markets for corporate control. It has evidently been the hope of the architects of the Russian program that the emergence of secondary capital markets would facilitate the entry of outsiders into the world of Russian corporate governance. It is, of course, not quite clear whether, as long as the easy money provided by the Central Bank makes subsidies more attractive than restructuring, the behavior of outsiders, should they gain a say in the running of Russian enterprises, would significantly

---

[15] This is not to say that our estimate of the Russian chances of success are entirely pessimistic. We shall see later that the program may be the best possible under the circumstances and constitute a political prerequisite for a more decisive policy of economic reform.

depart from the 'normalcy' or present enterprise behavior. But the corporate governance problems of Russian enterprises, especially those with a heavy proportion of labor (as opposed to managerial) ownership, transcend the issue of macroeconomic environment, and even if the latter changes, they are unlikely to disappear without the introduction of a significant measure of outside control. In this context, it is important to examine the chances that robust secondary markets for the securities of the privatized companies might develop in the foreseeable future.

There are two aspects of the development of secondary markets that need to be considered separately. The first concerns the potential for the emergency of a market for corporate control, i.e. for the stakes that allow active monitoring and intervention in the management of the enterprise. The second aspect concerns the emergence of a stock market at which minority stakes, entitling the owners to streams of income, but not to effective voice in corporate matters, are regularly traded.

With respect to the development of a market for corporate control, there are some obvious obstacles. To begin with, given the pre-dominance of Variant II, the insiders of most enterprises are likely to have an outright majority of the shares, and will be well-nigh impossible to dislodge, unless some of them are willing (and able) to sell their shares to outside investors. Furthermore, both the property funds, which hold the shares owned by the state, and the insiders restrict the supply of shares available for outside acquisitions. The property funds have reportedly been reluctant to sell the shares in their custody and a special presidential decree was necessary to expedite the process. Anecdotal evidence also points to the fact that the insiders often go to great lengths to buy up the shares of their companies (in addition to those they acquire on preferential terms) and to prevent other insiders from selling their shares.[16]

On the demand side, markets for corporate control are still more difficult to develop than ordinary stock markets, since they require large concentrations of capital that are not likely to emerge for some time in any East European country. This is even more true in Russia, where the law, apparently passed to assuage precisely the insiders' fears that outsider holdings would be too concentrated, restricted the scope of permitted activities of privatization investment funds, which are used in other countries, such as Poland and the Czech Republic, to exercise

---

[16] The methods used in this connection are said to include outright prohibitions and efforts to buy up the shares of workers through the company itself or through third parties acting on management's behalf.

supervising and monitoring functions on behalf of small shareholders. The Russian funds cannot own more than 10 percent of the shares of any one company, which effectively encourages them to remain passive and play a subsidiary role in the governance of the privatized enterprises. The well-known valuation difficulties and other doubts concerning the viability of most Russian enterprises make these properties risky and unattractive, thus reducing the demand even further.

But even leaving aside all these obstacles, the incentive for outside investors to acquire control positions in the privatized Russian enterprises are problematic precisely because of the already described indeterminacy of the rights available for purchase. As long as there are doubts concerning the credibility of the state's commitment, and indeed ability, to enforce the rights of a control group to engage in a type of restructuring that an outside investor might contemplate, there will be few prospective buyers. Moreover, even if there are some reasons to believe that insider owners might be able to engage in a certain amount of restructuring, there are additional doubts whether such ability can be effectively transferred together with the title to ownership. For much of the power the Russian managers do have may in fact come from their *status as insiders*, rather than from their position as owners, and an outsider must bear the additional risk that his title may prove worth no more than the paper on which it is certified. And since a buyer of control rights, unlike most buyers of minority stakes, has greater difficulty diversifying his risks (because of the size of the transaction), the demand might dwindle even further.

Finally, the ability of an outside investor to acquire control rights in a Russian enterprise depends on the existence of effective markets for *minority* positions, because it is unlikely that a viable market for corporate control could develop independently of a market for minority stakes. This is because the most important function of a market for corporate control is not the conveyance of such control from one party to another, but a *takeover*, i.e. a *formation of a cohesive majority out of a number of dispersed minority positions* in order to dislodge the existing incompetent or dishonest management. A friendly transfer of power from one cohesive control group to another does not usually occur under normal conditions, except for synergistic mergers or anti-competitive arrangements. In fact, in the absence of such special factors, there are important reasons to believe that a transfer of control from one cohesive group to another is not likely to occur, since the prospective buyers and sellers have asymmetric information concerning the real value of the firm. This means that the fact that a large stakeholder, with access to inside information, wants to sell his position sends a signal to prospective buyers that the firm may be in trouble. As a result, exit from large holdings may involve a loss to the insiders, and the expected 'control premium' might in fact become a significant liability. As opposed to this, a hostile takeover is much more likely to lead to genuine restructuring and the introduction of far-reaching changes in the business.

Thus, the two aspects of the development of secondary markets – the formation of the markets for minority and majority stakes – are in fact intimately linked to one another. And the examination of the chances for the development of a market for minority positions in Russian privatized enterprises also raises significant doubts.

The question of minority rights. It is a rather common wisdom that the development of secondary capital markets is a long and complicated process, and that the restructuring of East European economies cannot afford to wait for it to take place. But the authors of the Russian program evidently thought that the process could be given a serious boost if a large number of securities were to be found in the hands of many small investors, and this is what the voucher program was supposed to accomplish. The jury is still out on the success of the Russian experiment, but it should be emphasized that a free distribution of minority interests to the public may well fail to convey effective property interests, unless the stakes acquired by the public are considered genuinely valuable and can themselves be traded. In other words, unless at least *some* investors (and probably a very significant number of them) are prepared to spend real money (and not just vouchers) for the purchase of shares in Russian enterprises, i.e. unless many people not interested in costly monitoring of their investments gain sufficient *confidence in the system* to be prepared to acquire minority stakes in Russian businesses, increasing the supply of securities and other financial obligations can only result in the collapse of the nascent market, not its invigoration. And we need not add that unless the shares of insider-dominated companies fetch an attractive price in terms of real currency, the insiders will have no incentives to sell their shares to outsiders.

Some reasons for skepticism as to whether a sufficient level of investor confidence in the Russian enterprises might be created in the near future are well known: Russian enterprises are famous for their wasteful and inefficient operation, many managers are widely considered incompetent, and any attempt at significant restructuring (which is bound to lead to labor-force reductions) is likely to encounter resistance from the employees threatened in the security of their employment. These types of reasons are similar to those for which an investor in the West would not want to acquire a minority position in a company that is perceived to be mismanaged. But in addition to this, there is also another reason, which is more systemic and specifically tied to Russian conditions, why an investor may shy away from acquiring minority stakes in Russian companies, namely, because *it is not clear what rights are effectively conveyed in such a transaction.*

Minority rights in a modern corporation are not a straightforward form of property. In fact, they are a rather delicate product of an institutional culture related to a very special form of financing. A minority shareholder provides often substantial funds and receives in exchange neither a firm commitment to a specified form of repayment (such as that promised to an ordinary creditor) nor any significant control rights. Instead, he relies on the majority stakeholders to conduct the business of the corporation in such a way as to both maximize its value *and share the upside potential with the passive investor.* To be sure, every legal system provides some protection for minority shareholders and puts certain fiduciary obligations on the majority. But these are, of necessity, only marginally effective: the legal system cannot, in the name of protecting the minority, tie the hands of the majority (and its management team) in the exercise of their best business judgment; indeed, the whole institution of minority shareholding relies on the ability of an investor to 'piggyback' on the often ineffable skills and efforts of the controlling party, without a need to look over its shoulder and second-guess important business decisions. Thus, the institution of minority shareholding does not primarily rest on the investor's ability to vindicate personally his or her rights. Instead, it rests nearly entirely on the *institutional background of the market system,* i.e. a combination of incentives and expectations that generate the confidence in the fact that, in an overwhelming majority of cases, the majority will honor its commitments to the minority without any complicated system of monitoring and sanctions ever being mobilized.

The basis of all the incentives and expectations responsible for the confidence level necessary for a viable institution of minority shareholding is the fact that most companies must come back to the market for more financing. Thus, if a firm does not make a credible commitment to outside investors or casts doubt on their right to participate in the income streams produced by the firm, the firm's access to capital markets will be closed and it will not be able to generate capital in the future.

But the connection between a firm's failure to commit to minority investors' rights and the severing of its access to finance is not a simple matter. To begin with, breaches of faith to minority investors are not a clear-cut issue; whether a minority investor is receiving sufficient returns, given the firm's performance, general market conditions, the balance between short-term income and long-term appreciation, etc., is a rather murky question in most cases. In addition, the market must assimilate this ambiguous information, analyze and disseminate it, and produce a spontaneous response from prospective investors in the future. It is precisely this complex institutional framework, which is not planned or coordinated by anyone, that constitutes a significant part of what we called the 'private property regime': a self-enforcing mechanism that provides a silent background for everyday behavior of agents in a market society.

Seen from this perspective, the prospects for establishing a viable system of minority shareholding in Russia are not self-evidently favorable. In the present situation, the financing of large enterprises in Russia is done largely through the banks, which extend extremely generous credits backed by the close-to-unlimited printing capacity of the Central Bank. The availability of this nearly unlimited credit means that the insiders have little incentive to worry about their access to the capital markets, and thus about the rights of minority investors. In fact, their incentive is to increase their own compensation, rather than dividends. To acquire minority stakes in Russian enterprises, therefore, is to place one's faith in a system in which the legal obligations of the majority are not backed up by an appropriate system of incentives. And since the law can only police marginal deviations from established norms, it is highly questionable whether a purely legal obligation of good faith toward the minority can make the minority rights really effective.

But even if the macroeconomic policy were to change, the translation of the firms' financing needs into an effective self-enforcing mechanism for the protection of minority rights will be far from accomplished. This is, of course, because of the absence of the already discussed background institutions of a private property regime: the market's ability to evaluate the good faith of the people in control of large enterprises and deliver a sufficiently tight coordination between enterprise performance and the willingness of minority investors to trust their money to the signals of the market. And until such institutions exist, it may be impossible for the state to confer *on anyone* certain crucial types of entitlements, even if the state is prepared to relinquish its rights free of charge. What we are facing here, in other words, is a limitation on the state's ability to make the core of its privatization policies 'stick'; the attempted 'bootstrap' may be too abrupt, and the rights the state is trying to convey cannot be effectively created in the very act of conveyance.

The politics of transition to a private property regime

We have seen that, if privatization is looked at as a redressing of the balance between private and state action, with the aim of creating a stable private property regime, the government may face significant difficulties in its attempt to disentangle itself from the position of control with respect to the productive assets of the society. The reason for this is that a genuine release of such assets presupposes an institutional background of private property that a privatization program may fail to establish. But the government's difficulties do not end here: there are also all kinds of parties outside the government that perceive their own interests to be intimately linked with the continued hypertrophy of state control, and these parties are prepared to use their political power to keep the government actively engaged in economic decisions. Moreover, what is not usually observed is that the government's privatization policies themselves may play an important role in keeping some of these forces alive.

Privatization as a redistribution of political resources

Privatization is often seen as a way of lessening certain noxious forms of state intervention and a process of depoliticization of economic decisions. State ownership, it is said, is inefficient because politicians and state bureaucrats, in addition to using the state sector as a source of patronage, are incapable of resisting demands for never-ending subsidies to the enterprises owned by the state, and are always ready to engage in regulations protective of the state sector. But governments in many countries subsidize private enterprises as much as those owned by the state, and various nominally private parties are extremely adept at the game of rent-seeking. Indeed, the cost of tariffs, trade quotas, price supports, tax exemptions, and protective regulations is often many times greater than the support provided to the state sector.

Looking at the same issue from the point of view of recipients of governmental largess, it will be useful to remember that achieving one's objectives through state intervention is always one of the possible strategies a party may pursue, along with such other methods as outperforming one's competition in the market or reaching a collusive agreement with one's competitors. Whenever an economic agent has some resources at its disposal, it will consider, at the margin, whether using those resources to secure favorable state intervention is more or less beneficial from the agent's point of view than any other course of action. While some parties may desire state intervention more than others, it must be remembered that *every* economic agent would like to obtain rents from the state, and if some do not pursue them actively, it is because the cost, given opposition from other parties, opportunity costs, etc., is too high. This proclivity of business to seek state support does not change if the resources at the disposal of a party are obtained through privatization: since privatization transfers valuable assets from the state to various parties, it is always possible that the recipient might use these additional resources to increase the pressure on the state to deliver some other goods to the recipient. Thus, instead of viewing it as an automatic way of restricting state activity, one should look at *privatization as a redistribution of resources from some parties to others who may generate demand for different levels of state intervention.* In this sense, privatization may lead to the lessening of political pressure for state intervention, but it may also lead to its increase, and there is no *a priori* reason to believe that the former result is more likely than the latter. Thus, for example, if privatization were to crystallize into formal property rights the somewhat inchoate entitlements of workers inherited from the last years of communism in Poland, it is likely that pressure for subsidization and state job protection policies would increase rather than decrease, since the resources at the disposal of the workers would become greater, while the state's ability to counteract worker demands by increasing the power of the management or threatening another form of privatization would correspondingly diminish. (Future corrections may also be made more difficult by the fact that inchoate entitlements are transformed into formal property rights.) Or suppose, for example, that as a result of privatization, the control of major industrial enterprises is concentrated in the hands of a few financial institutions and that the state is perceived by the electorate as responsible for their establishment and proper functioning. Consequently, the new financial institutions may turn out to be politically much more powerful than the old state-sector lobby composed of workers and the management of state enterprises. It is quite likely that in such a situation, the dominant business strategy of the large private institutions might be to pressure the state to allow them to form monopolistic cartels that would be even less efficient than before privatization, or to threaten the state, which has no way of knowing how unprofitable the privatized enterprises really are, with massive factory closings and huge layoffs, in order to extract higher levels of subsidization than those prevailing prior to privatization. In fact, certain forms of privatization might even modify the incentives of existing actors in the direction of increasing the waste of the resources under their control, since such waste might, say, by expanding employment, increase their leverage in demanding larger subsidies from the government.[17]

It is clear, then, that not every ownership constellation produced by privatization will result in a greater depoliticization of economic decision making. What assures a degree of protection against rent-seeking behavior of special interests, and gives *credibility* to the state's commitment to withdraw from a range of ordinary economic decisions, is not so much the absence of direct state ownership as the existence of an arrangement that tilts the balance of political power away from reliance on excessive state intervention. It is thus one of the criteria of a successful privatization program that it redistributes resources in such a way as to contribute to a new alignment of political forces which in turn provides a basis for the sustainability of market-oriented economic policies.

Elements of a theory of political action

The development of a full-fledged theory of political arrangements associated with a private property regime is a matter of great complexity that cannot be fully attended to in the present context. We shall therefore limit our discussions to identifying the main components of such a theory and indicating the rough mode of their interaction.

The starting point of our analysis lies with the individual agents facing a decision concerning the best use of their assets. In particular, we would like to focus on the agents' incentives to demand assistance from the government or to pursue their goals through other means, such as excelling in the marketplace. It is these incentives that are affected by different privatization policies, and the analysis may permit us to assess the effectiveness of different programs on the basis of their impact on the overall demand for state intervention.

The incentives of the agents facing a decision among political

---

[17] For a related analysis, see Boycko, Shleifer, and Vishny (1992).

action, entrepreneurial endeavors, and other private arrangements depend on the type of resources at the disposal of the agent and the relative costs and benefits of the different courses of action.

Differential productivity of assets. Agents facing a choice among different strategies of maximizing their welfare have different assets at their disposal, and privatization may increase or decrease their stock of assets of different kinds. It is important to realize in this context that not all assets have the same productivity with respect to empowering their holders to realize their different objectives: some assets may be very productive when deployed toward the achievement of a superior market position, but much less adequate for achieving a desirable political objective. Other assets may have the opposite characteristics.

Two examples may make this clear. Suppose the state conveys to a private party a steel mill employing a large number of people and located in a 'company town,' dependent for its livelihood on the continuation of the steel production. Given how investment decisions had been made under communism and the technological obsolescence of steel production in Eastern Europe, it might be extremely difficult, if not impossible, to turn such properties around. Even to the extent that the steel mill might contain some divisions that might be salvaged, the necessary restructuring will probably involve large-scale layoffs, cuts in production, social dislocations in the surrounding community, etc. When all is said and done, the returns from restructuring are questionable at best, and the political cost of success might be considerable. But precisely because of this, the *political value* of the same assets is much greater, since the state might not be able to afford the closing of the mill and the assets might prove to be a tremendously effective tool in extracting rents from the budget.

Contrast this with another asset: a chocolate factory with a relatively established name, some foreign markets, and a potential Western investor. The transfer of such an asset to a private party offers a good chance of a rapid increase in value that may outstrip any returns from continued state involvement. Moreover, the restructuring involves few layoffs, and this makes the asset not very productive from the point of view of its ability to attract state support. Indeed, as we shall see shortly, attracting such support may be quite costly, since any subsidies may have to be dressed up and rationalized in ways that decrease the returns from investment in political activity.

The differential productivity of various assets with respect to their political and economic uses is in large part responsible for the fact that state intervention is more likely to redistribute resources from stronger, more efficient firms to those that are weaker and less able to compete. *Ceteris paribus*, stronger firms, being richer, might be expected to be able to secure more benefits for themselves in the political market. But in practice, the viability of the stronger firms itself makes their threats of imposing harms on politicians less credible and diminishes their ability to extract special favors from the government.

The idea that assets have differential productivity with respect to different objectives may also facilitate the understanding of the concept of the private property regime, which constitutes the constant background of our discussions. *For it is one of the main features of the private property regime that the political productivity of most assets is rather low and that there is no strong inverse relation between the economic and political value of a given asset.* This does not mean, of course, that in a well-functioning capitalist society, firms with large amounts of money do not manage to extract important rents from the state. Nor is it unknown that a large firm in trouble can obtain special assistance. But, overall, it is a dominant strategy for most asset holders to deploy most of their assets in the marketplace and to use only a fraction of them to provide a favorable political framework for economic operations. It is also generally (although not universally) true, that falling economic performance results in a decreasing, rather than increasing, ability to obtain political support. It is this state of affairs that may be very difficult to achieve in the conditions prevailing in most postcommunist societies.[18]

Costs and benefits of political activity. In addition to the differential productivity of the assets controlled by various parties, the same parties may also face other differential costs and benefits of political and economic activities.

• Some parties may face higher costs of collective action than others in

---

[18] It is important to realize that more is involved here than just saying that East European governments should be firm in their resistance to political pressures. Nor is the reason why assets have low political value in a private property regime merely a function of a changed political system. Instead, what is implied is that the stock of assets of a society must satisfy certain conditions before a durable establishment of a private property regime. In effect, as long as the capital stock contains too much that is economically worthless, so that its improvement involves serious social costs, the government is always subject to being held up for ransom by the holders of economically worthless assets. *Only when the winnowing out of the bad assets is a marginal, rather than the normal, economic problem, can the political system effectively resist pressures for large-scale redistribution.*

the pursuit of their political objectives, be it the securing of political rents or protecting themselves from exploitation by other groups. Benefits flowing from political action (or restraint) are often 'public goods,' i.e. they cannot be withheld from those who did not contribute their share of the cost of their achievement. If, further, a group of potential beneficiaries from governmental action (or restraint) is large and diffuse, the cost of organizing the members of the group and making sure they contribute their share of the expense of political action may be heavy, while the stakes of each individual member of the group in the success of the required political action may be quite small. Elementary social choice theory tells us that, in such situations, public goods will be suboptimally provided, and certain groups will be handicapped in their access to political largess.[19]

- For quite similar reasons, certain groups may face differential costs of political action because the *opposition* to their goals is better or less well organized. Thus, for example, if a labor union puts pressure on the government to prevent the closing of a loss-making factory, the losers from such a subsidy will most likely be the taxpayers, who will have to foot the bill. But it is extremely unlikely that the taxpayers will do anything about it, since each of them has only a miniscule interest at stake (although the aggregate sum might be quite considerable) and most of them are not even likely to know about the existence of the subsidy. If, on the other hand, a union's pressure for a job-saving program conflicts with the employer's ability to realize much higher rates of return on investment, the resistance to the union's political demands is likely to be much stronger.

- Certain firms (the healthier ones, in fact) might incur special costs related to governmental intervention, even if it is supposed to favor them, because of the need to hide or rationalize most forms of redistribution in an open political system.[20] Subsidies, to the extent they transfer resources from some parties to others, are clearly never 'naked;' they always require some form of justification in terms of 'public' or 'general' interest, such as health, safety, job maintenance,

---

[19] The classic presentation of this theory can be found in Olson (1965).

[20] The need to hide subsidies and clothe them in all kinds of public-interest sounding forms is much greater in democratic regimes. This, contrary to many public choice theorists, seems to indicate that democracies are less, not more, prone to redistribution, since the winners from government intervention gain only a relatively small fraction (smaller than under authoritarian regimes) of what they must take from the losers. Hence, the case is similar to that when externalities prevent the capture of a large fraction of the gains from a given activity, and the production of subsidies is 'inefficient' (in addition to the inefficiency involved in the act of redistribution itself), so that they will be 'suboptimally' produced.

support of independent producers, national defense, etc. But these embellishments usually come at an additional cost: the jobs 'saved' must be maintained later, whether or not they are efficient, the detailed pseudo-safety regulations that keep out foreign competitors may also restrict flexibility, wasteful government contracts may introduce additional managerial and organizational rigidities, etc. It is thus possible that the opportunity cost of politicization for the healthier firms includes not only the economic profits forgone because of the efforts that go into lobbying, but also losses in their own productivity that are likely to ensue upon politicization. Also, the need to disguise subsidies may make it more difficult to capture them without sharing with other groups, and this externality makes them less attractive. This may be one more reason why subsidization tends to redistribute more in favor of the weaker than the stronger firms.

• While everyone likes to receive rents from the state, there is some reason to believe that once a political system opens itself to arguments in favor of one kind of subsidies, it may find it difficult to resist demands for other kinds as well. This is because it may be easier to produce a general argument against redistribution than a number of special arguments against particular kinds of subsidies; not only because such arguments may be more subtle, but also because policing government officials may be easier in a system in which a blanket disapproval of subsidies is in force. Now, certain parties may clearly have greater stakes than others in opposing a system in which subsidies become common and easy to secure. Again, this is likely to be true about firms that generally outperform their competitors in the market. These firms know that they do well in the market system, but have no way of knowing whether their skills would turn out to be equally useful in the competition for political favors. They are, therefore, likely to oppose a system in which subsidies are easy to get, even if the cost of such a position may be to weaken their argument in favor of particular rents that may accrue to them under the present system.

The politics of postprivatization regimes

In light of all these considerations, one may attempt an assessment of the difficulties that East European governments face in the process of privatizing various state assets. The difficulties we considered previously, in connection with the problems of establishing a regime of clear property rights, concerned the tendency of the state to define too narrowly the sphere of private activity, the failures of enforcement, and the temptation to continue invading the putative rights of the private parties. The common feature of all these problems was the fact that the authorities, in one way or another, continued to crowd out and restrict the private sector. The difficulties we are now considering, by contrast, stem from the fact that the political forces in the post-transfer period combine to drag the state back to help (rather than restrict) them through its coercive power of redistribution. While this process comes in at the urging of the private parties, its ultimate effect is very similar: the state fails to redress the balance between private action and its own sphere of administration and continuously fails in its effort to establish a viable private property regime.

Strategies of asset allocation. The primary reason for the state's potential failure to withdraw from the administration of the economy, despite a formal privatization of its enterprises, is that the very nature of the assets in the hands of the state makes it difficult for the state to relinquish its control. The worst case scenario is that the capital stock inherited from the communist period, as well as the organizational form of the state sector, are, by and large, so distorted that it may be questionable whether any significant part of it is salvageable at all. (We are talking, of course, about assets held in large industrial enterprises, since there is no doubt that some other state assets, such as real estate and the capital stock that may be used by small businesses, are of significant value.) If this is the case, the state sector has no real chance of becoming a fully viable part of a market economy, and the only hope for the future lies in the new emerging private sector.

It is important to realize that even under this scenario, privatization may also be necessary, although it will probably lead to very little restructuring and much liquidation. To begin with, liquidation is also a complex business operation involving decisions concerning the disposition of assets, the speed of the process, etc. Privatizing this process in some form may greatly increase its efficiency. But above all, privatization of nonviable assets may be necessary for political reasons. The nonviable assets may be of little economic value, but they have considerable political value, and privatization may diffuse it under certain conditions. In particular, a well-designed privatization program in favor of enterprise insiders may sever some of the organizational links among the various insider interests, as well as those between the enterprises and the state.

It is thus not a precondition of every meaningful privatization program that the assets to be privatized be capable of being significantly improved and producing in a competitive market environment. But even if a significant portion of state assets is known to be viable, privatization faces a number of other pitfalls that may make much of the effort fruitless. The reason for this is that neither the privatizing authorities nor anyone else really knows which of the assets held by the state can and which cannot be successfully restructured, and this very fact may significantly raise the political value of the privatized assets for their postprivatization owners: since they can always claim that the privatized businesses will have to be closed or dramatically shrunk, they can hold the state to ransom and demand that it come in to the rescue. As a result, even if the businesses might, under certain circumstances, be restructured, their political value may become dominant in the eyes of the new owners.

What are, then, the strategies that the authorities may use to minimize the political value of the privatized assets and ensure as much as possible that their economic value is maximized? Much of the answer to this question has to do with the structure of ownership after privatization, and we shall consider this matter shortly. At this point, we would like to focus on two strategies of asset allocation that may play an important role.

Given that the very uncertainty concerning the viability of the capital stock of privatized enterprises is a factor that significantly enhances their political value, it is very important to try to find out how much and which part of the capital stock available for privatization is not viable, and to handle it separately from the privatization of the viable portion of the state sector. In this way, the new owners of assets initially determined to be viable will lose some of their bargaining power vis-à-vis the state and will have greater difficulties arguing for state support. The authorities, in turn, will have more confidence that resisting calls for subsidies will not lead to massive failures of the privatized industries, with the concomitant political consequences.

We have examined elsewhere in some detail a method by which the viability of the capital stock to be privatized may be assessed prior to privatization.[21] The gist of our proposal was that only by using a properly designed auction mechanism can the state benefit from a

---

[21] See Chapter 3 in this volume.

decentralized process during which private parties interested in the purchase of state assets invest significant resources into finding out which of these assets may be turned around through a restructuring effort, and which have probably negative value.

Another strategy for reducing the political value of the privatized assets is to ensure that most owners of such assets are diversified over a broad range of holdings, so that a system of subsidies would be likely to affect them negatively as well as positively (since they would be likely to own firms that pay the cost of subsidies as well as those that receive them). If it is believed, for example, that most privatized assets are generally of lower quality than the assets in the hands of the new private sector, it might be important to encourage owners of new firms to participate in the privatization process and try to provide incentives for the purchasers of state assets to acquire stakes in the new private sector as well. Also, to the extent that assets in the state sector are of uneven quality, even after those with negative value have been separated from the rest, the state might try to assure that new owners do not concentrate their holdings in certain areas. When all is said and done, however, the fact remains that the nature of the capital stock in the postcommunist economies of Eastern Europe remains a serious limiting factor not only with respect to the restructuring effort, but also with respect to the very ability of the state to privatize its enterprises in such a way as to contribute to the establishment of a genuine private property regime.

The role of the postprivatization ownership structure. We have seen that the ability of a given party to achieve its political objectives depends heavily not only on the assets in its portfolio, but also on the collective action problems faced by that party and by its opposition. Indeed, very few individuals or firms can single-handedly influence important actions of the government. Consequently, whether a party will be successful in lobbying for state support very often depends on the level of its political organization and the political organization of its opposition. Since privatization may well affect this factor, its political consequences must be carefully considered.

One of the main questions facing the authorities in devising a privatization program is how to structure the ownership of the privatized firms in the wake of the transfer. Unfortunately, there are a number of considerations here that may pull in different directions. In particular, the demands of effective corporate governance after privatization may speak for rather concentrated holdings in the hands of certain parties, such as the financial intermediaries in the Czech or Polish mass privatization programs, while political considerations may at least raise some doubts about such arrangements.

From the point of view of postprivatization politics there are dangers to both excessive dispersal and excessive concentration of ownership. One of the purposes of privatization must be to diffuse the power of pressure groups centered around state enterprises and to create new political forces opposed to continued state intervention. Thus, if privatization succeeds in weakening the unity of the management and the workers, i.e. the coalition which controlled the enterprises in the preprivatization period, they may also weaken the political pressures in favor of continued state involvement. But if, in the process, the authorities decide, in the name of management account-ability, to assure that the ownership of the privatized firms is sufficiently concentrated in the hands of powerful new intermediary institutions, they run the risk of creating new and even more effective lobbies for state intervention. Indeed, under certain circumstances, the privatization intermediaries may simply become an instrument of further political coordination of the forces in control of the privatized enterprises, and lead to an increased politicization of economic decision making. A similar effect may follow upon a privatization that conveys the ownership of state enterprises to other politically well-organized groups, such as labor, which have a vested interest in preventing serious restructuring.

This is not the place to propose a full-fledged solution to the problems of postprivatization politics. Indeed, our primary purpose here is to point to the insufficiently stressed difficulties and obstacles to effective privatization than to offer positive solutions. But if there is an answer to the problem of postprivatization politics, the solution must be conceived dynamically as coming from a *competition* among owners, each of whom might want subsidies for himself, but is ready to oppose similar demands by others. This means that a number of owners must see themselves as sufficiently benefiting from a system in which private activity is allowed to proceed without undue governmental inter-vention, and they must expect to be worse off in a system of wide-spread subsidization. These agents, even if they would like to receive state support, provided it could be limited to them, are at the same time not inclined to enter into any coalitions in favor of general economic activism by the state, and are not averse to support coalitions opposed to generalized state intervention. If the collective action problems standing in the way of such 'blocking power' are not too great,[22] a stable private property regime might be successfully established.

The paradox of transition

A fundamental problem underlies most of the obstacles on the path of economic transition in Eastern Europe. The capital stock of East European economies is obsolete and its corporate and industrial structure is largely dysfunctional. This, as is well known, requires a socially costly period of transition. Moreover, much of the restructuring of the state sector involves not so much a readjustment to new conditions as simple *shrinkage*, both in absolute terms and relative to the rest of the economy. What this means is that, rather paradoxically, privatization is to a large extent not so much a process by which assets in the state sector become revitalized, but rather a more or less managed process of *decline and retirement* of an *ex ante* unknown, but likely substantial, portion of these assets.[23] Some of this decline may be an effect of down-sizing the existing firms, with some viable portion of the business remaining at the end, but much may involve complete liquidation. The problem of choosing an appropriate path of privatization is thus largely how much of this decline can be absorbed by the economy, without overly distorting the whole process of transition, either by undermining political stability or preventing an effective establishment of a private property regime.

The very size of the transformation of the state sector means that the *change involved in the process of transition must be global, rather than marginal*. The changed mode of operation expected from the privatized units implies their being embedded in a new background of normalcy, and until this new background – which we called the private property regime – is created, the apparently transformed units are drawn back into the old mold. In other words, until a sufficiently critical mass of change is achieved, incremental steps remain largely ineffective.

But global change raises fundamental difficulties as well, on both

---

[22] Another factor of importance may be the existence of a political system in which blocking government action is easier than moving the authorities to do something positive. The American legislative system, with its proliferation of veto powers in various committees, is a good example. But the price of this system is, of course, that desirable legislation may be equally easily blocked as the undesirable.

[23] It seems clear that at least the heavy industry, overbuilt by the communist authorities, will have to be substantially reduced.

technical and political levels. On the technical levels, the market mechanism that is supposed to be established in the process of transition is paradigmatically a system of evolutionary, marginal changes, and cannot handle global transformations. When a system of rigid constraints is abolished at one fell swoop, the swings of the readjustment might be tremendously costly, and the state is drawn back in to manage the process. A very similar mechanism operates on the political level: since the speed of transition must be managed in order to prevent a disintegration of the social order, the degree of state intervention remains at a level that is too high and impedes the emergence of a normally functioning privately-based market economy. Thus, to the extent that privatization is not just a conveyance of state assets into private hands, but also a process of the management of the shrinkage of the state sector, the latter interferes with the former and restricts its effectiveness, with the result that the state comes back into economic decision making normally left to the private sector. All in all, the activism of the state, attempting to manage the process of the state sector's decline, prevents the establishment of a private property regime, which is the whole purpose of the transition.

Given the obstacle course on the way to establishing a genuine private property regime in Eastern Europe, there may be a number of strategies for the period of transition, each specifying a different path to a market economy. We would therefore like to conclude by reviewing the most important alternatives and analyzing their peculiar difficulties in the light of our earlier discussions.

The perils of evolution

If privatization yields so many paradoxes and contradictions, is it not simpler to abandon the whole idea and manage the transition by controlling the state sector directly until its demise? Some distinguished economists have come to this conclusion and argued that, instead of privatization, the future of the East European economies lies in spontaneous development, *ab ovo*, of the new private sector.[24] In essence, the 'evolutionists' claim that the complex institutional structures necessary for a functioning market economy, which have always and everywhere emerged in an evolutionary manner, cannot be brought about through a 'planned' restructuring of the state sector. Consequently, all attempts at

---

[24] The first to take this position was Kornai (1990). A similar point of view is argued by Murrell (1992).

finding a magical shortcut to a true market environment are much more likely to create malignant growths on the vital organs of the economy than to achieve their desired objective.

The evolutionists also believe that the postcommunist state sector is so deeply dysfunctional that any attempt at improving its working is likely to be more costly than building from scratch. While some fixed capital in the state sector might perhaps be usable by private entrepreneurs, its privatization should not be attempted with undue speed, and it should be sold only if it can be extracted from the organizational framework of the state enterprises within which it is now imbedded. Insofar as most of the state sector is concerned, it should simply be allowed to die its natural death, and leave room for new and better organizations of the capitalist economy. The only reason for not closing the state sector down right away is that a move of this kind would lead to too many social dislocations. For this reason, the state sector should be allowed to coexist for an indefinite (but potentially long) period of time with the emerging private sector, and state control over it should be *increased* in many cases to assure that more resources are not squandered. With time, when new businesses are able to absorb the labor force now employed by the state, the state sector will shrink and wither away.

In light of our previous discussions, the assumptions from which the evolutionists start are quite plausible, although their diagnosis of the extent to which the state sector is beyond any hope of redemption is on the most pessimistic side of the spectrum. Still, the solution proposed by the evolutionists is highly unrealistic. Indeed, the contrast between the plausible starting point and the implausible conclusions may be symptomatic of the paradoxical nature of the East European transition.

There are at least three reasons why the evolutionist story is implausible. First, the vision of a restrictive regulation of the state sector during a prolonged transitional period is highly unrealistic. Second, the idea that a healthy private sector can develop while the state sector continues to exist is very questionable. And third, unless privatized, the state sector is very unlikely to shrink over time. Instead, it is likely to become an ever-increasing drain on state resources.

The evolutionists believe that illusions concerning the effects of privatization on the restructuring of state enterprises may be responsible for a new infusion of scarce resources into the old state sector. To avoid this, they propose that the state increase its control over its enterprises and hem them in with a set of restrictive policies, such as price and wage controls, direct credit restrictions, and exchange controls.[25] But even apart from ever-present political considerations, which make it unlikely that the weak East European states will have the fortitude required to starve the state sector to death, the controls that the evolutionists expect the governments to exercise over the state sector do not seem to be feasible. To begin with, there is a tension between the policy of starving the state sector to death and doing it slowly. Presumably, the authorities will have to exercise some discretion in not allowing the state sector to collapse at one fell swoop, and the decisions involved here are precisely the ones that governments are extremely ill-equipped to make. Also, even if most of the state sector is not viable in the long run, this is not true about some (presumably not completely insignificant) portion of state enterprises, and it would be a dogmatic and wasteful policy to try to choke them to death together with the rest. But then, again, discriminations will have to be made between viable and nonviable enterprises, and the government will have to start making exactly those decisions it had proved itself incapable of making over the past forty years: setting prices at levels corresponding to efficient production costs, limiting wages to levels reflecting true productivity, providing credit on the basis of reliable risk estimates, permitting investments promising reasonable rates of return, etc. To state these requirements is to refute *any* state's ability to meet them, to say nothing of the barely competent East European states.

Nor is it likely that a healthy private sector will develop alongside a large state sector, since the publicly-owned enterprises, especially if the state is not fully successful in hardening their budget constraint, will constitute a corrupting influence, perverting the incentives and objectives of private entrepreneurs. Experience under communism is instructive in this respect: much of the private business activity in the old days was parasitic on the inefficiency of state enterprises, deriving exorbitant profits from an arbitrage of scarce goods purchased (with a heavy use of bribery and illicit connections) at controlled prices and resold on the free market. Equally instructive is the experience of military contractors around the world, with their ability to provide shoddy goods at exorbitant prices. The private–public symbiosis is not

---

[25] See Murrell (1992, p. 63). Kornai (1990, pp. 65–6) proposes a system in which discipline over state enterprises is imposed by the banking system and state control over investment. It is interesting to note that some of the practices of state control proposed by the evolutionists are reminiscent of the methods of old communist planning. In fact, Murrell specifically advocates the use of old planning bureaucracies to control the state sector (p. 66).

likely to be radically different in the postcommunist economies in which the state sector is not privatized. As long as private businesses are likely to be intertwined with the public sector, buying its outputs, providing parts and services for state-owned enterprises, entering into joint ventures with them, etc., the dominant business strategy of the new entrepreneurs will be to seek rents from the state sector rather than competing for the finicky private customers.

Finally, the evolutionists' hope that government policy will lead to a slow strangulation of the state sector flies in the face of everything we know about the behavior of the states around the world. Governments do not kill state industries when they are inefficient. They subsidize them, 'modernize' them, 'preserve jobs' in them, protect them from 'unfair competition,' give them a monopoly position, ensure their 'fair returns,' help them fix prices, extend 'job security' to their employees – in a word, nurse them rather than kill them. Only when state-owned firms can be sold for large amounts of cash, do states occasionally get rid of them, but that is not a prospect for the 'lemons' of Eastern Europe. The likely result of the evolutionist policy, therefore, is a prolonged period of *increasing* subsidization of the state sector. In the initial stages, a rationalization of the economic environment may lead to some improvements in public sector performance, but as time goes by, state enterprises are likely to require ever more significant amounts of state support.[26] The resulting drain on the budget will have to be covered either through increased taxation of the new private sector, or through deficit financing, which will undermine the macroeconomic stabilization policies necessary for the development of the private sector.

The path of mass privatization

At the other extreme of the paths of transition is the strategy of mass privatization. It relies heavily on free distribution of state assets to the general public, with a mechanism for a concentration of power of the dispersed owners through the introduction of special financial inter-mediaries.[27] These intermediaries, which hold significant stakes of the

[26] As pointed out by Kornai (1992a), there are signs that a number of nonprivatized enterprises are already failing to meet their tax obligations, which is, of course, equivalent to receiving subsidies. According to Kornai (p. 7), 'the sum of . . . unpaid taxes and social-security contributions [in Hungary] in mid-1991 was greater than the entire budget deficit planned for 1992.'

[27] For early examples and an elaboration of mass privatization programs, see Frydman and Rapaczynski (1990), Blanchard and Layard (1990), Lipton and Sachs (1990), and Chapter 1 in this volume.

privatized companies, and which in turn issue their own shares to the public, are often seen as the main force of postprivatization restructuring. Being locked into their holdings (because of the large blocks of shares they own and the absence of robust secondary markets for the shares of the privatized companies), the intermediaries are expected to maximize their return on investment by the exercise of 'voice' rather than 'exit,' and to become active investors, monitoring the performance of the management and stepping in when companies get into trouble. They are also often encouraged to have a significant foreign component among their own management, thus bringing badly needed expertise and perhaps access to foreign sources of capital.

To the extent the privatization intermediaries facilitate effective exercise of ownership rights by dispersed small stakeholders, they may have a serious positive effect on the establishment of viable property rights. But as we noted already, the main danger of this privatization strategy is that the intermediaries, instead of engaging in active restructuring, may become a new and powerful source of political pressure for more state subsidies. Under certain scenarios, the mass privatization programs could indeed introduce a very effective coordinating mechanism for the diverse forces opposed to the demise of the old state sector and lead to a lasting increase in state intervention.

Whether the dominant strategy of the privatization intermediaries will be to engage in active restructuring of the companies in their portfolio or to lobby for subsidies and other forms of state support, depends, according to our previous analyses, on the state and the distribution of the capital stock conveyed to the intermediaries and on the degree of competitiveness of the environment in which the intermediaries are made to operate.

We have said that privatization in Eastern Europe is, in large measure, a process of managed decline and retirement of state assets. It is questionable whether the intermediaries can be seen as potential managers of this process, since saddling them with nonviable companies is liable to increase too much the political value of their portfolios. Instead, the intermediaries can best be used to identify firms with positive value and to turn them around, especially if the social cost of such actions is not too high. For this reason, the choice of the path of rapid privatization with the use of intermediaries crucially depends on the assessment of the state of the capital stock available for privatization. If the state sector is seen as containing a large number of firms that can be turned around, and if an appropriate procedure can be found to allocate these firms to the intermediaries (so that few nonviable companies find their way into the program), then mass privatization raises a prospect of effective economic transformation. If, on the other hand, the capital stock is seen as mostly worthless, then conveying it to the intermediaries, in a situation in which the government cannot afford a rapid closing down of the old state sector, may only strengthen the pressure for government support.[28] Also, even if the firms in the state sector are thought to be viable, they might be, on the average, of lower quality than new firms. In this case, it might be a good strategy to encourage the intermediaries to acquire a mix of the shares of the privatized and the new companies in order to give them an interest in the health of the more dynamic part of the economy.

On the whole, however, there is a trade-off between the degree to which the intermediaries are diversified, either across the whole economy or within the old state sector, and their role as active investors. If the intermediaries have significant stakes in a limited number of firms, the economic value of their assets is likely to be higher for them, since they will have more incentives and be able to devote more attention to restructuring and streamlining the firms in their portfolios. At the same time, a lower degree of diversification increases the likelihood that weaker firms might represent a disproportionate part of some intermediaries' portfolios, and make it more tempting for them to politicize their activities.

But in all cases, the competitiveness of the environment in which the intermediaries operate is the most crucial condition of success of this path of development. We have considered in detail elsewhere what mechanisms may be used to try to prevent the ossification of the intermediaries into lobbying institutions, and this is not the place to recount these discussions.[29] Suffice it to say that unless the state manages to disassociate itself from the responsibility for the success or failure of the intermediaries, it will irreversibly strengthen their incentives to rely on its assistance. For this purpose, it might be necessary to make sure that there is a sufficiently large number of the intermediaries, that their entry is free, that the citizens have a free choice of whether or not to use the intermediaries for their investment,

---

[28] The Polish government has attempted to examine *ex ante* the economic viability of firms included in its mass privatization program. However, the economic value, if any, of the postcommunist state enterprises predominantly depends on their value after restructuring, rather than their historical performance evaluated at distorted prices in a nonmarket environment. It might be better, therefore, to rely on an evaluation of the viability and relative value of state assets by their prospective owners, along the lines proposed in Chapter 3 in this volume.

[29] See Chapter 3 in this volume.

and that the intermediaries themselves have as much choice as possible in structuring their portfolios. This last factor may be especially important for the enhancement of the economic value of the privatized assets for the intermediaries, and thus directing them toward the achievement of high returns from restructuring as their primary objective.

As we have pointed out, however, the road of mass privatization with the use of intermediaries is useful for the viable portion of the state sector, where rapid restructuring will not produce socially unacceptable costs. While the extent of the ultimately viable portion of the state sector in all East European countries is not known, it is a safe statement that every one of these economies contains a very substantial amount of 'dead wood' that needs to be removed if the economy is ever to become truly healthy. How this can be accomplished, once it is seen that a dynamic mass privatization program may not be an appropriate vehicle, is a very important question.

We have argued already that the nonviable part of the state sector must be separated from the rest if mass privatization is not to degenerate into a political bureaucracy. The question concerning the nonviable part of the state sector is how it can best be wound down, without exploding the political system or ruining the chances of establishing a genuine private property regime. On the one hand, preventing a political crisis may necessitate temporary subsidization, until the rest of the system can absorb the labor released through the shrinking of the state sector. On the other hand, subsidization is rarely temporary, and its presence in the economy constitutes a drain on valuable resources in other sectors and creates distorted incentives for all firms, even those that may be viable in a regime of hard budget constraints. Creating a special liquidation program, and 'privatizing' it through the use of private liquidation funds may perhaps be an appropriate solution. These liquidation funds may be made to bid for the companies in the program together with a predetermined and gradually (but quickly) decreasing amount of subsidies, in exchange for commitments concerning maintenance of certain levels of employment or social services. But instead of maintaining firms that cannot survive in the market, a probably much more effective solution is to counteract the unemployment resulting from the closing down of nonviable parts of the state sector by a targeted program of public works designed to improve the substandard infrastructure of the East European economies. Foreign assistance could perhaps be used to defray some of the budgetary cost of such projects, as well as for a limited subsidization of the restructuring of potentially viable large enterprises which, because of investors' risk aversion, cannot attract sufficient private investment.

Mass privatization without intermediaries

The Russian program, briefly described earlier, may provide an example of a 'third way' in which the state attempts to relinquish its ownership control over state enterprises, but does not put in place any 'constructivist' solutions to the governance problems of the privatized businesses. The essence of this approach is to convey title to state enterprises to a combination of insiders and dispersed outside owners, without the creation of any institutional mechanism for the exercise of outside control over the privatized firms. As we have indicated, there is some doubt as to the effectiveness of such a transfer of title, not only with respect to its impact on future restructuring, but also with regard to the creation of genuine property rights themselves. Nevertheless, a mass privatization program of this type may, under certain circumstances, constitute a transitional stage toward the establishment of a market economy, especially if it is combined (as it unfortunately is not in Russia) with an effective macroeconomic stabilization policy and a strong tightening of the budget constraint of the privatized enterprises.

The assumption we make here is that Russia, perhaps more than any other country, is characterized by an imbalanced development of industry, and a highly irrational allocation of productive resources even within the overgrown industrial sector. The tremendous military industry is only one of the elements of this misallocation; the huge 'prestige' projects, often constructed more for political than economic reasons, are another. Under these conditions, transition to a market economy in Russia is bound to require more intersectoral reallocation than a merely intra-enterprise restructuring. This, in turn, means that the social dislocations to be expected from the transition process may be much greater in Russia than in the 'Western rim' economies, and that privatization will, in large measure, be a way in which the former state sector shrinks, rather than is revitalized. Under these conditions, the Russian plan does offer certain significant advantages.

The price paid for not providing a basis for new corporate governance arrangements in a Russian-type mass privatization program is, of course, a reduced rate of restructuring that is likely to take place for some time after the change. The reliance on secondary markets to produce new ownership arrangements is likely, as we have seen, to proceed slowly and with difficulties. To the extent, therefore, to which the state sector contains a large number of potentially viable enterprises, the program may lead to significant welfare losses as a result of inefficient utilization of the existing resources. But if privatization is seen as primarily a program of managed decline of the state sector, a mass privatization program without effective intermediary institutions may play an important role in lessening the effectiveness of political resistance to the shrinkage of the former state sector. To be sure, under certain circumstances, such as those prevailing in some Central European countries, the absence of the effective external monitoring and control over the management and the workers strengthens both the political and economic power of these already too powerful groups of special interests. But in the Russian situation, the main opponent of an effective transition to a private property regime was the power of the central industrial *nomenklatura*, organized around branch ministries and industrial associations, and allied with local state apparatus. Now, if the Russian program accomplishes anything, it undermines this very powerful lobbying interest by cutting from under it the lower echelons of the economic bureaucracy and removing the source of its economic power. The plant-level management, together with the workers, are constituted as a separate interest by the program, and this new group, when cut off from the centralized institutional structures of the old regime, is much more dispersed and less well organized than the industrial lobby prior to privatization. Moreover, the group is probably not homogeneous itself, since those insiders who happen to work in potentially viable enterprises have an interest in some degree of restructuring and the reform process, while those who could not survive in a market system would like to continue state subsidization. Consequently, macroeconomic tightening of the belt, if it becomes politically viable, might encounter less well-organized political resistance and may result in a significant shrinkage of the old state sector, before the forces of the status quo have the time to organize.

BIBLIOGRAPHY

P. Aghion and P. Bolton (1992), 'An Incomplete-Contracts Approach to Financial Contracting,' *Review of Economic Studies*, vol. 59, 473–94.

A.A. Alchian (1950), 'Uncertainty, Evolution and Economic Theory,' *Journal of Political Economy*, vol. 58, 211–21.

—— and H. Demetz (1972), 'Production, Information Costs and Economic Organization,' *American Economic Review*, vol. 62, 777–95.

K.J. Arrow and E.S. Phelps (1991), 'Proposed Reform of the Economic System of Information and Decision in the USSR: Commentary and Advice,' *Rivista di Politica Economica*, vol. 81, no. 11.

A. Aslund (1991), *Gorbachev's Struggle for Economic Reform*, Ithaca, Cornell University Press.

C. Bandyk (1991), *Privatization in Poland*, Warsaw, Ministry of Ownership Changes.

W.J. Baumol (1993), 'Perils of Privatization,' mimeo.

D. Begg and R. Portes (1992), 'Enterprise and Economic Transformation: Financial Restructuring in Central and Eastern Europe,' mimeo.

J. Bentham (1931), *The Theory of Legislation: Principles of the Civil Code*, 6th ed., London, Trubner, 1st ed. 1890.

A. Berg (1992), 'The Logistics of Privatization Poland,' paper presented at the NBER Conference on Transition in Eastern Europe.

O.J. Blanchard and R. Layard (1990), 'Economic Change in Poland,' London, Centre for Research into Communist Economies Research Report.

O.J. Blanchard, R. Dornbusch, P. Krugman, R. Layard, and L. Summers (1990), 'Reform in Eastern Europe,' Report of the Wider World Economy Group, mimeo.

J. Blasi and D.L. Kruse (1992), *The New Owners*, New York, Harper-Collins.

M. Boycko, A. Schleifer, and R.W. Vishny (1992), 'Property Rights, Soft Budget Constraints, and Privatization,' Harvard University, mimeo.

G. Calvo and F. Coricelli (1991), 'Stagflationary Effects of Stabilization Programs in Reforming Socialist Countries: Supply-Side vs. Demand-Side Factors,' World Bank and International Monetary Fund, mimeo.

G. Carroll and D. Vogel, eds (1987), *Organizational Approaches to Strategy*, Cambridge, Mass., Ballinger.

A.D. Chandler Jr and H. Daems, eds (1980), *Managerial Hierarchies*, Cambridge, Mass., Harvard University Press.

D. Chelminski et al. (1992), 'Spoleczne bariery prywatysacji,' (Social Barriers to Privatization), Warsaw School of Economics, mimeo.

R.H. Coase (1960), 'The Problem of Social Cost,' *Journal of Law and Economics*.

J. Coffee (1991), 'Liability versus Control: The Institutional Investor as Corporate Monitor,' *Columbia Law Review*, 1277–368.

S. Commander, ed. (1991), *Managing Inflation in Socialist Economies in Transition*, Washington, DC, World Bank.

J.R. Commons (1934), *Institutional Economics*, Madison, University of Wisconsin Press.

J. Corbett and C. Mayer (1991), 'Financial Reform in Eastern Europe: Progress with the Wrong Model,' *Oxford Review of Economic Policy*, vol. 7, no. 4.

V. Corbo, F. Coricelli and J. Bossack, eds (1991), *Reformed Central and East European Economies*, Washington, DC, World Bank.

G. Csaki (1992), 'East–West Corporate Joint Ventures: Promises and Disappointments,' mimeo.

L. De Alessi (1983), 'Property Rights, Transaction Costs and X-Efficiency: An Essay in Economic Theory,' *American Economic Review*, vol. 73, 64–81.

J.B. DeLong (1991), 'Did Morgan's Men Add Value?' in P. Temin, ed., *Inside the Business Enterprise*, Chicago, University of Chicago Press.

H. Demsetz and K. Lehn (1985), 'The Structure of Corporate Ownership: Causes and Consequences,' *Journal of Political Economy*, vol. 93, no. 6, December.

J. Earle and D. Sapatoru (1993), 'Privatization in Romania,' in Earle, Frydman and Rapaczynski, eds, *Privatisation in the Transition to a Market Economy*.

J. Earle, R. Frydman and A. Rapaczynski, eds (1993a), *Privatisation in the Transition to a Market Economy*, London, Pinter Publishers, and New York, St Martin's Press.

——, ——, and —— (1993b), 'Notes on Voucher Privatization in Eastern Europe' in *The New Europe: Evolving Economic and Financial Systems in East and West*, Dordrecht, Kluwer.

T. Eggertsson (1990), *Economic Behavior and Institutions*, Cambridge and New York, Cambridge University Press.

J. Esser (1990), 'Bank Power in West Germany Revisited,' *Western European Politics*, vol. 13, no. 4.

E. Fama and M. Jensen (1983a) 'Separation of Ownership and Control,' *Journal of Law and Economics*, vol. 26, 301–25.

—— and —— (1983b), Agency Problems and Residual Claims,' *Journal of Law and Economics*, vol. 26, 327–49.

T. Faur (1993), 'Foreign Capital in Hungary's Privatisation' in Earle, Frydman and Rapaczynski, eds, *Privatisation in the Transition to a Market Economy*.

J. Franks and C. Mayer (1990), 'Capital Markets and Corporate Control: A Study of France, Germany and the UK,' *Economic Policy*, vol. 5, 191–231.

M. Friedman (1962), *Capitalism and Freedom*, Chicago, University of Chicago Press.

R. Frydman (1982), 'Towards an Understanding of Market Processes: Individual Expectations, Learning, and Convergence to Rational Expectations Equilibrium,' *American Economic Review*, vol. 72, 652–68.

—— and E.S. Phelps, eds (1983), *Individual Forecasting and Aggregate Outcomes: 'Rational Expectations' Examined*, Cambridge and New York, Cambridge University Press.

—— and A. Rapaczynski (1990), 'Sprywaryzowac Prywatyscje: Nowa Propozycja Przemian Wlasnosciowych w Polsce' (Privatizing Privatization: A New Proposal of Ownership Transformation in Poland) *Res publica*, September.

—— and S. Wellisz (1991), 'The Ownership-Control Structure and the Behavior of Polish Enterprises during the 1990 Reform: Macroeconomic Measures and Microeconomic Responses' in Corbo, Coricelli, and Bossack, eds, *Reformed Central and East European Economies*.

——, A. Rapaczynski, J.S. Earle et al. (1993a), *The Privatization Process in Central Europe*, London, Central European University Press.

——, ——, and —— et al. (1993b), *The Privatization Process in Russia, Ukraine and the Baltic States*, London, Central European University Press.

R. Frydman, A. Rapaczynski et al. (1994), *Small Privatization: Transformation of Retail Trade and Services in Poland, the Czech Republic and Hungary*, London, Central European University Press.

M. Gerlach (1987), 'Business Alliances and the Strategy of the Japanese Firm,' in Carroll and Vegel, eds.

A. Gerschenkron (1962), *Economic Backwardness in Historical Perspective*, Cambridge, Mass., Harvard University Press.

R.A. Goldsmith (1983), *A Financial History of the New Japan, 1868–1977*, New Haven, Conn., Yale University Press.

I. Grosfeld (1991a), 'Privatization in Eastern Europe: An Evolutionary Perspective,' mimeo.

—— (1991b), 'Privatization of State Enterprises in Eastern Europe: The Search for a Market Environment,' *East European Politics and Societies*.

—— and D. Hare (1991), 'Privatization in Hungary, Poland and Czechoslovakia' in R. Portes, ed. *European Economies*, Luxembourg, European Communications, Directorate General for Financial Affairs.

S.J. Grossman and O.D. Hart (1986), 'The Costs and Benefits of Ownership: A Theory of Vertical and Lateral Integration,' *Journal of Political Economy*, vol. 94, no. 4.

E. Hankiss (1990), *East European Alternatives*, Oxford, Oxford University Press.

H. Hansmann (1990), 'When Does Worker Ownership Work? ESOPs, Law Firms, Codetermination, and Economic Democracy,' *Yale Law Journal*, vol. 99, no. 8.

O. Hart (1993), 'The Market Mechanism as an Incentive Scheme,' *Bell Journal of Economics*, vol. 14, no. 2, 366–82.

—— and J. Moore (1989), 'Default and Renegotiation: A Dynamic Model of Debt,' MIT, Working Paper no. 560.

—— and —— (1991), 'A Theory of Debt Based on the Inalienability of Human Capital,' MIT, Working Paper no. 592.

J. Havel (1992), 'Basic Problems Connected with Statistical Data on Privatisation Process in Czechoslovakia,' mimeo.

—— and E. Kukla (1992), 'Mass Privatisation Programs in Czechoslovakia 1991–1992,' mimeo.

F.A. von Hayek (1948), *Individualism and Economic Order*, Chicago, University of Chicago Press.

—— (1955), *The Counter-Revolution of Science*, New York, The Free Press.

M. Helwig (1991), 'Banking, Financial Intermediation and Corporate Finance' in A. Giovanini and C. Mayer, eds, *European Financial Integration*, Cambridge, Cambridge University Press.

E.S. Herman (1981), *Corporate Control, Corporate Power*, Cambridge and New York, Cambridge University Press.

M. Hinds (1991), 'Issues in the Introduction of Market Forces in Eastern European Socialist Economies,' in Commander, ed., *Managing Inflation in Socialist Economies in Transition*.

A. Hirschman (1970), *Exit, Voice, and Loyalty: Responses to Decline in Firms, Organizations, and States*, Cambridge, Mass., Harvard University Press.

J. Hirschmeier and Tsunehiko Yui (1981), *The Development of Japanese Business, 1600–1980*, London and Boston, Allen & Unwin.

T. Hoshi, A, Kashyap, and D. Scharfstein (1991), 'Corporate Structure, Liquidity, and Investment: Evidence from Japanese Industrial Groups,' *Quarterly Journal of Economics*, vol. 106, no. 1.

M. Jensen (1986), 'Agency Cost of Free Cash Flow, Corporate Finance and Takeovers,' *American Economic Review*, vol. 76, no. 1, 323–9.

—— and Meckling (1976), 'Theory of the Firm: Managerial Behaviour, Agency Costs and Ownership Structure,' *Journal of Financial Economics*, vol. 3, 305–60.

—— and K.J. Murphy (1991), 'Performance Pay and Top Management Incentives,' *Journal of Political Economy*, vol. 98, no. 2.

—— and R. Ruback (1983), 'The Market for Corporate Control: The Scientific Evidence,' *Journal of Financial Economics*, vol. 11, 5–50.

W. Joyce and A. van de Ven, eds (1981), *Organizational Design*, New York, Wiley.

J. Kocka (1980), 'The Rise of Modern Industrial Enterprise in Germany,' in Chandler and Daems, eds.

J. Kornai (1990), *The Road to a Free Economy: Shifting from a Socialist System: The Example of Hungary*, New York, Norton.

—— (1992a), 'The Postcommunist Transition and the State: Reflections in the Light of Hungarian Fiscal Problems,' *American Economic Review, Papers and Proceedings*.

—— (1992b), *The Socialist System*, Princeton, NJ, Princeton University Press.

M. Lindsay (1992), *Developing Capital Markets in Eastern Europe: A Business Reference*, New York, New York University Press.

D. Lipton and J. Sachs (1990), 'Privatization in Eastern Europe: The Case of Poland,' *Brookings Papers on Economic Activity*, no. 1 (Spring).

J. Locke (1963), *The Second Treatise of Government*, ed. Peter Laslett, Cambridge, Cambridge University Press.

K. Meszaros (1993), 'Evolution of the Hungarian Capital Market: The Budapest Stock Exchange' in Earle, Frydman, and Rapaczynski, eds, *Privatisation in the Transition to a Market Economy*.

K. Mizsei (1990), 'Experiences with Privatisation in Hungary,' mimeo.

—— (1992), 'The Hungarian Transformation,' mimeo.

J. Mladek (1993), 'Alternative Paths to Privatisation in Czechoslovakia' in Earle, Frydman, and Rapaczynski, eds, *Privatisation in the Transition to a Market Economy*.

R. Morck, A. Schleifer and R.W. Vishny (1988), 'Management Ownership and Market Valuation,' *Journal of Financial Economics*, vol. 20, 293–315.

H. Monissen (1978), 'The Current Status of Labour Participation in the Management of Business Firms in Germany,' in Pejovich, ed.

P. Murrell (1992), 'Privatization versus the Fresh Start' in V. Tismaneanu and P. Clawson, *Uprooting Leninism, Cultivating Liberty*, Philadelphia, University Press of America.

R.R. Nelson (1991), 'Capitalism as an Engine of Progress and Why Do Firms Differ, and How Does It Matter?'; unpublished, Columbia University.

—— and S.G. Winter (1982), *An Evolutionary Theory of Economic Change*, Cambridge, Mass., Harvard University Press.

D.C. North (1981), *Structure and Change in Economic History*, New York, Norton.

M. Olson Jr (1965), *The Logic of Collective Action*, Cambridge, Mass., Harvard University Press.

S. Pejovich, ed. (1978), *The Codetermination Movement in the West*, Lexington, Mass., Lexington Books.

E.S. Phelps (1991), 'Privatisation Processes in Eastern Europe: Concluding Remarks,' *Rivista di Politica Economica*, vol. 81, no. 11.

M. Polanyi (1962), *Personal Knowledge*, Chicago, University of Chicago Press.

K. Popper (1961), *The Poverty of Historicism*, London, Routledge & Kegan Paul.

Radio Free Europe (1992), *Privatisation*, Research Report, April.

M. Roe (1991), 'A Political Theory of American Corporate Finance,' *Columbia Law Review*, vol. 91, no. 10.

Kazvo Sato and Yasuo Hoshino, eds (1984), *The Anatomy of Japanese Business*, London, Croom Helm.

A. Schonfield (1965), *Modern Capitalism*, London, Oxford University Press.

A. Schleifer and R.W. Vishny (1986), 'Large Shareholders and Corporate Control,' *Journal of Political Economy*, vol. 94, no. 3, 461–88.

—— and —— (1991), 'The Take-over Wave of the 1980s,' *Science*, 17 August.

—— and —— (1992), 'Privatization in Russia: First Steps,' mimeo, National Bureau of Economic Research, Cambridge, Mass.

H. Siebert, H. Schmieding, and P. Nunnenkamp (1991), 'The Transformation of a Socialist Economy: Lesson of German Unification' in G. Winckler, ed., *Central and Eastern Europe*.

H. Simon (1957), *Models of Man*, New York, Wiley.

G. Soros (1987), *The Alchemy of Finance: Reading the Mind of the Market*, New York, Simon & Schuster.

J. Staniszkisz (1991), *The Dynamics of the Breakthrough in Eastern Europe: The Polish Experience*, Berkeley, University of California Press.

D. Stark (1990), 'Privatisation in Hungary: From Plan to Market or Plan to Clan,' *East European Politics and Societies*, vol. 4, no. 2.

—— (1992), 'Path Dependence and Privatization Strategies in East Central Europe,' mimeo.

I. Szelenyi (1990), 'Alternative Futures for Eastern Europe: The Case of Hungary,' *East European Politics and Societies*, vol. 4, no. 2.

J. Szomburg (1993), 'The Decision Making Structure of Polish Privatization' in Earle, Frydman, and Rapaczynski, eds, *Privatization in the Transition to a Market Economy*.

P. Tamowicz (1993), 'Small Privatization: An Inside View' in Earle, Frydman, and Rapaczynski, eds, *Privatization in the Transition to a Market Economy*.

L. Urban (1993), 'Role and Impact of the Legislature in the Hungarian Privatization' in Earle, Frydman, and Rapaczynski, eds, *Privatization in the Transition to a Market Economy*.

J. Vickers and G. Yarrow (1986), 'Telecommunications: Liberalisation and the Privatisation of British Telecom' in J. Kay, C. Mayer, and D. Thompson, eds, *Privatisation and Regulation*, Oxford, Oxford University Press.

E. Voszka (1993), 'Spontaneous Privatization in Hungary' in Earle, Frydman, and Rapaczynski, eds, *Privatization in the Transition to a Market Economy*.

M. Weisbach (1988), 'Outside Directors and CEO Turnover,' *Journal of Financial Economics*, vol. 20, 431–60.

P.J.D. Wiles (1984), *Economic Institutions Compared*, Oxford, Basil Blackwell.

O.E. Williamson (1975), *Markets and Hierarchies: Analysis and Antitrust Implications*, New York, The Free Press.

—— (1985), *The Economic Institutions of Capitalism: Firms, Markets, Relational Contracting*, New York, The Free Press.

—— and W.G. Ouchi (1981), 'The Markets and Hierarchies Program of Research: Origins, Implications, Prospects,' in Joyce and van de Ven, eds.

G. Winckler, ed. (1991), *Central and Eastern Europe: Roads to Growth*, Washington, DC, International Monetary Fund and Vienna, Austrian National Bank.

J. Zieleniec (1990), 'Microeconomic Categories in Different Economic Systems: The Firm' in R.E. Quandt and D. Triska, eds, *Optimal Decision in Markets and Planned Economies*, Boulder, Colo., Westview Press.

INDEX